# ENCYCLOPAEDIA OF
# INDIAN GOVERNMENT:
## PROGRAMMES AND POLICIES

# ENCYCLOPAEDIA
# OF
# INDIAN GOVERNMENT:
# PROGRAMMES AND POLICIES

## Vol. 36
## Telecommunications

*Edited by*

**Satish Tiwari**

**ANMOL PUBLICATIONS PVT. LTD.**
**NEW DELHI - 110 002 (INDIA)**

**ANMOL PUBLICATIONS PVT. LTD.**
4374/4B, Ansari Road, Daryaganj
New Delhi - 110 002

*Encyclopaedia of Indian Government: Programmes and Policies*

First Edition, 2000
ISBN 81-261-0515-1 (Set)



PRINTED IN INDIA

Published by J.L. Kumar for Anmol Publications Pvt. Ltd., New Delhi - 110 002 and Printed at Mehra Offset Press, Delhi.

# Contents

# Preface

Encyclopaedia of Indian Government: Programmes and Policies contains authoritative information on about fifty departmental policies and their future developmental programmes.

Organised to be completed in 40 volumes, this gigantic work covers Agriculture; Atomic Energy; Chemicals and Fertilizers; Coal; Commerce; Communication; Culture; Defence; Education; Environment and Forests; External Affairs; Finance; Food & Consumer Affairs; Food Processing Industries; Health and Family Welfare; Home Affairs and Internal Security; Human Resources; Industry; Information and Broadcasting; Labour; Law, Justice and Company Affairs; Non-conventional Energy Sources; Ocean Development; Parliamentary Affairs; Personnel, Public Grievances and Pensions; Petroleum and Natural Gas; Planning and Programme Implementation; Planning and Statistics; Posts and Telegraphs; Power; Rural Development; Science and Technology; Social Justice and Empowerment; Space; States Affairs; Steel; Steel and Mines; Sugar and Edible Oils; Surface Transport; Textiles; Tourism; Urban Development; Water Resources; Women and Child development etc.

Based on the information derived from authoritative sources, this work contains authentic facts and figures. I am deeply beholden to all the scholars whose writings are cited or substantially made use of in the present work. I am also thankful to Anmol Publications Pvt. Ltd. for undertaking publication of this encyclopaedia. I am solely responsible for shortcomings in presentation of matter.

Encyclopaedic in nature, this will prove a dependable reference work for scholars and academics besides those appearing for different competitive examinations.

—**Satish Tiwari**

# 1

# Service Directly Under Telecom Commission

**Major achievements**

During the year 1997-98, a record number of 32.59 lacs new telephone connections were provided. This achievement was 22.40% more than the achievement of 25.64 lacg new connections provided during the preceding year.

*Civil telephones*

Telephone facilities in villages is an essential prerequisite for the development of rural sector. As against the target of 83,000 villages, 42855 villages have been covered with telephone facility during the year, bringing the total number of villages provided with telephone facilities to 310687. This represents a growth of 16 per cent over the previous year.

*STD stations*

The direct dialing facility is very useful for accessing distant stations instantly. The Department has, therefore, been constantly increasing the number of STD stations in the country. It was decided to increase the number of NSD/STD stations at a faster rate and, accordingly, 2799 new stations were added during 1997-98. There were 16019 NSD/STD Stations in the country as on 31.3.1998.

*Accessibility*

Since there is a long waiting list for telephone connections and also considering the fact that telephone facility is needed by general public who cannot afford to have a telephone of their own, it was decided that the accessibility should be improved by providing a large number of PCOs for general public. Accordingly, a total number of 210495 local PCOs, 213385 NSD/STD PCOs and 4060 High way NSD/STD PCOs have been provided up to 31.3.98.

*Telephone metered call units*

The number of metered call units (accounting for local and STD/ISD calls) increased to 11770.9 crores during the year compared to 9329.6 crores during 1996-97 representing an increase of 26-18%. The number of Telex metered call units declined to 9.12 crores in 1997-98 from 12.86 crores in 1996-97, representing a decrease of 29.08 %.

*Rural communications*

Improvement in Rural communications is evident from the following facts

*Type of rural exchanges commissioned during the year 1996-97*

| SI. No. | Type of Equipment | No. of gross lines |
|---|---|---|
| 1. | 64 Port MILT | 23494 |
| 2. | 128P C-DOT RAX | 113718 |
| 3. | 256P C-DOT RAX | 664304 |
| 4. | 200L E PAM | 1148 |
| 5. | 512Port C-DOT SBM | 121808 |
| 6. | 1000L C-DOT SBM | 406288 |
| 7. | 1200/1400L C-DOT SBM | 49396 |
| 8. | 512P ILT/2048 Port ILT | 38305 |

| | | |
|---|---|---|
| 9. | 200L E-PAM | 1148 |
| 10. | Upgradation Kits (128P-256P) | 81974 |
| 11. | NEAX 61/S | 1524 |
| 12. | Other Exch | 28822 |
| 13. | Line Module-I | 101551 |
| 14. | Line Module-II, | 91926 |
| Total | | 1724258 |

***Mission better communications***

An intensive drive was launched under "Mission Better Communications" to enhance subscribers satisfaction by improving quality of existing services, accessibility to Telecom services in rural and urban areas, specially in hilly and backward areas through replacement of fault prone and worn-out equipments, computerisation of services, upgradation and modernisation of technology and motivational training of staff. Steps taken under "Mission Better Communications" brought fruitful results which are evident from the following:

| | Target 1997-98 | Achievements 1997-98 |
|---|---|---|
| (i) Faults/100 stns/month Telephones | 12.0 | 16.8 |
| (ii) Trunk efficiency (%) | 87.7 | 81.5 |
| (iii) Call completion rate (%) (Live) | | |
| a) Local | 60.0 | 57.4 |
| b) Junction | 50.0 | 45.2 |
| c) STD | 43.0 | 40.5 |

Telecom Directorate Observation Team carried out 16 observations of telephone systems during the year. Factors which adversely affected the performance of telephone systems were analysed and brought to the notice of the concerned field units and remedial action taken. The achievements are as indicated below:

| SI. No. | Activity | Achievements 1997-98 | |
|---|---|---|---|
| (i) | Additions | | |
| | Net equipped Capacity | 35.19 | lacs lines |
| | Direct Exchange Lines | 32.59 | lacs lines |
| (ii) | Accessibility | | |
| | Total Public Telephones | 427940 | |
| (iii) | Modernisation | | |
| | Optical Fibber Cable System commiss-ioned | 17995 | RKMs |
| | Microwave (including UHF) Systems commissioned | 23822 | RKMs |
| | TAX Lines added | 314.3 | K |
| | Digital Trunk Automatic Exchanges | 32 | |
| | Digital Trunk Automatic Exchange Lines | 1251.5 | K |
| (iv) | Rural CommunicationVillages provided with the Telephone facility | 42855 | |
| | Small sized Electronic Exchanges | 12.0 lakhs | |
| | Motivational Training to Staff | 69084 | |

**Financial review**

*Revenue expenditure and surplus*

On a cash basis the revenue realisation of DOT in 97-98 (excluding Delhi and Mumbai Telephone Districts) was Rs. 14586.91 crores which includes, inter-alia Network charges from MTN Land VSNL. The net working expenses were Rs. 7554.06 crores inclusive of depreciation. The net surplus was Rs. 6746.35 crores as against Rs. 5884.95 crores in the previous year.

*The status of telecommunication services as indicated by various service parameters is given below:*

| | Status as on | |
|---|---|---|
| | 1.4.97 | 1.4.98 |
| A) Accessibility | | |
| —Direct Telephone Exchange Lines working (lakhs) | 145.43 | 178.02 |
| —Trunk Automatic Exchange | 347 | 379 |
| —Computerised Directory Enquiry (Station) | 721 | 1077 |
| —Computerised Fault Repair Service (Station) | 699 | 1008 |
| —Telephone facility in villages | 267832 | 310687 |
| —International Subscriber Trunk Dialing (ISD) facility to other countries | 236 | 236 |
| —Stations provided with approved NSD facility | 7958 | 11157 |
| —District H.Q. provided with approved STID facility | 522 | 547 |
| B) Quality of Service | | |
| (a) Telephone fault rate per 100 stations per month | 17.2 | 1.7.4 |
| (b) Percentage delivery of telegrams within 12 day light hours | 94.0 | 95.8 |
| (c) Effective percentage of trunk calls | 80.6 | 81.5 |

*Capital investm ent*

During the year the plan expenditure was Rs. 8733.57 crores and this was met from the following sources:

| | |
|---|---|
| Internal Resources | Rs. 8733.57 crores |
| Market Borrowings | Nil |
| Budgetary Support | Nil |

Out of the above plan outlay the capital investment on the fixed assets was Rs. 8646.1 0 crores. With this addition, the total investment on gross fixed assets of the Department at the end of year stood at the level of Rs. 53847.21 crores out of which dividend bearing capital is Rs. 2644.26 crores.

*Tariff*

— Clarification in respect of Data Circuits on Digital Transmission Media leased by DOT to Press subscribers issued vide order No.4-8/92-R&C dated 17.4.97.

— Orders for introduction of STD facility on Public Telephones provided in villages (VPTs) issued vide order No. 3-15/97-R&C dated 7.7.97

— Tariff for certain special services for Electronic Telephone Exchanges partially modified vide order No. 3-22/92-R&C dated 1.9.97.

— Clarification with regard to tariff for 64 kbps Satellite Based TDM-TDMA Network in C-Band of frequency issued vide order No. 4-10/93-R&C dated 12.11.97.

**Telephone services**

*Access to telephone system*

All the cities (300) and Towns (4689) in the country as per 1991 census have access to the telephone network through telephone exchanges.

Out of total target of 83000 villages, 42855 villages

*Revenue*

(Rs. in Lakhs)

| | Telephone | Telex | Phone Circuit | Telegraph Circuit |
|---|---|---|---|---|
| (a) Total amount billed for (including MTNL) (As on 31.3.98) | 1594254.00 | 6645.06 | 32723.84 | 3478.03 |
| (b) Total amount collected (As on 31.3,98) Phone Telegraph Circuits Circuits | 1560948.02 | 6855.89 | 30040.06 | 3059.51 |
| (c) Three months old Outstanding as on 30th June, 1998 | 177191.78 | 1945.09 | 13440.44 | 3664.24 |
| (d) Percentage of item (c) w.r.t. item (a) above (As on 31.3.98) | 11.11% | 29.27% | 41.07% | 105.35% |
| (e) Average Monthly Revenue during the year (including MTNL) (As on 31.3.98) | Rs. 879.36 | - | - | - |
| (f) Percentage of excess metering complaints over the No. of bills issued during the year. (1997-98). | 0.19% | - | - | - |

*Telex, phone circuits and telegraph circuits revenue*

(Rs. in lakhs)

| | Telex | | Phone Circuit | | Telegraph Circuits | |
|---|---|---|---|---|---|---|
| | 1996-97 | 1997-98 | 1996-97 | 1997-98 | 1996-97 | 1997-98 |
| (a) Amount billed for excluding MTNL | 4942.26 | 6645.06 | 13150.02 | 32723.84 | 252.29 | 3478-03 |
| (b) Amount Collected | 4883.73 | 6855.89 | 12054.67 | 30040.06 | 2660.38 | 3059.51 |
| (c) Three Months old outstanding as on 30th June of next financial year. | 1256.30 | 1945.09 | 6946.96 | 13440.44 | 2917.73 | 3664.24 |
| (d) Percentage | 25.42 | 29.27 | 52.83 | 41.07 | 115.77 | 105.35 |

*Telephone revenue*

| | Year 1996-97 | Year 1997-98 | %age increase |
|---|---|---|---|
| (a) Amount billed for excluding MTNL | 969372.39 | 1170954.37 | 20.80 |
| (b) Amount collected | 944912.28 | 1147850.27 | 21.48 |

were covered with village telephone facilities during 1997-98.

1192 new telephone exchanges (net addition) were commissioned during the year raising the total number of departmental exchanges to 23392. This represents a growth of 5.36% over the previous year. The equipped capacity of telephone exchanges rose to 212.6 lakh lines with the net addition of 35.19 lakh new lines during the year representing an increase of 19.83% during the previous year.

During the year a record number of 32.59 lakh new telephone connections (Net DELs) have been added, bringing the total number of DELs to 178.00 lakhs. This represents a growth of 22.40% during the year.

### *Participation of private sector in basic telephone service and the licensing process*

#### *Policy provisions*

In accordance with National Telecom Policy, 1994, the private operators are permitted to operate Basic Telephone Services in addition to the Department of Telecom (DOT). The monopoly position of DOT is, thus, changing to deploy where one private operator will provide Basic Telephone Services in each circle along with DOT/MTNL.

Only Indian registered companies are permitted to operate Basic Telephone Services. Foreign equity in these companies is permitted only up to 49%.

The prospective operators need to have an experience of providing 5 lakh lines of Basic Telephone Service.

The new National Telecom Policy is presently under consideration of the Government.

*Achievements*

Three rounds of tenders have been invited since Jan. 1995 in respect of 21 Telecom Circles in the country.

Based on these biddings 9 companies were issued Letters Of Intent (LOI) for 13 Telecom Circles. Six companies have signed the Licence and Interconnect Agreements for six circles.

Out of four companies which had filed Civil Suits in High Court of Delhi, two private companies have entered into an out of court settlement with the Government. Based on this M/s Essar Commission has already signed the Licence Agreement for Basic Telephone Service in Punjab Circle. M/s Techno Telecom, the second company, have also agreed to pay the licence fee and other required guarantees and sign the Licence Agreement.

The Court cases of two companies which were given Letters of Intent for 5 circles are still pending in the High Court of Delhi.

M/s Huges Ispat Ltd. which was issued LOIs for Maharashtra and Karnataka circles have signed the Licence for Maharashtra circle and have applied for creation of a separate legal entity for Karnataka Circle. The case is under consideration of the Government and likely to be finalised soon.

M/s Bharati Telenet Ltd., the Licensee for Basic Telephone Services in Madhya Pradesh Circle have started service in the city of Indore on 4.6.98 and in Bhopal on 9.10.98. M/s. Hughes Ispat Ltd., the Licensee for Basic Telephone Service in Maharashtra Circle has started service in Navi Mumbai on 30.10.98.

*Issues raised by private operators*

The Basic Service Licensees have raised various issues like deferment of IInd year Licence Fee, increasing the licence period from 15 to 25 years, relaxation of licence condition in respect of use of copper cable etc. All these issues are under consideration of a recently constituted Group on Telecommunications. These have been, resolved with the approval of the Government.

***Incentives announced by the Government***

Telecom Sector has been declared as "Infrastructure" with all the attendant benefits like five year Tax Holiday and after five years from the start of operations, the projects would get exemption for the balance number of years within a twelve year period. Telecom Sector would be exempt from the Minimum Alternate Tax (MAT).

The limits on External Commercial Borrowings for the Telecom projects have been made flexible, raising the ECB limits from the level of twice the equity to 50% of the Project Cost. Moreover, rupee expenditure, including the Licence Fee, has been permitted to be met from the External Commercial Borrowings.

Amortisation of Licence Fee has been permitted from the Accounting Year 1996-97. The investments made in debentures and equity shares of a public company providing telecommunication services are made eligible for tax rebate under section 88 of the Income Tax Act.

***Participation of private sector in value added telecommunication services***

Telecommunication has been identified the world over as a basic infrastructure essential for socioeconomic development. Modernisation and expansion of existing telecom services and introduction of new services is of utmost importance for further growth of telecommunication services in the country.

Franchise for certain value added services is being given on a nonexclusive basis. Proposals for permission/

operation of these services on a licence basis is considered by DOT for following Value Added Services:

(i) Electronic Mail Service.

(ii) Voice Mail/Audiotex Service.

(iii) Closed User Group Domestic 64 kbps Data Network Service via INSAT.

(iv) Videotex Service.

(v) Video Conferencing Service.

(vi) Credit Card Authorisation Service.

(vii) Internet.

Following services are franchised on a tender basis:

(i) Radio Paging Service.

(ii) Cellular Mobile Telephone Service.

Proposals were also invited at one time in January, 1995 for the operation of "Public Mobile Radio Trunked Service" on nonexclusive basis due to limitation in frequency spectrum in discrete service areas of 300 KMs. radius without connectivity to PSTN.

Proposals for grant of licenses for other Value-Added Services may also be considered on nonexclusive basis on submission of detailed technical and commercial proposal.

*Status*

(i) Electronic Mail: The licences for this service have been issued on all-India basis to 15 companies. All companies have started the operation of the service in the country.

(ii) Voice Mail/Audiotex Service:- The licence for this service is issued on a city-wise basis. Licences have been issued to 14 companies for operation of this service in 40 cities. The service has been started in 11 cities.

(iii) Closed User Group Domestic 64 kbps Data Network via INSAT The licence for the service is issued on all-India basis. 12 companies have been granted licence to operate this service. Ten companies have started operation of this service in the country.

(iv) No licence has been awarded for operation of Videotex Service, Video-conferencing and Credit Card Authorisation.

(v) Public Mobile Radio Trunked Service:- 139 License Agreements signed with 25 companies for operation of PMRTS in 54 cities are current. The service has already started in 21 cities by 17 companies.

(vi) INTERNET:- Policy for privation of INTERNET Services along with Guidelines and Terms and Conditions of the Licenses was announced in January, 1998. TRAI in its order dated 17.2.1998 has held that the INTERNET Policy formulated and announced by the Government without obtaining TRAI's recommendation regarding terms and conditions of the licenses to such service provider cannot be held valid. This has delayed the entry of private sector in the field of INTERNET Services.

(vii) Cellular Mobile Service:-The service is available in four metro cities of the country by two operators in each city. 33 Licences have been issued to 13 Indian companies for the franchise of the service in 18 Territorial Telecom Circles. The service has already started in selected cities of 17 Telecom Circles. The total number of Cellular customers in the Country are approximately 8.5 lakhs.

*Telecom regulatory authority of India*

The Telecom Regulatory Authority of India (TRAI) was

established through an Act of Parliament in early 1997, inter alia, to regulate the Telecom Services in the country and for matters connected therewith. As per the Act, the Authority shall consist of a Chairperson and not less than two but not exceeding six members to be appointed by the Central Government. At present, the Authority has a Chairperson and 5 members. The Head Office of the Authority is at New Delhi.

The powers and functions of the TRAI include recommending the need and timing for introduction of new service provider, the terms and conditions of licence to a service provider, ensuring technical compatibility and effective interconnection between different service providers, ensure compliance of terms and conditions of licence, and revocation of licence for noncompliance of terms and conditions of licence.

It is also required to facilitate competition and promote efficiency in the operation of telecommunications services, protect the interest of consumers of telecom services, monitoring the quality of service provided by service providers, conduct periodical survey of such services, settle disputes between service providers and ensure effective compliance of universal service obligations.

Another important function which has been entrusted to the Authority is to notify the rates at which the telecommunications services shall be provided both within and outside India.

### *Telephone demand*

A record number of 32.59 lakhs additional new telephone connections were provided during the year 1997-98.

### *Quality of service*

Telecom Directorate Observation Team carried out 16 observations of Telephone systems during the year.

Factors which adversely affected the performance of Telephone system were analysed and brought to the notice of the concerned field units.

***Public grievances***

There are several means for redressing public grievances, including Customers Service Centers, Public Grievances Cells, Telephone Adalats, Open House Sessions. During 1.4.97 to 31.3.98, 8940 complaints were received by PG Cell of Headquarters; 8518 complaints were disposed off.

***Long distance services***

Subscriber trunk dialing:- There has been an addition of 32 Nos. Trunk Automatic Exchanges during the year bringing the total to 379 TAXs in the country. The equipped capacity increased by 314300 lines bringing the total to 1261500 lines. The number of stations connected to the National Subscriber Dialing Network through these TAXs increased by 2799 bringing the total to 16019.

There is an increase of 26.18% in the number of telephone metered call units, the figures for the year under review being 11770.9 crores as against 9329.6 for the previous year.

***Trunk services***

94299 Trunk Circuits were added in the Telecom Network during the year 1997-98, bringing the total number of trunk circuits to 326851 as on 31.3.98. The percentage increase in the trunk circuits during the year was 40.54%. The number of trunk calls booked touched a total of 7.18 crores of which 5.62 crores were effective.

***Computerisation of group dialing scheme***

As on 31.3.97,17 ITI make SFK Digital systems (also called CTMX) were operational at various stations in the country. With further commissioning of one system each at Jodhpur, Guwahati and Agra, during the year, the figure has now gone to 20.

*Implementation of group dialing scheme*

As on 31.3.97, Group Dialling scheme was fully available in 1893 SDCAs in the Country. With the implementation of the scheme in another 92 SDCAs during the year, the figure has gone to 1985.

*Home country direct service*

In the year 1991, in association with Videsh Sanchar Nigarn Ltd. (VSNL), Home Country Direct Service was first introduced to eight countries. As on 31.3.97, this service was available for 31 countries. With the introduction of this service to Bahrain, Norway and Poland during the year, the figure has gone to 31.

*"90" Service*

To enable the STD barred subscribers to have an access to their District as well as Tehsil headquarters within a Long Distance Charging Area (LDCA), the Direct Dialling facility with Dynamic control and Detailed Billing using "90" as dialling code has been introduced during the year. All the Telecom Circles and Districts are making their best efforts to introduce the service in all the exchanges wherever it is technically feasible.

*National sanchar doot awards*

National Sanchar Doot Awards for the year 1995-96 and 1996-97 were given away to the meritorious employees of Department of Telecommunication by the Hon'ble Minister for Communication on 17.05.97, on the World Telecommunication Day. The amount of Cash Award for Sanchar Doot was also enhanced from Rs. 10,000/- to Rs. 51,000/- for each of the categories.

*Transmission system*

17995 RKMs of Microwave system were added with 8250 number of channels during the year. The total RKMs and total number of channels working on microwave media are 72592 RKMs and 129322 respectively at the end of the year.

23822 RKMs of optical fibre systems with 277110 channels were commissioned during the year bringing the total to 76261 RKMs and 576465 channels as on 31.3.1998.

8009 Speech channels on Open Wire Carrier Systems were commissioned during the year raising the total number of channels to 90928 as on 31.3.98.

36388 channels have been added on PCM systems raising the number of channels to 560716 as on 31.3.1998.

***Wireless links***

During the period 1.4.97 to 31.3.98 DOT commissioned 4 Nos. of low power point to point single channel H.F. Wireless Stations on Rent and Guarantee with a route kilometer of 506 KMs. At the end of March, 98, the total number of point to point single channel H.F. Wireless Stations were 446 with a route length of 64,000 KMs.

**Telex service**

Due to introduction of FAX, better STD facilities and other new technologies, telex demand is being reduced continuously. At all the stations sufficient capacities are available to meet telex on demand. The demand of telex connections is reducing day by day so much that at some places working exchanges are being closed due to withdrawal/surrendering of telex connections. In fact telex has become an obsolete technology now.

Equipped Capacity of the network has reduced from 60376 lines to 60026 lines. The number of telex working connections were 25188 as on 31st March, 1998. The number of Telex metered calls decreased to 9.12 crores during 1997-98 compared to 12.86 crores in. 1996-97 representing a decrease of 29.08%.

**Public telegraph services**

All the cities (300) and towns (4689) as per 1991 census and a large number of villages have access to Public Telegraph Services through Telegraph Offices.

There were 957 Departmental Telegraph Offices, 44622 Combined Offices and 981 Telecom Centres as on 31.3.1998.

*Telegraph traffic*

A total of 512.18 lakhs inland telegrams were booked during the year compared to 538.8 lakhs during the previous year which represents a fall of 4.94%. Of the total telegrams booked, 9.73% were on state business and 0.60% on press business.

4.09 lakhs international telegrams were booked during the period as against 5.72 lakhs in the previous year showing a decrease of 28.49% over the previous year.

*Modernisation of telegraph network*

— SFMS-32 lines systems was commissioned at Bhubaneswar (Orissa) on 18.5.97

— 32L SFMS at Shillong installed & kept on traffic trials.

— Five FTCS have been commissioned at Bareilly, Moradabad, Meerut, Delhi and Kanpur. Sixteen FTs in Delhi and 10 FTs in U.P.(W) have been installed.

*Quality of service*

95.8% of telegrams were delivered within 12 day light hours during the period 1997-98 against the yearly target of 94%.

*Developmental activities*

Six Telegraph Offices and seventeen Telecom Centres

were opened during the period 1997-98 and status of TOs/T.Cs. on 31.3.98 was 957/981.

***Customer's facilities***

Express Money Transfer Service is working well in Andhra Pradesh and Tamilnadu and now introduced in Maharashtra and Kerala circles with limited transactions within state.

*Particulars of EMTs (1997-98)*

| | |
|---|---|
| i) No. of EMTs booke | |
| a) A. R | 1,67,049 |
| b) Tamilnadu | 58,872 |
| ii) EMT Transactions | |
| a) A. R | 14,76,38,069 |
| b) Tamilnadu | 4,85,71,091 |
| iii) EMT Revenue (Commission) | |
| a) A.R | 40,14,175 |
| b) Tamilnadu | 13,96,891 |

Total No. of bureaufax centres on 31.12.97 was 1,283. Total no. of fax messages booked up to 31.3.98 was 32,34,466. No. of fax messages delivered (incoming fax message) up to 31.3.98 was 5,29,591. Total revenue earned from booked fax messages up to 31.3.1998 is Rs. 13,19,39,662.

Total revenue earned from incoming fax messages up to 31.3.1998 Rs. 52,35,187.

***Policy matters***

Decision has been taken for decentralisation of equipments used in Telegraph network and power delegated thereto.

The project for establishment of three repair centres

to maintain the SFMSS-32 lines & 64 lines (AEM make) has been approved by Telecom Commission. The Heads of circles of the concerned centres have been requested to respond to the project proposal.

The proposal of franchising of Telegraph services through franchised PCO holders stands approved by Telecom Commission in principle.

**New technologies and projects of special significance**

Installation of Multichannel per carrier very small aperture terminals (MCPC-VSATs). 49 number of MCPC-VSATs were made operational from 1.4.97 to 31.3.1998 at various places in country. Under this scheme, the stations which cannot be provided long distance media through terrestrial system, are provided STD facility through INSAT system. Such stations are mostly located at remote, hilly and inaccessible places including Islands having small telephone exchanges with low traffic areas.

***Installation of remote area business message network (RABMN)-VSATs***

Only 2 number of RABMN-VSATS were commissioned during the period 1.4.97 to 31.3.1998. These VSATs are low speed terminals and entry of private sector with High Speed Terminals have badly affected the commissioning of RABMN-VSATS. RABMN-VSATs are directly purchased by the customers from suppliers. These terminals are also able to switch on to the Telex network of the country, I-NET (i.e. terrestrial packet switched public data network) and to GPSS (i.e. Gateway Packet Switching System) for international connectivity.

***Installation of high speed VSAT network (HVNET)***

A satellite based network using Very Small Aperture Terminals (VSATs) to provide high speed 64 Kbps switched data service known as HVNET was made operational by 31.3.1998 along with 14 nos. of VSATs provided temporarily for Amarnath Yatra. This network also has been badly affected by the entry of private sector in this field. The network has access to DOT's Packet Switched Public Data Networks (INET/RABMN) and International data networks through the Gateway Packet Switching System of VSNL. The Network envisages voice facility amongst VSATs including connectivity to Public Switched Telephone Network (PSTN). The Hub station is co-located with satellite earth station at Mumbai.

### *New works*

#### *Digital satellite facility*

Purchase Order was issued for supply of IDR (Intermediate Data Rate) equipment for providing digital facility at 14 stations in different parts of the country. Supply of equipment was not received during 97-98.

#### *INSAT -Mobile Satellite Services (INSAT-MSS)*

Installation of INSAT-MSS equipment had been completed at Jayanagar Earth Station (Bangalore), but service could not be commissioned due to level variation in INSAT-MSS transponder observed during Nov. 1997 which is still continuing. This system shall provide encoded voice service between land portable, maritime users & fixed users on public switched telephone network (PSTN). This shall also support data, fax, massaging & reporting services. The project is being executed by CDOT on behalf of Deptt. of Telecom. Mobile Terminals shall be purchased by the customers directly from the identified indigenous manufacturers.

#### *Digital Circuit Multiplying Equipment (DCME)*

Field trial for DCME facility to be provided at 4 stations namely Delhi, Mumbai, Calcutta and Chennai had been started at Delhi and Mumbai.

*Ku-band facility*

Ku-band digital facility was to be provided at 3 places namely Delhi, Bangalore and NOCC at Sikandrabad in U.P. The equipment had been procured from Ms. ISL. Antennae had been installed and alignment completed. DOT/QA testing had been completed and installation of equipments had been started at respective sites.

*Data communications service*

Inet Phase-II network was planned to provide data services in 89 cities, including 8 cities of Inet Phase-I. The target was extended to 102 cities. These cities have been categorised in 3 groups on the basis of business activity and demand for different types of connections and facilities. This network will have a capacity of high speed data transmission at maximum speed of up to 64 KBPs between computers as well as interactive access from public switched telephone network (PSTN).

The following were the activities for the period

(i) Type I location at Mumbai-II was commissioned.

(ii) 14 locations have been upgraded (earlier covered by ACX-40 concentrators) to type-II nodes with PSX. These are Belgaum, Chandigarh, Jabalpur, Ludhiana, Madurai, Mangalore, Mysore, Panjim, Trivandrum, Vijayawada, Bhopal, Guwahati, Patna and Vizag.

iii) Following type-III locations were commissioned:- Ahmadnagar, Ajmer, Bikaner, Durgapur, Faridabad, Gandhinagar, Gorakhpur, Haldia, Jodhpur, Kakinada, Kalyan, Karnal, Kota, Mathura, Moradabad, Muzzafarpur, Ooty, Pathankot, Quilon, Raipur, Rohtak, Rourkela, Sambalpur, Shillong, Sholapur, Siliguri, Tirupur and Trinelvelly.

*Integrated Services Digital Network (ISDN)*

The ISDN services have been introduced in six more cities

during this year and now the facilities are available at seventeen towns viz Hyderabad, Ranchi, Ahmedabad, Rajkot, Bangalore, Indore, Jabalpur, Pune, Nagpur, Jaipur, Tuticorin, Kanpur, Lucknow, Delhi, Mumbai, Chennai and Calcutta. The total number of ISDN subscribers at the end of March, 98 is 1211.

*Introduction of Internet in Rural area - "Tele-Villages"*

To commemorate the 50th Anniversary of India's Independence and to popularise and create awareness amongst the rural populace, Internet demonstration services were inaugurated in 15 rural centres, named "Tele-Villages", spread over 14 Telecom Circles on the birthday of the Father of the Nation, i.e. 2nd October, 97. These free of cost demonstrations were initially introduced for a period of three months. It was further extended by another three months. These demonstrations of Internet have been received well by the rural masses.

**Major achievements in computerisation**

*Customer related activity*

— 350 (Three Hundred Fifty) more towns have been computerised for Directory Enquiry (DO).

— 276 (Two Hundred Seventy Six) more towns have been computerised for Fault Repair Service (FRS).

— 24 (Twenty Four) more towns have been computerised for Commercial Service (CS).

**Standardisation of software packages**

*Fault repair service (FRS) and directory enquiry (DO):-* COMMANDIR Package for Fault Repair Service (FRS) & Directory Enquiry Services (DQ), standardised by *DOT*, has been implemented in 222 SSAs for Directory Enquiry and in 219 SSAs for Fault Repair Service. The COMMANDIR Package for DQ services has been tested for ten lacs lines with 150 operators under simulation conditions. The Package has also been modified and its upgraded version 1.3.1 has been released by TEC, which contains number of new features like import of data from Commercial Service etc.

*Nation wide directory enquiry services (NDQ):-* As decided in 1995 to implement ONLINE Nation Wide Directory Enquiry Service using X-25 and X-28 INET connections. 127 SSAs have been provided Host connectivity with data of whole SSAs.

*Computerised commercial service system (CSS):-* Commercial Service System (CSS) Package developed at Chandigarh by M/s dde-ORG have been modified to incorporate additional features and ver. 1.2 has been validated.

The Package has been made over to C-DOT for maintenance, upgradation, integration with other Packages and for distribution to field units.

The instruction Manual for installation & operation of CSS Package was prepared and circulated to the field units. The guidelines for Acceptance Testing (A/T) of the CSS package by T&D circle were prepared & circulated to the field units.

Regular Training is being imparted in this package. During this period, six training courses have been organised at BRBRAITT Jabalpur. Training in SCO UNIX and ORACLE is also being imparted.

*Computerisation of TR buiilling and accounting (TRBA):-* Trichur package for TR Billing and Accounting (Trichur), Standardised in DOT, has been made over tc C-DOT along with source code and documentation for further maintenance, development and integration of this package with other customer related packages.

*Inventory management:-* Inventory Management

Package for use in CTS and CSD has been tested and Version 1.1 has been standardised for implementation in CTSs/CSD. A Steering Committee constituted under the Chairmanship of Advisor (production), Telecom Commission completed its work and submitted its report. The package (IMTC) has already been implemented in 7 CTSs/CSDs and it is under implementation at other places. The Draft specifications for procurement module for CGM TS, Calcutta and MM Cell of DOT has been finalised for making over to C-DOT for the development of software package.

*Software for project management:-* MS Software package for Project Management has been standardised for use in DOT 40 copies of the software have been purchased and distributed one copy each to all field units. Training to field staff has been imparted for its use.

*Computerised Facilitation Counters:-* As a measure of responsive and effective administration, it has been decided by the Cabinet Secretary to set up Computerised Facilitation Counters (CFC) at the Reception of all the Ministries/Departments of the Government of India for disseminating information to the citizen/user regarding schemes/procedures of the organisation, forms and applications, and about individual applications.

CFC at the Reception of Sanchar Bhawan has been made operational. All the Telecom Circles and PSUs of DOT have been asked to setup similar CFC at their Headquarters, in response of which CFC has already been made operational at the HQ of Maharashtra Telecom Circle and Kerala Telecom Circle and at other places action is being taken to set up such Facilitation Counters.

*Interactive voice response system (IVRS):-* Rajasthan Telecom Circle, who had been nominated for the development of Software for Integrated Interactive Voice Response System (IVRS), has awarded the tender for development & implementation of Software at Alwar, as a pilot project. The Company has developed the software and TEC/C-DOT has been asked to validate the software. The software is expected to be available for distribution to the field units during the first quarter of 1998-99.

*Integrated Customer Management Software Package:-* TEC/C-DOT has recently tested an Integrated Software Package "AP-SOFT" for DQ, TRB&A and Commercial Service System. This package is being developed indigenously by AP Telecom Circle.

*Zonal meeting in computerisation:-* Four Zonal Meetings were organised under the Chairmanship of Adv(T) in New Delhi, Mumbai, Chennai and Calcutta during the year, in which all the field units participated, for reviewing the progress in computerisation and to discuss various problems being faced both in the computer Hardware and software front.

*Workshop in Computerisation:-* Two workshops were organised during the year by Information Technology Cell, one for TRA Billing at C-DOT Bangalore and another on Computerisation at ALTTC, Ghaziabad to discuss computerisation in DOT.

*Activities in Sanchar Bhavan*

(i) LAN Server working in Sanchar Bhawan and Dak Bhawan have been upgraded to Pentium Pro. Connectivity between Sanchar Bhavan and Dak Bhavan Server has been established.

(ii) During the period 39 more Pentium PCs, printers & 5 servers have been added and another 53 Pentium PCs with latest MS Office '97 software is being procured.

(iii) Computerisation Gate Pass has been introduced at the Reception of Sanchar Bhawan to issue gate pass to visitors since Dec. 97.

(iv) DOT-MAIL facility has been made operational in the Sanchar Bhawan through which data and file can be transferred. E-mail facility is also available through Internet on DOT-MAIL.

(v)Admn. IV section has been selected as one of the sections in TCHQ for full computerisation working. For this a private vendor "Prodata" has completed the system study, the report of which is under approval.

(vi) Microsoft Corporation of India Ltd. has been associated for system study of TCHQ working with an objective of bringing Office Automation and modernising the way of working in Telecom Directorate.

(vii)A Quarterly News Letter on Information Technology has been started from the IT Cell to disseminate the information on Information Technology. First issue of this News Letter has been published and distributed in Feb., 98.

(viii) Additional Books on computer and IT has been added in the computer library for use of the Officers of DOT A list of computer books available in the Computer Library is made available on LAN for accessing by the users.

(ix) The report of the Committee set up for scrapping, the old version computers of the type PC XT286/ PCAT-286 working in Telecom Directorate has been finalised. Case is being processed to replace the old Computers of configuration - PC AT/286 and its earlier versions.

(x) Internet Connections are being provided to all senior officers, of the level of IDDG & above of Telecom Directorate.

(xi) LAP-TOP Computers are being procured for providing to Senior officers of Telecom Commission.

***Future plan***

(i) Standardisation of Integrated Package for Customer related service like Commercial Service, TRBA, DO, FRS etc.

(ii) Establishment of Call Center.

(iii) Upgradation of LAN at TCHQ, New Delhi.

(iv) Creation of DOT web site and Wide Area Network.

(v) Creation of Multimedia Center.

(vi) Computerisation of Material Management System of DOT by development of a Software package for Procurement Module of Accounting modules of M. M. System.

(vii) Replacement of old Computers and Printer Working in Telecom Directorate and providing state of art Pentium Computers, Printer, UPS and latest Software for office working.

***C-DOT***

*Projects in the field*

*MAX-XL*:- The infrastructure assessment for M/s ITI was completed by QA and the type approval was given to Mis. ITI. After commissioning of Indira Nagar exchange, the MAX-XL switches are now being installed at more sites namely, Bihar (Madhubani), Karnataka (Chikmaglur, Yelahanka, Gadag, Mandya)), Tamil Nadu (Dindigal, Namakkal, Kumbakonam, Nagercoil), Kerala (Affingal), Punjab (Abhor). TOT training program was completed for nine more manufacturers namely, BEL, BHEL Crompton Greaves, Keltron, IL-Kota, Hindustan Teleprinters, Punjab Communication, United Telecom and ECIL. Order for two lakh lines of MAX-XL exchanges (including 40K lines for Jayanagar, field trial site with ISDN and 800 K BHCA capability) was placed with the M/s Indian Telephone Industries (ITI). So far, 10 exchanges (One lakh lines) were commissioned in the field.

Technology for C-DOT SBM-RAX based on "XL" hardware and MAX-XL has also been offered to the C-DOT switching products manufacturers.

*ISDN CPEs:-* Functional evaluation of ISDN customer premises equipment, namely, Network Termination (NT310) and Terminal Adapter (TA210) by TEC was completed successfully and TEC approval has been accorded. The interworking of these equipment with all the new technology exchanges has been satisfactorily proven Technology transfer for NT310 and TA210 to M/s ITI model plant was completed.

*TAX-XL:-* The TAX-XL at Ratfam was commissioned with CCS #7 signalling towards OCB TAX at Bhopal and Siemens EWSD TAX at Indore. Bhopal TAX was synchronized with national clock and the field trial was completed successfully.

*CCS #7 SIGNALLING SYSTEM:-* CCS #7 (SS7) field trial for MAX-L was completed at Kharagpur. Environmental tests of Signalling Unit Module (SUM) were also carried out at Bangalore C-DOT SBM RAX MAX-L and MAX-XL exchanges have become capable of supporting IN and ISDN services.

*Non A/C RSU:-* The development of non-A/C RSU (Remote Switching Unit) capable for QM333 category B operation was completed. After the successful field trials at Ratnagiri (Maharashtra and Vapi (Gujarat), TEC clearance was obtained.

*Detailed billing and bulk billing:-* The detailed billing and bulk billing facilities on junctions for C-DOT exchanges were tested satisfactorily. The bill monitoring software package was developed, tested and TEC clearance was obtained after successful field trials.

Network Synchronization Equipment (NSE):- The Network Synchronization Equipment (NSE) developed for level 2 operation in the synchronization network was successfully tested for clock stability and jetters transfer function by TEC. This equipment fully satisfies ITU-T standards and can be used for network synchronization of E-10B and C-DOT SBM RAX, as well as MAX-L exchanges. The equipment was offered to TEC and after field trial with E-10B exchanges clearance for production has been obtained Transfer of Technology is in progress to M/s ITI, Mankapur.

*Regional access barring ('90') facility:-* Testing of regional access barring '90' facility in C-DOT exchanges (256P RAX/SBM/RAX/MAX-L/MAX-XL) was completed by TEC. C-DOT organized 30 workshops in different telecom circles and about 900 DOT officials were trained on retrofitting the facility The new versions of the software are being ported on all the existing exchanges in the field.

*SBM RAX:-* With the commissioning of 317 exchanges (4.68 lakh lines) during the year, the total number of the same commissioned in the field so far has gone up to 2300 exchanges (21.64 lakh lines).

*MAX-L:-* With the commissioning of 47 exchanges (2.97 lakh lines) during the year, the total number of the same commissioned in the field so far has gone up to 310 exchanges (12.53 lakh lines).

*256P RAX*

— Country adaptations for Ethiopia, Colombia, Gambia,

Bangladesh were completed. RAX software version (DOT version) 2-1 -1 was released with following enhancements

— Dynamic O/G restriction matrix.

— Regional STD (90) facility

— STD/ISD restrictions on CCB subscribers.

— Total number of RAXs (256P & 128P RAX) operational in the network is 19,000.

*TDMA PMP:-* The validation of the equipment including environmental testing was completed by TEC. The field trial of the equipment was successfully completed with Mysore as a base station and remotes; at Harohalli, Doora and Varuna. After the formal technology approval the equipment would be ready for bulk production.

*MCPC VSAT:-* The MCPC VSAT equipment in C-Band was evaluated by TEC. The equipment was installed for a field trial with hub at Jaynagar and remote at Maralwadi (Bangalore).

*INSAT mobile satellite system (INSAT MSS):-* This project was undertaken for providing mobile satellite services through indigenous satellite INSAT-2C. Hub equipment, portable and maritime terminals were developed jointly to meet these requirements by C-DOT and COMSAT laboratories of USA. The installation and testing of the system was completed at Jayanagar, Bangalore with satellite simulator and INSAT 2C satellite during its availability. The system supports voice, data and fax communication between the mobile terminals and also between mobile and PSTN subscribers with hub as gateway. The transfer of technology (TOT) process for these terminals to the indigenous manufacturers is proposed after commissioning.

***Progress in the development of key projects***

*Integrated services digital network (ISDN):-* C-DOT has developed Integrated Services Digital Network (ISDN) capability for its exchanges. The ISDN interfaces, bearer services and supplementary services have been developed according to ITU-T and national standards. The basic functions of ISDN interfaces, supplementary services, fax, and video calls were demonstrated to the Telecom Commission during August, 1997. The ISDN capability can be retrofitted on existing exchanges by deploying the ISDN Terminal Unit (ISTU) in addition to SS7 Signalling Unit Module (SUM).

***Intelligent Network (IN) Services***

Service logic was develop for Service Control Point (SCP) for creation of a number of services using SSP on C-DOT switches. IN services hold immense value-addition and revenue earning potential for the service providers. Besides, the subscribers would be able to get improved service flexibly and economically.

The trial for SSP (SSP functionality implemented in C-DOT SBM Exchange) with Toll - Free Phone Service was launched in MTNL (Delhi) network at Karol Bagh on the occasion of the 50th Anniversary of India's Independence and subsequently in Calcutta Network. The toll-free phone service aims at providing the subscribers charge-free access to MTNL officers. IN services based on C-DOT technology are now proposed to be provided at Ahmedabad, Chennai, Bangalore, Hyderabad, Jaipur, Lucknow, Patna and Pune.

*V 5.1/5.2 interface for C-DOT Switches:-* C-DOT worked on V5.2 interface which is an emerging concept for connecting Access Network Product (ANP) to the main exchange. This interface can serve different type of interfaces including radio system of the "Wireless In Local Loop (WILL)"

C-DOT is implementing the standardized protocols related to V 5. 1 /V 5.2 to interface access network with C-DOT switches. This will help in interconnecting various access technologies to C-DOT exchanges. Currently, the product is under system validation and its interface with C-DOTs composite MUX to provide remoting features for POTs and ISDN (basic rate) subscribers has been established in the lab.

*Composite MUX (remote line concentrator):-* A 120 line unit is under development which will serve both analog and ISDN subscribers. This remote line concentrator has connection to the C-DOT main exchange or remote BM (Base Module) using V 5.2 interface. Another version of the unit with V 5.1 interface can function as a multiplexer. The equipment will be available in two versions- Wall mounted and Desktop.

*Asynchronous transfer mode (ATM) system:-* The Asynchronous Transfer Mode (ATM) is an emerging technology for meeting broadband transmission and switching requirements. The first prototype ATM cross-connect switch has been designed.

*Fibre access system (FAS):-* Lab realization work progressed further. The equipment would provide Fibre To The Curb (FTTC) and Fibre To The Home (FTTH) solutions in the access part of the telecom network. Some hardware sub modules were tested and other modules are in various stages of design. Software subsystems are under development.

*Synchronous digital hierarchy (SDH) system:-* These projects constitute a series of products namely, STM-1, STM-4, Digital Access Cross-connect (DACCS) and Network Management System. The development of these products are in different stages of product cycle. While, the STM is in the internal validation stage, the STM-4 and DACCS are in the lab realization stage.

Digital Enhanced Cordless Technology (DECT) System:- This system provides Wireless In the Local Loop (WILL) solutions both in the urban and in the rural scenarios. While on solution uses Base Station Controller (BSC), Base Station Units (BSU) and remote radio units, the other uses an interface card in the remote line of the TDMA system the later can serve wireless subscribers instead or wired subscribers usually supported by TDMA. Both the systems are in the final stages of lab integration.

*Field & manufacturing support*

To reassure its manufacturers on C-DOT support, many workshops and discussions were held with the manufacturers. C-DOT continued to provide product support to 21,000 switches with 5.8 million lines of C-DOT technology in the network in terms of upgradation, retrofitting and training to field staff. C-DOT continued its interaction with the manufacturers and field installations for providing all types of maintenance support.

***TEC clearance received***

Bulk production clearance was received for ASIC Based Signal Processing (ISP - Integrated Signal Processing) card after field trial at Ambala and other sites in Haryana. This card will replace the existing Signalling Processor Card (SPC) being used in 256P RAX, SBM RRAX, MAX-L and MAX-XL.

Bulk production clearance was received for high performance version of existing IOP (after field trials at Haldwani MAX-L) used with SBM RAX, MAX-L and MAX-XL exchanges (IOP-VII) developed with the entire control circuitry implemented on a single PCB and more powerful CPU. This will make the equipment more reliable and easy to maintain.

Clearance for the S/W link 1-4-5.43-3 was received after successful field trials at Hoshiarpur (MAXL), Dasua

(MAX-M) and Indira Nagar (MAX-XL). Some of the features supported in the link are:

— Regional ('90' level) barring.

— 16 PCM connectivity between RSU and the main exchange.

— IOP booting from the unix cartridge.

Clearance for the S/W link 1-4-2.25-4 was received after successful field trials at Sonepat (Haryana). Some of the features supported in the link are :

— Metering and detailed billing on junctions.

— Call saving on bus failure.

— Calling line identification.

— Centralised Automated Message Accounting (CAMA).

Clearance for the S/W link 1-4-8.1-3 was received after successful field trials at Ratlam (M.P.) and Kharagpur (West Bengal). The release supports

— SS7 and Network Synchronisation

— Clearance was received for SBM RAX based on "XL" hardware.

— Non-A/C RSU was accorded clearance after successful field trial.

— Technology approval was accorded for C-DOT NSE (Network Synchronisation Equipment) after successful field trial for use as standalone equipment in E-10B exchanges.

— Technology approval was accorded for C-DOT NSC (Network Synchronisation Controller) after, successful field trial for integration and use in C-DOT MAX-XL and TAX-XL exchange configurations.

— Clearance for the SM link 2-1 -1 was received for 256P RAX.

— ESL card supporting 16 PCM connectivity between the main exchange and the RSU (MAX-L) was given clearance.

— Functional clearance was received for Enhanced Subscriber Unit (ESU), used as Calling Line Identification (CLI) unit with PC interface.

— Clearance was received for ISDN CPEs (Customer Premises Equipment) namely, NT310 (Network Termination) and TA210 (Terminal Adapter).

— Clearance was obtained for propagating COMAC (Centralise Operation and Maintenance Centre) software package for 256PRAX in field.

— Clearance was obtained for propagating BMON (Bill Monitoring) software package for bill monitoring function for MAX.

**Standards and specifications**

*GRs finalised:-* PTC Thermistor for use on MDF; Digital Loop Carrier System (DLC) on SDH; Bill Processing system for INET Phase II; Frame Relay switch; Router; Internet Service Provider; Frame Relay Access Device; Smart Card Payphones; Smart Card Pay Phone Control Unit; Smart Card Pay Phone Management System; Boss-Secretary Telephone System; Pocket sized Card Reader for Smart card Payphone systems; Key Telephone System; Intelligent Network Application Part-National standard; NT1 for interface approval; C-DOT Trunk Automatic Exchange-XL; Noise Figure Meter; Digital Radio Measurement System; Stand Alone Synchronisation Equipment; Electromagnetic Compatibility Standard; Multi Protocol Frame Relay Concentrator; Managed Leased Line Network; 2048 KBPS Line Driver;

ATM/Frame Relay Protocol Analyser; Aerial Optical Fibre; National Internet Backbone; Store and Forward Fax Service; Line Jack Unit; Indian Script Code for Language Paging; Indian Script Code for Language Paging Devanagri/Marathi; Indian Script Code for Language Paging Gujarati; Subscriber Service Unit for calling Line Identification Purpose.

*GRs revised/amended/Errata:-* Saddles for fitting Cl brackets and struts of tublars poles; Angle Iron Ties; Caps for tublar poles; Mole Skin; Iron line stores; Bracket and Plastic insulated telephone stalk; HDPE pipes; Brace Angle Iron; Saddle for fitting Angle Iron Guard Bracket on Hamilton Tubes A & B; Coupling of different types of Clamp for couplings; 10/20 pair DP with 10 pair Quick connection (IDC) Drop wire module and casing; GD Tubes for Internal/External use; FRP Moulded DP Box 10 & 20 pairs with moulded tag block; Discrete Connectors; Intelligent Network Services; TR Billing Hardware; VSAT based distance Education system; V.32 bis modem card; Voice band data modem (V.29); ISP equipment dimensioning/configuration; Amendment No.1 to Single pair/10 pair Screened PCM Cable for Inter bay digital equipment wiring; Additional climatic and environmental tests for Electronic Push Button Telephone for 98-99 procurement; ISDN Customer Premises Equipment; Large size local cum Tandem Digital Switching system; National routing, switching and numbering plan; Wireless local loop System; PCM MUX equipment; 2/ 8 Mb/s Direct Digital MUX; Third Order Digital MUX. equipment; Fourth Order Digital MUX. equipment: 2/34 Mb/s Direct Digital MUX; MDF for 512 lines and above; Commercial System; TR Billing and Accounting System.

*GRs withdrawn:-* Cable paper core unit twin lead sheathed armoured; Cable paper core star quad trunk armoured; Cable paper core star quad local armoured;

Cable paper insulated PE sheathed Al moisture barrier with steel tape armouring and PE jacket; Cable lead sheathed PCUT PE protected un-armoured; Copper wire for UG cable 1955 spec.; Insulating or wrapping paper used in telephone cables; Lead sheath for UG telephone cables; Steel tapes used in UG telephone cables; Jute (hessian cloth) used in dry Core telephone cables; Bitumen base filling compound; Copper strips for wires, copper and copper weld; House Bracket; Compression sleeve for making crimped joint for 2.12 mm GI wire and drop wire; RCC sockets forming the bottom sockets - section of hamilton poles; CT Box Intl 6 pairs; Cable Terminal Box 20 pairs External; Asbestos cement ducts; Self supporting PVC Drop Wire with integral barrier; PE insulated and sheath with GI wire as integral barrier; Voice band data modem (V.29); 2400/1200/300 bps voice band data modem cards with addendum; Videotex terminal; Add-on unit to Coin box Telephone (CBT-80); Single Channel VHF system; 2/15 Shared Radio System (Issue-02); 2/15 Shared Radio System (Issue-04); 4/36 Analogue MARR; Development spec. for PCM cable for 2 Mb/s digital line; Development spec. for PCM cable for 2 MB/s digital system; Programming Loading Coil; General specification for all testing instruments; Digital Multimeter; Base Band Data Modem; STD Coin Collection Box; Line Jack Unit for Termination Telephone Line amendment; Quarter Modular Line Cord; Electronic Telephone Instrument; Add on Unit to Coin Box Telephone; Card Vending Machine; Disposable Smart Card; Monitoring and Control System for Direct Exchange Line.

*Engineering guidelines issued for:-* Frame Relay Service through Inet Phase II; Integration of INET Phase-I equipment into INET Phase II network; For X.75 gateway for connecting other Data networks to Inot: PSTN Access Procedure in Inet Phase 11; Digital Satellite Phone

Terminal (DSPT); CCS-7 implementation; Internet connectivity for DOT, Space/power requirements for ATM equipment; 18 GHz Digital M/W system; "90" dialling scheme within LDCA; INMARSAT-VPT numbering, routing plan; Switching and Routing Plan for Cellular Mobile Telephone Services.

*Test schedule prepared for:-* SDH Analyser 1/4/16; NT interface approval; SSU (Subscriber Service Unit); CLIP (Calling Line Identification Presentation); ISDN Customer Premises Equipment; PTC Thermistor; FRP DP Box 10/20 pairs with moulded tag block; ISDN Protocol tester; 16 KHz Metering PUIse Analyser; Key Telephone System; CMTS Monitoring for circles; Point of interconnection test; Public Mobile Radio Trunking Service; Cellular Mobile Telephone Services; Network Termination Equipment; Installation of Accessory and Fixure for installation of self Supporting Metal Free Aerial Optical Fibre Cable; Terminal Adapter; Multipath Fade Simulator; IR between PSTN and Network of licensed service providers interface at 2048 kbps.

***Testing, field trial and validation of new technology system and products***

Barring and detailed billing for 90/98 level in C-DOT SBM, RAX and MAX-L exchange and for level 90 in new technology exchanges; Software link 1-4-5, 43-3 supporting dynamic barring and detailed billing over level 90 for C-DOT, SBM, MAX-L, MAX-XL exchange; C-DOT MAX-XL software with link 1-4-8.1-3 with dynamic barring and detailed billing for level 90; C-DOT ISP and IOP card; Synchronisation of C-DOT MAX-XL exch. to increase the modem Data rate of Subs; C-DOT exch. for bill monitoring functionality (BMON), C-DOT NSE 2.0 (Network Synchronisation Equipment); Non-A/C RSU of CDOT, CLI P facility in C-DOT MAX-L at Sonepat with software Link 1-4-2.25-4; 16 PCM RSU connectivity for

C-DOT MAX-L; Environmental testing of C-DOT Network Synchronisation Equipment (NSE); Environmental testing on CCS-7 unit of C-DOT, Technology approval for C-DOT-NSC (Networking Synchronisation Controller) in MAX-XL exchanges; 10 digit CLI in FETEX 100L switching system; Software patch for 1/3 tariff for FETEX 150; Pending points of validation in 5ESS Exchange; Tandem working for 5ESS system; PRI interface in 5ESS; Software patch in EWSD switching systems; Software version 9 in EWSD local exchange; ISDN PC card of M/s CMC; Line parameter measurements on ISDN lines; CCS7 and ISDN interworking of NEAX-61 E; International ISDN; national and International roaming for Mobile Services; IIT developed WLL system based on DECT Technology; Field trial of DECTWLL system of M/s Ericsson at New Delhi; VSAT services; Ku band Hub Station Equipment except HPA in association with QA at ISL, Bangalore tested; STM-4 in ring Configuration and Point to Point of M/sAlcatel at Hyderabad; ADM-1 of M/s Fibcom. completed; ADM-4 of M/s Fibcom. Gurgaon; Field trial of STM-16 of M/s Fibcom at Bombay; Optical fibre Splicing machine of M/s Seven Hills Optic Communication, Calcutta; Pending points of CDTMX at Chennai; New features of CTMX system of ITI; Testing of AMS (Alarm Management System), DEL (Digital Error Logger) and DPM (Digital Performance Monitoring) in the Telestra NMS system at Chennai; Voice Mail/Audiotex services of M/s Sawarkar Telecom Pvt. Ltd.; Video conferencing over ISDN at 128 Kbps between TEC, N.D. and BRBBRAITT, Jabalpur; Video Conferencing at 364 Kbps; CSMS (Customer Services Management System) offered by MTNL at Bhikaji Cama Place for commercial and billing modules; Credit Card Authorisation service; 20 GHz Signal Generator and VSWR test set of M/s Meera Agencies; Frame Relay Access Device (FRAD) of M/s PCL, New Delhi; 2.7 GHz synthesized Signal Generator of M/s HP India; ISDN feature Phone in OCB-283 and F-150 exchanges; New features for EWSD technology against 1.3 m tender; Validation of NEAX-61 E exchange at Modinagar; Validation of FETEX-1 50 exchange Version 4.0 for CCS7, Supplementary Services, Charge Band and ILT features; STM-1 6 of M/s Fibcom; Chandigarh Commercial System; Commercial modules and TRA modules of APSOFT of A.P Telecom Circle at Hyderabad; Digital Line Concentrator of M/s MIC; C-DOT SBM RAX based on XL hardware with software 1-4-5.43-3 with IOP-VH; Validation software developed by Indore Telecom District for recording of traffic measurements in EWSD TAX on hourly basis for CCR study; DCME equipment installed between Delhi and Mumbai; C-DOT, TDMA-PMP system; WLL, CDMA technology field trial; Validation of 11 GHz, 140 Mbps Microwave equipment of M/s NATELCO Nasik.

*Network planning/engineering*

Planning of PON network based on optical fibre technology in rural communication; Proposal identified to provide reliable Telecom Services to the rural sector with high demand and potential growth at Ludhiana Telecom Distt.; Memorandum to Telecom Commission in respect of pilot project on "Distance Learning and Remote Library access" as Asia Pacific Telecommunity Bangkok Project prepared; Engineering guidelines for x TDMA PMP System; Data Analysis for the Propagation Measurement at Mumbai; New Humidity and Temp. Sensor procured from USA tested at Chingelputte; Data Analysis for the Propagation Measurement at Mumbai.

*Field support*

Distributed COMMANDIR package to various places and provided support for installation; Enquiry Module of Commandir (2 Exch. Ver.) modified as per the requirements given by Bhavnagar Telecom Distt.;

Synchronisation of OCB Jullandhar with OCB TAX Karolbagh, N.Delhi; Synchronisation of Bhopal OCBTAX with Bombay EWSDTAX and OCI3 TAX Karolbagh, N.Delhi; Supplied IMA Ves. MS software of El OB exchange to different places; Distributed E-1 OB maintenance Advisor package to various field units; Developed and tested and provided assistances for implementing E-10B software for 8 digit depth analysis; Provided technical support in E-10B upgradation of 2L version software; Supplied Exec., Real data and SDF tapes to Chirala, Okhla and Pathankot El OB exchanges; Provided technical assistance in upgration of local EWSD exch. at CUFF Prade to patch status 17V; Implemented upgraded software in EWSDTAX at Raipur and Ahemdabad; Modified FOCIN command for Network Management System implemented at Delhi Gate exch. for field trial; CCS7 introduced between Ratlam, Bhopal and More; Instructions on ISDN testing; CLIP software supplied to Calcutta Telephones; BNRC (Back up National Reference Clock Centre) at Karol Bagh, handed over to MTNL, New Delhi; Issued Implementation procedure of CLI in E10B exchange; Status of CCS7 links in New Technology exchange consolidated addressed.

*Field problem solved*

International ISDN access from Kanpur; Call failure on C7-R2 interworking at Bhopal OCB-283 DTAX; Analysis of nature of Address indicator in OCB Tandem Exchange-, CCS7 interworking between EWSD MSG and OCIB -Tandern; Creating CCS-7 signalling link over satellite media in OCB TAX Calcutta; CCS7 interworking between C-DOT, SEIM and OCB 283 exchanges at Shimla; Signalling Transfer Point (STP) function introduced in MTNL Delhi Network for CCs-7 working in AXE-10 exch. at Nehru Place; in EWSD TAX at Ahemdabad; Disconnection of Dial tone at Delhi Gate E1013 exch.; False alarm from BT rack at Nehru Place El

08 exch.; Non-functioning of status for dynamic STID at Jammu E10B exch.; For OCHALA printout at E-10B exchange Bhatinda; Creation of new file by data correction in MTR file at E-1 08 Guwahati exchange; Corruption in ADB in E-10B exchange Dehradun by data correction in TR files; Restored DI Nehru Place exchange OMC by using OMC backup; File creation at Dilshad Garden E-10B exchange Delhi by data correction in catalogue file; Prepared Exec. tape for Hoshiarpur E-1 OB exchange; Unstable link between E-10B exchange and OMC at Gorakhpur; Non-supression of Directory nos. and wrong announcement on incoming calls at Karolbagh E-10B exch.; Initialisation of TR due to corruption in Catalogue file solved by disk data correction in E-10B Kanpur; Creation of SR5 subscriber due to corruption in TMNE file solved by OMC data modification in E-10B Kotakapura.

*Tender evaluation*

Procurement of solid state disk drive/Winchester drive for the replacement of UD50 disk drive at E-10B software centre; Procurement of PCM analyser; Procurement of software for TEC LAN; Assisted Telecom Commission in evaluation of the tender 6 GHz and 11 GHz SDH Microwave equipment; ADB tender for Rural communication for Eastern U.P; For procurement of Line Drivers and stand alone enclosure; Procurement of UPS system and laser printer; Assisted MTNL Delhi in evaluation of the tender for Managed Leased Data Network (MLDN); Router; 1.69 million line tender for local exchange.

*Other activities*

13 GHz 34 Mbps digital radio system installed at MTNL Mumbai; Impact of Y2 K problem in DOT reviewed; Technical paper prepared on "Spectrum issues for Radio based PCS"; Test report for Roaming in CMTS using STP

sent to VAS cell; Seminar on ISDN, OCB 283, ATM, INET and SDH Network on Video Conferencing between BRBRAITT Jabalpur and New Delhi as part of distance learning; List of specifications and equipments finalised for Multimedia Project; Multimedia Kit installation completed; Presentation on TEC LAN on UTP demonstrating access to TEC Web pages on Intranetware, Unix Server and Internet was given at TEC computer Lab. to ADET Trainees of ALTTC Ghaziabad; Multiparity Video Conferencing demonstration among TEC Delhi, MTNL Bombay, TTC Jabalpur and Bangalore Telephone District; Updated the Internet TEC Web Pages; Analysis of Ku band propagation data for calculation of Annual exceedance and worst month statistics completed; Seminar on ATM was organised at Bombay, in coordination with MTNL, Bombay; Specifications for Pentium PCs, Laserjet, Printers, Modems and UPS System; The PSX loaded with new software release supporting Frame Relay and their configuration updated at ALTTC; Modified guidelines for Inet Ph I and Ph II connectivity and sent for field trial.

*Comments provided on*

National Preparatory Committee (NPC) to the World Radio Communication Conference; Final report of the working group on fixed services for allocation of exclusive bandwidth for higher density fixed services in 40 GHz and 50 GHz band.

*Type approval issued*

| | |
|---|---|
| Type Approvals | 646 |
| Interface Approvals | 318 |
| Source/Compatibility Approval | 23 |
| Service Test Certificates | 268 |

Telecom factories

The Telecom factories previously known as P&T

Workshops are as old as Indian Telegraph itself. The oldest workshop was set up at Alipore, Calcutta as a repair workshop in 1855. It gradually started production of Telegraph and Telecom equipments required by the Department. At present there are seven Telecom Factories located at Mumbai, Calcutta (Alipore & Gopalpur), Jabalpur (Wright Town & Richhai), Bhilai and Kharagpur. The factories are Central Government units like Ordnance factories and Railway workshops.

*Production*

The main products of the factories are as under

(a) Telecom factory, Mumbai

(i) C.D. Cabinets

(ii) C.T Box

(iii) Support Bracket

(iv) Private Wire Relay Set

(v) D.P. Box

(vi) MDFs

(vii) Line Jack Units

(viii) Modems

(ix) Electronic Relay Plates

(x) Pay Phones

*(b) Telecom factory, Culcutta (Alipore)*

(i) Bracket Channel Iron

(ii) Buttenski Telephone

(iii) C.D. Cabinets

(iv) C.TBox

(v) D.P.Box

(vi) Line Jack Units

(vii) MDFs

(viii) Microwave Towers/TTH Tower

(ix) Mast 40/15 Meter

(x) Personal Computer (Supply and Maintenance)

(xi) Repair of E-1 OB/C-DoT Cards

(xii) Repair of Telephone Instruments

(xiii) Stalks

(xiv) Support Bracket

(xv) U-Back

*(c) Telecom factory, Calcutta (Gopalpur)*

(i) Galvanising Operation

(ii) Microwave Towers

(iii) Masts

(d) Telecom factory, Kharagpur

(i) Sockets.

(ii) Sole Plates

(iii) Saddles.

(iv) Special Alloy Castings for Exports

*(e) Telecom factory, Jabalpur (wright town)*

(i) Tubes (Riveted).

(ii) Bracket Channel Iron.

(iii) Stalks.

(iv) C.D.Cabinets.

(v) Line Jack Units.

(vi) Microwave Towers/TTH Towers

(vii) Repair of C-DOT Cards

(viii) Masts 40/15 Meter

(ix) Repair of Telephone Instruments

(x) Support Bracket

(xi) U-Back

***(f) Telecom factory, Jabalpur (Richhai)***

(i) Tubes (Welded)

(ii) Galvanising Operation

***(g) Telecom factory, Bhilai***

(i) Microwave Towers/TTH Towers

(ii) Mast 15 Meter

Telecom factories are under the charge of Chief General Managers in Senior Administrative Grade. CGM, Telecom factory, Mumbai is incharge of Mumbai factory. CGM, Telecom factory, Jabalpur is incharge of Wright Town (Jabalpur) and Bhilai Units. CGM, Telecom factory, Calcutta is incharge of Alipore, Gopalpur & Kharagpur Units. CGM, Telecom factory, Richhai is incharge of Richhai (Jabalpur) unit.

***Staff strength***

The staff strength of the factories as on 31-3-98 is as the next page:-

| Unit (TF) | Gr'A' | G r'B' | Gr'C' | G r'D' | Sub-Total | Indus-trial | Total |
|---|---|---|---|---|---|---|---|
| Mumbai | 17 | 2B | 287 | 117 | 449 | 1096 | 1545 |
| Alipore | 13 | 26 | 267 | 134 | 440 | 1106 | 1546 |
| Gopalpur | 2 | 4 | 12 | 1 | 19 | 96 | 115 |
| Kharagpur | 6 | 10 | 31 | 23 | 70 | 261 | 331 |
| Wright Town | 16 | 22 | 197 | 132 | 367 | 994 | 1361 |
| Richhai | 11 | 11 | 67 | 58 | 147 | 478 | 625 |
| Bhilai | 4 | 6 | 32 | 35 | 77 | 152 | 229 |
| Total | 69 | 107 | 893 | 500 | 1569 | 4183 | 5752 |

*Financial Achievement of Telecom Factories for the year 1997-98.*

(Figures in Crores)

| Sl. No. | Telecom Factory | Target 1997-98 | Turnover 1997-98 |
|---|---|---|---|
| i. | Mumbai | 45.00 | 41.00 |
| ii. | Calcutta | 56.00 | 64.60 |
| iii. | Kharagpur | 4.00 | 2.86 |
| iv. | Wright Town (Jabalpur) | 55.00 | 47.08 |
| v. | Richhai (Jabalpur) | 27.00 | 21.19 |
| vi. | Bhilai | 11.00 | 11.76 |
| Total | | 198.00 | 188.49 |

Physical Performance: Achievement in respect of important items is as indicated below:

| SL.No. | Items | Achievements 1997-98 |
|---|---|---|
| (1) Telecom factory, Mumbai | | |
| i. | C.D.Cabinets of Sorts | 8525 |
| ii. | C.T. Box 100 Pairs | 61670 |
| iii. | D.P.Boxes 10/20 Pairs | 136400 |
| iv. | Line Jack Unit | 770000 |
| v | Pay Phones | 3240 |
| vi. | MIDFs | 1635 |
| vii. | Modems | 450 |
| (2) | Telecom factory, Calcutta and Gopalpur | |
| i. | D.P. Boxes of sorts | 96050 |
| ii. | C.T. Box 100 pairs | 70668 |
| iii. | 15 M Masts | 4918 |
| iv | Bkt.Ch. Iron 4 Wire | 832500 |
| v | Microwave Towers | 1362 |
| vi. | Buttenski Telephone | 8225 |

| | | |
|---|---|---|
| vii. | MDF of Sorts | 1783 |
| viii. | Stalks of Sorts | 370000 |
| ix. | C.D.Cabinets of Sorts | 3179 |
| x. | U-Back | 1116500 |
| xi. | Line Jack Unit | 700890 |
| xii. | CBT - 80 | 2039 |
| xiii. | Support Bracket | 267000 |
| (3) | Telecom factory, Khagarpur | |
| i. | Socket'B | 32083 |
| ii. | Saddles | 815000 |
| iii. | Sole Plate | 124000 |
| (4) | Telecom factory (wright town), (Jabalpur) | |
| i. | Tubes B-8 Equv. (Rivetted) | 310260 |
| ii. | C.D. Cabinets of Sorts | 3563 |
| iii. | Stalks of Sorts | 378000 |
| iv. | Bkt. Ch. Iron 4 Wire | 469000 |
| v. | Microwave Towers | 2837 M.Tons |
| vi. | Line Jack Unit | 336400 |
| vii. | U-Back464000 | |
| viii. | Masts 15 M | 958 nos. |
| ix. | Masts 40 M | 101 |
| x. | Support Bracket | 183750 |
| (5) | Telecom factory- Richhai, Jabalpur | |
| i. | Tubes B-8 Equivalent (Welded) | 336530 |
| (6) | Telcom factory, Bhilai | |
| i. | Microwave Towers | 3025 M Tones |
| ii. | 15 M Masts | 705 Nos. |

***Role of telecom factories***

As in-house production units, Telecom factories are a source of uninterrupted supply and can be depended upon for extra supplies in the event of shortfall in supply from private sources apart from ensuring fair price in respect of certain items being supplied both by Telecom factories and the private manufacturers. Telecom factories have adapted modern production processes to achieve quality production and cost reduction so as to stand in competition with private companies. Product diversification is given due emphasis to utilise the available infrastructure and manpower. Factories have now entered new areas like Repair of cards, Telephone Instruments, Computers etc.

Following new items have been productionised during 1997-98:

i. CBT-95

ii. Support Bracket

iii. **TTH Towers**

Telecom quality assurance

The Telecom Quality Assurance Organisation of the Department of Telecommunications was formed in 1979 as a part of Technical and Development Circle but later became as an independent Telecom Quality Assurance Circle in 1986. Telecom Quality Assurance Circle has been one of the most vital Organisations covering all aspects of Quality-Assurance work thereby enabling standardisation and uniformity of approach and procedures. It is entrusted with the responsibility of assuring quality on a wide range of products and equipments inducted into Telecom network. To carry out the above work, the Telecom Quality Assurance Circle with Headquarters at Bangalore, functions with 84 Quality Assurance Centres located all over India and two Apex Laboratories namely, the Telecom Testing Laboratory (TTL) and Component Approval Centre for

Telecom (CACT). The TTL has also three branches at New Delhi, Hyderabad and Calcutta.

*Activities*

(i) Value of stores accepted during 1997-98 is Rs. 55,326 Millions.

(ii) One new QA Centres opened at Hyderabad (M/s. XL Telecom Ltd., Mallapur, Hyderabad-74).

(iii) 148 Infrastructure Assessments carried out for conventional products and 140 for TEC products.

(iv) 528 Type Approval Certificates issued.

(v) 11 nos. of Major Quality problems identified based on QA testing/Field feedback.

(vi) Approved Inspection Scheme introduced for 6 products.

(vii) Delegated Inspection Scheme introduced for 8 products.

(viii) First Product Qualification testing completed for 163 products.

(ix) 52 Telecom products taken up for Maintenance Approval.

(x) No. Important Meetings held - 21 and No. of Meetings where Senior QA Officers participated - 35.

(xi) 4 Documents issued during the year as Quality Manuals on various Telecom Products.

(xii) Rs. 1080.95 Lakh of Non-plan and Rs. 64.81 Lakh of Plan expenditure incurred during the year.

*New facilities added in TTL/CACT*

— Profile Projector has been procured and installed for inspection of PCBs.

— Tensile test machine of OFC Lab has been installed.

— Columns of High Performance Liquid Chromatography System have been added.

— Test programme has been done for testing 59 new components.

— Maintenance free battery for 3 KVA UPS System has been received to install at FA lab. of CACT

— Flash point and drop point tester for testing PHF/OF Cables Jellies has been installed in FA Lab. of CACT.

*Activities of CACT*

— 24,333 Components tested as part of Surveillance/ Approval/FA activities.

— 477 Component Approvals issued.

— 14 Component Manufactures infrastructure Assessed.

— 27,995 Chamber hours utilised for climatic and environmental tests.

— 240 components were subjected to failure analysis.

— 45 reports generated by SCRAM.

— 82 Source Approval Certificate for raw material issued.

— 630 Nos. of Components/Equipments subjected to environmental tests.

*UNDP project*

Six Numbers of ITU-UNDP seminars were conducted at CACT, Bangalore with the help of foreign experts.

*Seminars and meetings*

QA Circle participated in 5 Seminars/Training programmes conducted by outside agencies. Training programmes on Quality and Reliability matters conducted by Telecom QA Circle, for the benefit of its personnel.

*World telecom day*

World Telecommunications Day was celebrated on 17th May, 1997. The CACT Laboratories were kept open for School/College students.

**Personnel**

*Staff employment*

The total number of staff employed and their distribution in different services is indicated in Table 14 of the Report. The total staff employed at the end of the year was 4.25 lakhs as compared to 4.29 lakhs during the last year. This includes staff in MTNL and industrial workers in the telecommunication factories also.

Scheduled castes and scheduled tribes

There were 74639 Scheduled Castes and 19920 Scheduled Tribes employees in the Department as on 31.3.1998. This includes 1579 sweepers.

*Women employees*

At the end of the year there were 53783 women employees out of total of 4.25 lakh employees in the Department.

*Human resource development- training*

Keeping in view rapid technological innovations and changes in the Telecom Sector, training programmes are organised so as to continuously upgrade and update the knowledge and skills of the telecom personnel. The strategy adopted by the Department in this direction comprises

(i) Strengthening and modernizing the training infrastructure.

(ii) Evolving appropriate training methodology for various cadres.

(iii) Deputing personnel for training to institutions in developed countries to acquire knowledge and expertise in latest technologies in Telecom field.

*Training infrastructure*

Presently the Department has 44 Telecom Training Centres comprising two apex level training centres namely, ALTTC, Ghaziabad and BRBRAITT, Jabalpur for training of telecom professionals and engineers, 15 Regional Telecom Training Centres (RTTCs) located at different regions in the country to provide training to supervisory staff of the Department and 27 CTTCs/DTTCs to cater to the training needs of field personnel.

In addition to above, temporary branch Telecom Training Centres in various circles were continued wherever necessary to expedite the training of staff in Restructured Cadres.

The training equipment at various training centres is upgraded continuously to keep pace with changing technology. Video Conferencing facility was also provided between BRBRAITT Jabalpur and TEC New Delhi during 1997-98.

*Personnel trained*

A total of 69,084 personnel were trained in various training centres during the year 1997- 98. This includes 144 foreigners trained in ALTTC, Ghaziabad and BRBRAITT Jabalpur. The details are given in Table 16. 67 Officers of the Department were deputed abroad during 1997-98 for training in modem switching, transmission technologies and management. 52 Officers of the Department were deputed for seminars and courses conducted by other departments and outside agencies.

***Training under restructure scheme***

Training for restructured cadres of Phone Mechanic, Telecom Technical Assistant (TTA) and Senior Telecom Operating Assistants is in progress. A total of 29531 Phone Mechanics, 4106 TTAs and 11224 Sr. TOAs were trained during the year 1997-98.

***Training development activities***

A UNDP Project in the area of Quality-Assurance to enhance Quality-Assurance capabilities of the Department of Telecom has just been completed. The project was widely appreciated by agencies including UNDP & ITU and above all by the manufacturers of Telecom components who have attained better confidence in production of Telecom components with much better quality.

A UNDP Project in the area of HRD & Management, which was launched in November-1 996, picked up momentum during the current financial year 1997-98 wherein the following achievements were made:-

(i) Officers deputed for Study Tour and Fellowships= 30

(ii) Experts/Consultants including CTA arrived in India = 15.5 manmonths

(iii) Equipment procured for ALTTC = Protocol analyser

**Progress of special sub-plan**

***Tribal sub-plan***

The Department has formulated Tribal Sub- Plan (TSP) as a part of the 9th Five Year Plan for providing telecom facilities in the tribal areas. For all round and faster development of Telecom facilities in tribal areas, the Department is treating these areas as special focus areas. The main objectives of the tribal sub-plan are:-

(i) To provide the telephone facility practically on demand in tribal areas by end of 9th plan.

(ii) To provide NSD facility to all exchanges in Tribal areas by end of 9th plan.

(iii) To provide public telephones in all tribal villages by the end of 9th plan.

*Financial outlay and actual expenditure*

The approved plan outlay for TSP for 1997-98 was Rs. 591.15 Crores (R.E.). The actual expenditure during 1997-98 was Rs. 468.74 Crores.

*Physical targets and achievements*

Statement showing the Physical Targets and Achievements during 1997-98 and Targets for 1998-99 are given in Table 12 of the Statistical Supplement.

*Special component plan for the development of north eastern region*

The Department of Telecom is giving special attention to the rapid development of telecom facilities in the NE Region of the country. During 1997-98 there was net addition of 78,614 lines of Telephone switching capacity, 59507 direct exchange lines and 2977 village public telephones. As on 31.3.98, all the 7 North Eastern States namely Arunachal Pradesh, Manipur, Meghalaya, Mizoram, Nagaland, Tripura and Assam had 100% electronic telephone exchanges. During 1998-99, 113200 lines of net switching capacity, 82000 direct exchange lines and 3900 village public telephones are planned to be provided in the North Eastern region.

*National capital region (NCR)*

In order to decongest the National Capital and to reduce the population pressure on it, National Capital Region consisting of 20 priority towns and 5 counter magnet towns spreading to 5 States surrounding the National Capital is getting special attention for development of infrastructure facilities including the telecom facilities in these towns. During 1997-98 Department of Telecom has provided 75656 lines of Telephone switching capacity and 83430 direct exchange lines in the Region.

During the 9th Plan period, all efforts will be made to improve the telecom facilities of NCR and to introduce various value added services to make it at par with Delhi, which is one of the demands of the NCR Planning Board. Also, it is aimed to make the telephone available on demand at the earliest during the 9th Plan period in the entire NCR region.

*Use of Hindi*

During the period under report O.L. Branch followed Rules & Regulations prescribed by the Department of Official Language. The main activities of the O.L. Branch were as given below:-

(i) Acquainted all the Telecom Circles/Administrative Off ices/Undertakings with the O.L. Act, Rules and instructions issued thereunder for their compliance for achieving the targets fixed by O.L. Department in their Annual Programme for the year under report.

(ii) Reviewed the Quarterly Progress Report regarding progressive use of Hindi received from all the Sections of DOT (Hq.) and all the Telecom Circles/ other Admn. Offices/Undertakings etc. and took necessary corrective measures in respect of those wherein defects were noticed.

(iii) Provided Hindi information through Hindi Vishesh Seva (177) and monitored thereof. Now this service has been extended by the Department in 30 cities.

(iv) Arranged nomination for Hindi training for those Officers/Officials who had not acquired working knowledge of Hindi. Similarly, Stenographers/

Typist who had not undergone training in Hindi Stenography/Typing were nominated for the above respective training courses.

(v) Carried out inspections of Telecom Circles/Admn. Offices/Undertakings to ensure as to what extent the provisions of O.L. Act/Rules and instructions issued thereunder were strictly adhered to. About 6 inspections were carried out during the year under review.

(vi) As usual Hindi Day/Week/Fortnight was organised from 1.9.97 to 15.9.97 which is a regular activity of every year prescribed by Deptt. of Official Language.

(vii) An Akhil Bhartiya Rajbhasha Sammelane was organised in D.O.T (HO) on 7th November 1997.

(viii) O.L. Branch works as a Co-ordinator from DOT (Hq.) during the course of inspections of Circles etc. by Committees of Parliament on Official Language which is also a regular feature every year. About 12 inspections were carried out by Committee of Parliament on Official Language during 97-98. Parliamentary Committee also inspected D.O.T (HQ) during the year under report.

(ix) Translated all the documents in Hindi/English specified in Section 3(3) of Official Language Act 1963 and Official Language Rule 1976, all the papers/reports to be laid by DOT on the table in both the Houses of Parliament.

(x) Four quarterly meetings of the Department Official Language Implementation Committee were held during the period under review.

(xi) A Hindi workshop for five days was conducted in D.O.T (HQ) to remove hesitation of officials in doing their daily official work in Hindi.

***Welfare and sports activities***

An amount of Rs. 4.75 crore has been provided for the Welfare & Sports activities to the Department of Telecommunications during the year 1997-98. An amount of Rs. 4,46,20,771/- has been disbursed to different Circles/U nits for meeting their Welfare& Sports expenditure from April '97 to March '98.

The following important schemes for grant of financial assistance from Welfare fund to the Telecom employees or their dependent have been formulated and are being enjoyed by our employees and their dependent as the case may be.

a) Financial assistance to the dependent of deceased employees.

b) Supply of sewing machines to the families of deceased employees.

c) Financial assistance in cases of death of casual labourers (temporary status mazdoor); in case of death of retired employees; in prolonged illness cases of employees; in serious illness/magi operations etc.; on account of prolonged illness of the dependent of employees; for nutritive diet for TB patients; by way of loans in emergency cases; to victims of natural calamities; handicapped for purchase of artificial limbs; to handicapped children on account of transport/ hostel mess charges; towards railway fares from headquarters to artificial limb centre.

d) Scholarships and awards.

e) Book awards and incentives to meritorious children.

f) Grant-in-aid to Recreation/Sports club.

g) Holiday excursion trips.

There is a Telecom. Women's Central Organisation (TWCO) for undertaking Welfare activities for Telecom women and their children which includes opening of creches, tailoring centres, nurs( schools and arts and crafts classes.

The annual grant to TWCO is Rs. 2 lakhs (and for its branch located in circles is Rs. 15,000/- ). Creches can now be opened in both office buildings or in Colonies depending upon the consensus and convenience of the user employees. In any case, building would not be rented specifically for this purpose.

Out of 33 holiday homes at present functioning in important hill stations/health resorts, 14 are under administrative control of Department of Telecom. These are utilised by employees of Department for holidaying purpose.

To develop sports among Sportsmen, tournaments in 17 disciplines are conducted at differ places during 1997-98 on all-India basis. An amount of Rs. 66,69,721/- was spent for Sports Cultural activities during 1997-98.

P & T Sports Control Board has sent combined P&T team for National in the Power Lifting Weight lifting, Chess, Wrestling, and Kabaddi tournaments.

*Work study*

15 norms studies and 11 work measurements studies were completed during the year 1997-98 i.e. from 1.4.97 to 31.3.98.

*Industrial assistance and export promotion group*

The Industrial Assistance and Export Promotion Group of Production Wing of DOT is responsible for the development and regulation of the Telecom Industry in the country. The main activities of the Group are:

i. Providing assistance in formulation of Import and Export policies for the Telecom Sector.

ii. Providing assistance in formulation of foreign investment policies and procedures for the Telecom Sector.

iii. Processing of applications for foreign investment and foreign technology in Telecom Sect

iv. Matters relating to promotion of Telecom Exports including sponsoring of trade delegation, of up of Indian pavilions in international Exhibitions and Organisation of Seminars etc.

v. Assistance in matters relating to Customs and Excise duties and other Direct and Indirect Taxes for the Telecom Sector.

vi. Assistance in matters relating to Trade and Industrial policies for the Telecom Sector.

vii. Assistance to various industrial units in the Telecom Sector for implementation of their projects.

*Manufacture of telecom equipments*

India is a major manufacturer of a wide variety of Telecom Equipments. The growth in Telecom equipments production in the country is as follows:

(Rupees in crores)

| | 1992-93 | '93-94 | '94-95 | '95-96 | '96-97 | '97-98 |
|---|---|---|---|---|---|---|
| Production | 3985 | 5500 | 7000 | 7750 | 8300 | 9960 |

*Export of telecom equipments and services*

Vigorous efforts are being made to increase the exports of Telecom equipments and services. India has now been recognised as a key supplier of products and technologies for rural Telecom by international organisations viz. ITU etc.

*Growth in Exports of Telecom Equipments and services is as follows:*

(Rs. in Crores

| | 1992-93 | '93-94 | '94-95 | '95-96 | '96-97 | '97-98 |
|---|---|---|---|---|---|---|
| Service | 282 | 456 | 598 | 1108 | 1458 | 2232 |
| Consultancy | 119 | 118 | 207 | 235 | 270 | 313 |
| Hardware | 24 | 58 | 131 | 310 | 240 | 296 |

***Approval in respect to direct foreign investment (DFI)***

An amount of Rs. 31466.11 Crore has been approved as Direct foreign investment from 1.8.91 to 31.8.98 in various Telecom manufacturing and services projects as per following details. The actual inflow during this period has been Rs. 3985.12 crores.

| S. No. | Category (Rs in Crores) | No. of Approval | FDI Approvals |
|---|---|---|---|
| i. | Radio Paging Service | 46 | 1166.39 |
| ii. | Cellular/Basic Telecom Service | 110 | 20724.59 |
| iii. | Manufacturing and other Telecom Services | 296 | 9575.13 |
| | Total | 452 | 31466.11 |

***Private investment promotion cell***

This group has recently been created to encourage, stimulate and facilitate private investment in telecom sector and to smoothen the implementation of these projects. Main activities of this group are:

*Promotional Activities:*

— Interaction with Business Councils/Industry Associations.

— Interaction with Indian Investment Centre and other

Government/Semi-Government bodies concerned with investment promotion.

— To recommend formation of policies to catalyse and stimulate private investment in Telecom Sector.

— Printing of Promotional Literature and their distribution.

— Organisation of investment Conferences/Seminars/ Exhibitions and dissemination of information, arrange publicity about avenues/scope of private investment in Telecom Sector.

— Deputation of officers from DoT for attending the National/International Conferences/Seminars/ Exhibitions concerned with investment promotion.

***Training***

During the year, as many as 441 Officers of various levels have been trained in vigilance functions.

***Other activities***

*Special CBI Cells:-* Special CBI Cells set up in metro cities to prevent leakage of telecom revenue continued to perform well and give encouraging results. Though it is not possible to quantify their gains in concrete financial terms, these Cells had registered 120 cases involving 130 Departmental officials and 33 outsiders.

*Special Squads:-* Special Squads were formed in the year 1995 for surprise visits to the subscriber's premises and Telephone Exchanges. The main job of these squads is random checking of equipments, telephone lines etc. to find out tempering, if any, with the equipments or lines in the Switch Room/external plant. Follow-up action was taken on various irregularities/omissions found by the special squads. This has resulted in considerable improvement in the services and preventing misuse of lines.

*Technical Solutions:-* A committee was set up in May, 1995 to study the technical and administrative aspects of revenue leakage. The Committee submitted its report in July, 1995. Several recommendations of the Committee on use of sensitive commands, carrying out of software modifications to stop misuse of certain commands for stoppage of metering etc. were implemented. Another committee was setup under the Chairmanship of Sr. DDG (Vig) in Dec., 1996 for carrying out detailed study on technical and administrative aspects to prevent revenue leakage. The Committee has submitted its report and its recommendations are under implementation by the field units.

***Management information system (MIS)***

MIS Cell helps in monitoring the performance of Telecom Circles, Metro Districts, MTNL & Mtce. Regions through various MIS Reports. The following Monthly statements are submitted to the Telecom Commission.

— Top management report.

— Status Report of Equipped Capacity, DELs and Waiting List of Telecom Circles/Metro Distts./MTNL in respect of Telephones.

— Achievement Report in respect of net increase in Telephone Equipped Capacity and DELs against the target fixed in respect of Telecom Circles/Metro Distts./MTNL.

— Special Monthly MIS Report.

(a) Service performance of Telecom Circles/Metro Distts./MTNL.

(b) Development activities on all-India basis.

(c) Financial Performance of Department on all-India basis along with Collection Efficiency circle-wise.

(d) Position of supplies from suppliers in respect of equipments for Department against the target of supplies for the month.

MIS publication on Telecom Network, Telecom Development & Financial Performance and other statistical information for each financial year is published every year. It contains information about performance of all the Telecom Circles, Metro Districts, MTNL and Telecom Maintenance Regions along with the information about Volume & Growth of various services provided by Department. The data compilation work for the publication of MIS book for the year 1997-98 is in final stage.

*Economic Research Unit (ERU) and Statistics (STT) Section*

The following studies/exercises were completed during 1997-98:

(i) Call Slab Wise Distribution Pattern of Subscribe rs/ Calls - A case study of 8/28 Telecom Districts : 1993-94 and 1994-95.

(ii) Impact of Tariff revision effective from 1.5.93 on subscribers calling pattern and revenue.

(iii) Telephone Demand Projections - Towns having exchanges with 200 lines and above 1997-2007.

(iv) Telephone Revenue - An analysis of Trends and An Examination of Determinants for 1993-94 and 1994-95.

(v) Examination of "Federal Communications Commission (FCC)" Document - Notice of Proposed Rule making (NPRM) - from economic angle.

(vi) Two Decades of studies in Telecom Economics.

(vii) Committee on "Metered Calls and Revenue per DEL per day".

**International co-operation/seminars/meetings**

***Bilateral Co-operation Meetings***

i) Joint Working Group/Joint Working Commission & Inter-Ministerial meetings.

ii) 26 Bilateral Co-operation meetings held in various Ministries from 1st April '97 to 31st March '98. 12.9.1.2. Delegation (Dignitories from Foreign Countries)

*(A) 9 delegations have visited DOT, as mentioned below:*

i) H. E. Mr. Mimoun Aoujil, Secretary General of the Ministry of Posts & Telecom, Morocco.

ii) Mr. Pitak Intrawideyanunt, Dy. Foreign Minister of Thailand.

iii) H.E. Mr. Wolfgang Boetsch, Minister of Posts and Telecommunications, Federal Republic of Germany along with a large German Government business delegation.

iv) H. E. Mr. Alyaksandr Lukashenka, President of Belarus.

v) Mr. V.Goncharenko, Minister of Communication of Belarus.

vi) Mr. Reed Hunt, Chairman, US Federal Communications Commission (FCC) and Chief Regulator of the Telecom Industry in the United States, along with his delegation team, has called on the Hon'ble Minister of Communications on 26th June 1997 & Chairman TC on 27th June '97 in Sanchar Bhawan, New Delhi.

vii) Mr. Vonya Mccann US Co-ordinator for International Communication& Information policy, along with a large American delegation of FCC officials and businessmen.

viii) Mr. William Daley, United States Commerce Secretary along with a large delegation of American businessmen.

ix) H. E. Dr. Peter Medgyessy, Finance Minister of the Republic of Hungary.

x) Ms. Rita Murrell, and Mr. Ashok Pasricha, Engineer from the U.S. Export-import Bank (EXIM) called on DDG(IR) to meet with EXIM Borrowers, guarantors and appropriate Government entities in India to discuss pending and potential business.

xi) Mr. David Brar of Agriteam Canada and Mr. Shabir Ahmad of JPs Associates called on DDG(IR) to discuss CIDA:s project, (a) establishment of radio advisory council and (b) Consumer watchdog facility regarding telecom services.

*(B) MOU Signed:-*

i) A Memorandum of Understanding was signed between Government of India & Germany in the field of Posts & Telecommunications in DOT Sanchar Bhawan at Ministerial level on 2.9.97.

ii) n agreement was signed between Government of India & Belarus in the field of Posts & Telecommunications in Vigyan Bhawan at Ministerial level on 27.9.97.

iii) A Memorandum of Understanding on Mutual Cooperation on Telecommunications between Deptt. of Telecom India and the Ministry of Industry, France was signed at Secretary level on 21.1.98 in Paris.

***Seminars/workshops/meetings/training - national level***

i) 35 DOT Officers participated in Seminar/Meetings etc. held in India organised by various International Organisations.

ii) Procured cases regarding grant of permission to foreign Telecom Companies for establishing their branch offices in India.

*Exhibitions (international & National):-*

*(A) International:-*

i) "Asia Telecom '97" in Singapore from 9-14 June, 1997. Department of Telecommunications participated along with its associated Public Sector Undertakings and private companies.

ii) Industrial and Technological Exhibition of India at Beijing (China), from 7-11 July '1997. C-DOT & TCIL participated in the exhibition. A delegation led by Chairman (TC) also visited the exhibition.

iii) "Telecom Expo '90" at Hanoi (Vietnam) from 2-6 December 1997: Department of Telecommunications participated along with Public Sector Undertakings such as C-DOT, ITI, and TCIL.

iv) "The Pride of India" Exhibition from 14-17 January, 1998 in Hanoi (Vietnam): Public Sector Undertakings of the Department of Telecommunications, ITI, HTL and C-DOT participated. The event was to commemorate 50 years of India's Independence.

v) An "Indian Trade Exhibition" was organised at World Trade Centre, Mexico City (Mexico), from 3-9 March '98.

vi) "Cebit '98" at Hanover (Germany) from 9-25 March, 1998.

*(B) National/regional:-*

i) Gateway '97 at Science City Calcutta, from 5-9 November 1997.

ii) Sishu Utsav '97 at Durgapur, West Bengal from 11 -25 November 1997.

iii) India International Trade Fair '97 was held at Pragati Maidan, New Delhi from 14-27 November 1997 DoT pavilion was inaugurated by Hon'ble Minister of Communications.

iv) COMMS India '97 from 9-11 December 1997 at Pragati Maidan, New Delhi.

v) 11th Industrial India Trade Fair at Calcutta 19-31 December 1997.

vi) All India Agriculture, Science and Industrial Trade Fair '98 at Kalyani, Nadia (West Bengal) from 1st to 15th January, 1998. It was organised by Jai Prakash Narayan Janmotsav Committee.

vii) "Sunderban Mela '98" at Canning Town, West Bengal, from 3rd to 12th January, 1998. It was organised by Bandhu Mahal.

Deputation of officers to foreign countries from 1st April '97 to 31st March 1998 is as follows:-

i) Deputation of 31 officers to Geneva, Singapore Cascais (Portugal), Manila, Tornoto & Seoul for different study groups of ITU-T/ITU-R/ITU-D.

ii) Deputation of 16 officers to Shanghai (China), Kathmandu, Tokyo, Bangkok, & Chaingmai (Thailand) for attending APT Meetings/Seminars.

iii) Deputation of 18 officers to Phuket (Thailand), Bangkok, Singapore, Geneva and Kathmandu for attending Meetings/Workshop/TCDC, Consultancies with UNDP/ITU Project.

iv) Deputation of 36 officers for attending miscellaneous International Meetings/Seminars/Conferences to Germany, USA, Seoul, London, Chicago, Copen hengon (Denmark) and Auckland.

v) A high level business delegation led by Sh.

R.N.Bhardwaj, DDG(IR), accompanied by Sr. officers of the level of Executive Directors from I.TI., C-DOT, & TCIL visited Hanoi (Vietnam) from 28-31st July, 1997, to explore the possibilities of business in Telecommunications.

vi) Indian delegation participated in Asia Pacific Telecommunity (APT) Regional meeting for WRC-97 organised by APT from 28th July to 1st August '97 at Seoul, Republic of Korea.

vii) Hon'ble MOC inaugurated the Conference of India Industry in association with US Trade and Development Agency & U.S. Department of Commerce.

viii) A four member DoT delegation headed by the Chairman, Telecom Commission visited France from 19th to 21st January 1998 to participate in the meeting of Indo-French Joint Committee on Posts and Telecommunications.

ix) A three member DoT Delegation headed by the Chairman, Telecom Commission visited Canada from 2nd to 6th February 1998 in connection with CIDA proposals in the session of Telecommunications.

x) A satellite Coordination meeting was held between Administrations of USA and India, during 9-13 February 1998 for Coordination of PANAMSAT and INSAT Satellite networks.

xi) Indo-Ethiopia Joint Trade Committee meeting was held on 25-26th February, 1998 in Addis Ababa. Sr. representatives from C-DoT, HTL and R&D attended the meeting.

— About 55 foreign delegates and 200 officers from DOT & other PSU's (TCHQ, C-DOT MTNL, TCIL, ITI, HTL, & TEC etc.) participated in "Asia-Pacific

Telecom Trade & Finance Colloquium" held in Vigyan Bhawan, New Delhi from 3-5 Nov. 1997. Hon'ble MOS(C) has inaugurated this event on 3.11.97.

— "A National Telecom Seminar' was held on 14th Jan. '98 in Hotel Ashok, Chanakya Puri, New Delhi to celebrate "50th year of our Independence." The seminar was inaugurated by Chairman Telecom Commission. Dy. Secretary General (ITU)), Geneva, Mr. Henry Chasia delivered a keynote address on the occasion.

**Network division**

*Meeting held*

(i) DSLCC: meeting was held with the representatives of Defence authorities and Deptt. of Telecom on 4-4-97 at Sena Bhawan, New Delhi.

(ii) Joint Study group meeting with officers of Defence authorities and Deptt. of Telecom were held on 23-9-97 and 10-11 -97 in Sena Bhawan.

(iii) Steering Committee meeting between representatives of Defence and Dir (NW), DOT was held on 19-8-97 in South Block, New Delhi.

*Miscellaneous activities*

(a) ATNs & Audit paras

(i) 17 ATNs have been vetted and cleared by Audit.

(ii) For one ATN of 95-96, the cell is vigorously taking up the case with CGMT (MHR) for want of detailed particulars of dues.

*(b) Territorial army cases*

(i) Additional benefits viz Best training Award among TA Trainees and introduction of TA medals among

TA Personnel are under process of sanction. The case has not yet been finalised by Finance.

(ii) Case of splitting of Annual Trg. Camp for TA personnel is under process.

(iii) Out of 14 proposed TA personnel, 7 have been trained in Satellite communication through NW cell. For the remaining personnel Trg. programme has been scheduled in this year.

*(c) War-contingent circuit*

Feasibility reports of War contingent circuits from pending units are being updated. Some more information has been received from different units.

*(d) Army HQRS*

Sanction of 13 STD, PCOs for the Border area of J&K has been obtained from MOD up to 28th Feb. '98. The case for extension up to 28-2-99 has already been processed.

**Civil wing**

The Civil Wing in the Department of Telecom came into existence in the year 1963. It is responsible for executing and maintaining the Buildings and services infrastructure for the Department. Its activities include planning and execution of:-

i) Technical Buildings for housing Telecom Equipment.

ii) Administrative Offices.

iii) Staff Quarters.

iv) Cable Ducts.

v) Civil Works for Transmission Towers.

vi) Air Conditioning.

vii) Substations Engine Alternator.

viii) Services such as Fire Fighting and Environmental Works.

It is also responsible for maintenance, rehabilitation and retrofitting of Building assets.

*Work load*

The activities of the Civil Wing have increased many folds over the years. The workload of the Civil Wing has progressively increased from a mere Rs. 4 crores in the year 1963 to Rs. 1,000 crores in the current financial year. In order to cater for the stringent requirement of high technology telecom equipment, the Civil wing is constantly upgrading the technology of designs, construction, air conditioning and other systems installed in the Buildings.

*Organisational setup*

The Civil Wing has three disciplines viz. Civil, Electrical and Architecture. All these three disciplines provide inputs for planning and construction of a Building Project. Each discipline is headed by a Sr. DDG in the headquarters reporting to Member (Production). The field set up is headed by Chief Engineers/Chief Architects located at various places.

*Achievements*

The physical achievements of the Civil Wing during the period 1997-98 are as follows:-

| Sl. No. | Type of Bldg. Completed During 1997-98 | No. of Building |
|---|---|---|
| i) | MAX-I | 62 |
| ii) | MAX-II | 500 |
| iii) | CTO/DTO | 10 |
| iv) | Transmission Buildings | 78 |

| | | |
|---|---|---|
| V) | Towers Foundation | 257 |
| vi) | Admn. Buildings | 16 |
| vii) | Staff Quarters | 2486 |
| viii) | Other Buildings | 212 |
| ix) | Cable duct (in route Kms.) | 124.94 |

***Staff***

P&T Building Works Service - Group "A"

*Gazetted*

| | Civil | Electrical | Architecture | Total |
|---|---|---|---|---|
| Higher Admn. Grade | 1 | 1 | 1 | 3 |
| Senior Administrative Grade | 20 | 9 | 4 | 33 |
| Junior Administrative Grade | 105 | 36 | 16 | 157 |
| Senior Time Scale | 250 | 97 | 38 | 385 |
| Junior Time Scale | 49 | 11 | 25 | 85 |
| Total | 425 | 154 | 84 | 663 |

**Telecom commission**

***Composition of Telecom commission***

The composition of the full-time Members of the Telecom Commission during 1997-98 was as follows:-

| | | | |
|---|---|---|---|
| Chairman | Sri A. V. Gokak | W. E. F. | 4.11.96 |
| Member (Finance) | Sri A. Prasad | W.E.F. | 31.07.97 |
| Member (Production) | Sri R.R.N.Prasad | W. E. F. | 01.10.97 |
| Member (Services) | Sri P. S. Saran | W.E.F. | 11.01.95 |
| Member (Technology) | Sri N. K. Sinha | W. E. F. | 15.11.95 |

# 2

# Statistical Supplement

*Table*

*Profit and loss account for the year 1997-98*

*(Rs. Millions)*

| *Particulars* | *1996-97 (Actual)* | *1997-98 (Provisional)* |
|---|---|---|
| Operating Income | | |
| Telephones | 1093.50 | 129548 |
| Telegraphs | 66.0 | 601 |
| Telex | 731 | 1490 |
| Railway Communications | 2636 | 2351 |
| Miscellaneous | 8482 | 11684 |
| Total (A) | 121859 | 145674 |
| Operating Expenses | | |
| Staff Expenses | 22614 | 31400 |
| Cost of other operation | 9416 | 7850 |
| Depreciation | 15244 | 18323 |
| Total (B) | 47275 | 57573 |
| Net operating income (A-B)=(C) | 74584 | 88101 |
| Add: Other Income (D) | 7929 | 8365 |
| Total Profit before payment of interests etc. (C + D) = (E) | 82513 | 96466 |
| Less: Interest Payment | | |

*(Contd....)*

| | | |
|---|---|---|
| To MTNL | 9979 | 10617 |
| To GOVT | 2923 | 2865 |
| Redemption of Bonds | 7526 | 7610 |
| Total (F) | 20428 | 21092 |
| Net profit (E-F) = (G) | 62085 | 75374 |
| Appropriation of profit to | | |
| Telecom Capital Reserve Fund | 59362 | 68916 |
| Telecom Revenue Reserve Fund | 666 | 775 |
| Own Resources | 2058 | 5683 |
| Ave. Plant-in-service | 301376 | 365665 |
| Operating Ratio | 38,8 | 40 |
| Rate of Return | 24.7 | 24 |

sources and application of funds (1997-98) provisional

*(Rs. in Millions)*

| *Particulars* | *1996-97 (Actual)* | *1997-98 (Provisional)* |
|---|---|---|
| Sources of funds | 0 | 0 |
| Internal Resources | 62088 | 73600 |
| Depreciations | 15244 | 18323 |
| Funds | 17829 | 981 |
| Repayment of Loan | 217 | 1085 |
| Total | 95379 | 93990 |
| Borrowed funds | 0 | 0 |
| Total Sources of Funds | 95379 | 93990 |
| Application funds | | |
| Construction Funds | 75302 | 86461 |
| Accounts with Government | 17829 | 981 |
| Accounts with MTNL | 19 | 175 |
| Working Capital | | |
| Stores | 187 | 859 |
| Others | 2042 | 5513 |
| Total Application of Fund | 95379 | 93990 |

*Table*

*Balance Sheet as at 31-03-1998 (Provisional)*

*(Rs. in Millions)*

| *Liabilities* | | *Assets* | |
|---|---|---|---|
| 1996-97 | 1997-98 | 1996-97 | 1997-98 |
| Actual (Exclusive of Mumbai & Delhi Phones) | Provisional (Exclusive of Mumbai & Delhi Phones) | Actual (Exclusive of Mumbai and Delhi Phones) | Provisional (Exclusive of Mumbai & Delhi Phones) |

Table

Financial working 1996-97 & 1997-98 (Cash basis)

*(Rs. in Crores)*

| 1996-97 | | 1997-98 |
|---|---|---|
| 12266.10 | Receipts | 14586.91 |
| | Expenditure | |
| 419.40 | General Administration | 575.94 |
| 685.61 | Operation | 896.19 |
| 0.08 | Stores & Factories | (-)12.38 |
| 6.07 | Research & Development | 7.99 |
| 29.04 | Accounts & Audit | 40.84 |
| 1879.81 | Engineering & Maintenance | 2488.77 |
| 22.66 | Amenities to Staff | 38.23 |
| 251.77 | Pensionary Charges | 412.85 |
| 17.65 | Stationery & Printing | 22.43 |
| 1524.45 | Depreciation on Historical Costs | 1832.33 |
| 1.66 | Social Security & Welfare programme | 1.10 |
| 1929.32 | Other Expenditure | 2089.30 |
| 6767.36 | Total Expenditure | 8393.59 |
| 678.55 | Credit to working Expenses | 839.53 |
| 6088.81 | Net working Expenses | 7554.06 |
| 6177.29 | Net Receipts | 7032.85 |
| 292.34 | Dividend to General Revenues | 286.50 |
| 5884.95 | Surplus | 6746.35 |

*Table*

*Summary of financial working for 10 years of dot exclusing MTNL (Cash basis)*

*(Rs. in Crores)*

| Year | Revenue | Expenditure | | | | |
|---|---|---|---|---|---|---|
| | Revenue | Net Working expenses excluding Depreciation | Depre-ciation | Dividend | Total | Surplus |
| 1988-89 | 2358.54 | 1139.07 | 235.94 | 160.66 | 1535.67 | 822.87 |
| 1989-90 | 2358.54 | 1300.26 | 302.48 | 180.37 | 1783.11 | 1058.03 |
| 1990-91 | 3404.79 | 1468.29 | 388.66 | 220.27 | 2077.22 | 1327.57 |
| 1991-92 | 3874.52 | 1652.90 | 491.71 | 246.61 | 2391.22 | 1483.30 |
| 1992-93 | 4757.71 | 1923.70 | 638.89 | 257.13 | 2819.72 | 1937.99 |
| 1993-94 | 6094.87 | 2960.71 | 777.31 | 230.33 | 3968.35 | 2126.52 |
| 1994-95 | 7799.12 | 2886.31 | 977.16 | 269.76 | 4133.23 | 3665.89 |
| 1995-96 | 9760.55 | 3066.35 | 1223.04 | 279.19 | 4568.58 | 5191.97 |
| 1996-97 | 12266.10 | 4564.38 | 1524.43 | 292.34 | 6381.15 | 5884.95 |
| 1997-98 | 14586.91 | 5720.02 | 1834.04 | 286.50 | 7840.56 | 6746.35 |

*Table*

*Capital outlay during and upto the end of 1997-98 (Fixed assets)*

*(Rs.in Crores)*

| Sl. No. | Other Assets | During the year | Total at the end of the year |
|---|---|---|---|
| 1. | Land | 59.73 | 412.04 |
| 2. | Building | 610.41 | 3541.06 |
| 3. | Cables | 4133.62 | 20656.48 |
| 4. | Telegraph & Telephone Lines Radio Masts & Aerials | 140.99 | 3805.25 |
| 5. | Apparatus & Plant | 2986.11 | 23071.10 |
| 6. | Motor Vehicles | 37.76 | 205.58 |
| 7. | General Admn./Directions & Execution Establishment & Other Charges etc. | 45.06 | 274.62 |
| 8. | Other Expenditure | 632.42 | 1881.08 |

*(Contd...)*

| | | | |
|---|---|---|---|
| 9. | Gross Fixed Assets | 8646.10 | 53847.21 |
| 10. | Deduct Receipts & | 0.83 | 20.45 |
| | Recoveries on Capital Accounts | 8645.27 | 53826.76 |
| 11. | Total Fixed Assets. | | |
| 12. | Deduct Amt. met from Advances Rentals under OYT & Other Schemes | -10.66 | 581.42 |
| 13. | Deduct Amt. met from Telex Deposit scheme | -0.88 | 30.54 |
| 14. | Deduct Expenditure met from Telecom. Capital Reserve Fund | 6801.85 | 30805.69 |
| 15. | Deduct Amt. from contribution from Revenue | — | 460.01 |
| 16. | Deduct Depreciation on Historical costs transferred from Revenue | | |
| 17. | Repayment of loan by MTNL. | 108.50 | 317.00 |
| 18. | Deposit by MTNL for financing Telecom. Projects (Bonds). | 0.00 | 8694.87 |
| 19. | Total deductions | 8731.14 | 50715.20 |
| 20. | Net fixed Assets (item 11 -19) | -85.87 | 3111.56 |
| 21. | Consumers co-operative Society | — | — |
| 22. | Stores and Manufacture Suspense | 95.55 | 508.22 |
| 23. | Civil Engg. Stores Transactions | -9.68 | -37.04 |
| 24. | Total Other Assets | 85.87 | 471.18 |
| 25. | Dividend bearing Capital Outlay (i.e. item 20 + 24). | 0.00 | 3582.74 |
| 26. | Deduct Amt. met by setting Off of the credit balance equivalent to the debit balance Under DOT in the P&T Revenue Reserve Fund as on 0 1 /04/1985. | 0.00 | 938.48 |
| 27. | Net Dividend bearing Capital Outlay (item 25-26). | 0.00 | 2644.26 |

*Table*

*Summary of stores suspense - 1997-98*

*(Rs. in Crores)*

| | *Opening Balance as on 1.4.97* | *Receipts during the year* | *Issues during the year* | *Closing balance as on 31.3.98* |
|---|---|---|---|---|
| Store & manufacture suspense | | | | |
| General Stores | 288.00 | 865.68 | 818.14 | 335.54 |
| Workshop Stores | 20.55 | 258.61 | 258.69 | 20.47 |
| Manufacture Suspense | 104.11 | 330.65 | 282.56 | 152.20 |
| Total Stores & Manufacture Suspense | 412.66 | 1454.94 | 1359.39 | 508.21 |
| Civil engg. stores | | | | |
| Civil Engg. Stores | -8.99 | 128.14 | 136.60 | -17.45 |
| Purchases | (-)54.32 | 62.07 | 65.53 | -57.78 |
| Misc. Civil Engg. Works Advances | 35.95 | 39.58 | 37.33 | 38.20 |
| Total Civil Eng. Stores | (-)27.36 | 229.78 | 239.46 | -37.03 |
| Total Stores Suspense | 385.30 | 1684.72 | 1598.85 | 471.17 |

*Table*

*Revenue reserve fund*

*(Rs. in crores)*

| *Balance as on 1/4/97* | *Appropriation from Surplus* | *Interest on the balance at the credit of the fund* | *Withdrawals* | *Closing balance as on 31/3/98* |
|---|---|---|---|---|
| 68.58 | 69.11 | 8.37 | 69.11 | 76.95 |

*Table*

*Capital reserve fund*

*(Rs. in crores)*

| *Balance as on 1-4-97* | *Appropriation from Surplus* | *Interest on the balance at the credit of the fund* | *Withdrawals* | *Closing Balance as on 31.3.98* |
|---|---|---|---|---|
| 1819.62 | 6677.24 | 214.39 | 6801.85 | 1909.40 |

*Table*

*Telex exchanges and telegraph offices as on 31-3-98*

| *Circle/Metro District* | *No. of Telex Exchanges* | *Telegraph Office Departmental* | *Combined* |
|---|---|---|---|
| Circle | | | |
| A& N | 1 | 1 | - |
| Andhra | 24 | 118 | 3833 |
| Assam | 6 | 29 | 448 |
| Bihar | 1 | 59 | 4219 |
| Delhi | - | 26 | 5 |
| Gujarat | 27 | 40 | 1732 |
| Haryana | 16 | 17 | 376 |
| Himachal Pradesh | 3 | 13 | 1242 |
| Jammu & Kashmir | 2 | 9 | 138 |
| Karnataka | 25 | 69 | 5036 |
| Kerala | 10 | 39 | 1985 |
| Madhya Pradesh | 12 | 67 | 2344 |
| Maharashtra | 27 | 100 | 2863 |
| North Eastern | 5 | 13 | 251 |
| Orissa | 20 | 29 | 3397 |
| Punjab | 9 | 24 | 587 |
| Rajasthan | 14 | 47 | 2258 |
| Tamil Nadu | 66 | 108 | 6546 |

*(Contd. . .)*

| | | | |
|---|---|---|---|
| Uttar Pradesh(E) | 8 | 60 | 3813 |
| Uttar Pradesh(W) | 15 | 45 | 1575 |
| West Bengal | 11 | 44 | 1974 |
| Total for Circle | 302 | 957 | 44622 |
| Metro Districts | | | |
| Mumbai | 12 | — | — |
| Calcutta | 1 | — | — |
| Delhi | 13 | — | — |
| Chennai | 6 | — | — |
| Total for Metro Districts | 32 | — | — |
| Total | 334 | 957 | 44622 |

*Table*

*Telephones as on 31-3-98*

| *Sl. No.* | *Circle/ Metro Distts.* | *No. of Telephone Exchanges* | *Total Telephone Stations* | *DELs including* Junctions |
|---|---|---|---|---|
| Circles | | | | |
| 1. | A & N | 25 | 8924 | 8272 |
| 2. | Andhra Pradesh | 2092 | 1230828 | 1167419 |
| 3. | Assam | 319 | 176792 | 161531 |
| 4. | Bihar | 851 | 412301 | 399093 |
| 5. | Gujarat | 1462 | 1333278 | 1292440 |
| 6. | Haryana | 794 | 434419 | 428395 |
| 7. | Himachal Pradesh | 611 | 184872 | 181886 |
| 8. | Jammu & Kashmir | 252 | 96076 | 89362 |
| 9. | Karnataka | 2171 | 1261448 | 1227683 |
| 10. | Kerala | 818 | 1113496 | 1084019 |
| 11. | Madhya Pradesh | 2728 | 828891 | 800784 |
| 12. | Maharashtra | 2832 | 1587392 | 1529555 |
| 13. | North Eastern | 269 | 123682 | 116479 |
| 14. | Orissa | 759 | 277174 | 266098 |
| 15. | Punjab | 1004 | 909145 | 890495 |
| 16. | Rajasthan | 1624 | 737394 | 755560 |

*(Contd...)*

| | | | | |
|---|---|---|---|---|
| 17. | Tamil Nadu | 1435 | 1192760 | 1165806 |
| 18. | U.P(E) | 1256 | 691794 | 686212 |
| 19. | U.P(W) | 874, | 669905 | 654547 |
| 20. | West Bengal | 727 | 322515 | 314426 |
| | Total for Circles | 22903 | 13593146 | 13220062 |
| | Metro Districts | | | |
| 21. | Mumbai | 132 | 2056998 | 1855629 |
| 22. | Calcutta | 136 | 731542 | 672278 |
| 23. | Delhi | 157 | 1688571 | 1551111 |
| 24. | Chennai | 78 | 549272 | 502616 |
| | Total for Metro Districts | 503 | 5026383 | 4581634 |
| | Grand Total | 23406 | 18619529 | 17801696 |

*Table*

*Tribal sub-plan (1997-98) - Targets and achievements*

| | | *1997-98* | | *1998-99* |
|---|---|---|---|---|
| *Sl.* | *Item* | *Target* | *Achievement* | *Target* |
| 1. | Telephone Exchanges (Nos.) | 100 | 114 | 120 |
| 2. | Switching Capacity (Lines) | 125000 | 196297 | 200000 |
| 3. | Direct Exchange Lines (Nos.) | 100000 | 161384 | 160000 |
| 4. | UHF Systems Microwave systems | 1500 | 1697 | 1500 |
| 5. | Village Public Telephones | 135000 | 5316 | 13000 |
| 6. | Satellite stations | 20 | 3 | 61 |

*Table*
*Personnel-actual strength*
(including those on deputation)
(as on 31.03.1998)

| *Gazetted* | *Group A* | *Group B* | *Total* |
|---|---|---|---|
| Chairman | 1 | — | 1 |
| Telecom. commission member | | | |
| Telecom. commission advisors | 4 | — | 4 |
| Telecom. commission | 4 | — | 4 |
| Additional Secretary | 1 | — | 1 |
| Joint Secretary | 1 | — | 1 |
| Deputy secretary | 1 | —1 Chief | General |
| managers | 44 | — | 44 |
| Total | 56 | — | 56 |
| Telecom. Accounts & finance service-group A | | | |
| Senior | | | |
| Administrative grade | 34 | — | 34 |
| Junior | | | |
| Administrative grade | 82 | — | 82 |
| Senior time scale | 207 | — | 207 |
| Junior time scale | 190 | — | 190 |
| Total | 513 | - | 513 |
| Telecome accounts & finance service-group B | | | |
| Account Officer | — | 1,510 | 1,510 |
| Assistant Account Office | — | 2,905 | 2,905 |
| Total | — | 4,415 | 4,415 |
| Telegraph Engineering Service-Group A | | | |
| Senior | | | |
| Administrative Grade | 298 | — | 298 |
| Junior | | | |
| Administrative Grade | 778 | — | 778 |
| Senior Time Scale | 2,860 | — | 2,860 |
| Junior Time Scale | 364 | — | 364 |
| Total: | 4,300 | — | 4,300 |

*(Contd...)*

## Personnel-Actual Strength (including those on deputation) [As on 31.03.1998]

| | | | |
|---|---|---|---|
| Telegraph Engineering Service-Group B | | | |
| Total : | — | 16,313 | 16,313 |
| * Telegraph Traffic Service-Group A | | | |
| Senior Administrative Grade | 1 | 1 | |
| Junior Administrative Grade | 13 | 13 | |
| Senior Time Scale | 65 | 65 | |
| Total : | 79 | 79 | |
| *Telegraph Traffic Service-Group A | | | |
| TTS Group-B | — | 215 | 215 |
| Total : | — | 215 | 215 |
| Central Secretariat Service | | | |
| Assistant Director | | | |
| General Grade | 10 | — | 10 |
| Section Officers | — | 99 | 99 |
| Senior Personnel Assistant (Grade'B | — | 71 | 71 |
| Total : | 10 | 170 | 180 |
| General Central Service | | | |
| GCS: | 994 | 2.328 | 3,322 |
| Total | 994 | 2,328 | 3,322 |
| Grand Total : | 5,952 | 23,443 | 29,395 |

## Personnel-Actual Strength (including those on deputation) [As on 31.03.1998]

| *Non-Gazetted* | *Non-Gazetted Group'B'* | *Group'C'* | *Group'D'* | *Total* |
|---|---|---|---|---|
| Telecom. Directorate | 387 | 980 | 840 | 2207 |

| | | | |
|---|---|---|---|
| Telegraph Engineering Service-Group 'C' | | | |
| Junior Engineers (including S.G. & Civil. Engg.) | 22,847 | — | 22,847 |
| Telephone Operators | 52,251 | — | 52,251 |
| Technician (including S.G.) | 28,187 | — | 28,187 |
| Line Staff | | | |
| (i) Inspectors | 741 | — | 741 |
| (ii) Sub-inspectors | 3,086 | — | 3,086 |
| (iii) Lineman | 21,338 | — | 21,338 |
| Telephone Inspectors | 2,232 | — | 2,232 |
| Telephone Supervisors | 6,440 | — | 6,440 |
| *Telegraph Traffic Service Group 'C' | | | |
| Telegraphists | 13,996 | — | 13,996 |
| Telegraph Masters (LSG, HSG) | 1,306 | — | 1,306 |
| Telegraph Overseer | 323 | — | 323 |
| Others | 117224 | — | 117224 |
| Total: | 269971 | — | 269971 |
| Telegraph Engineering Service Group D | | | |
| TES | — | 100975 | 100975 |
| *Telegraph Traffic Service Group D | | | |
| Telegraph-man (Indoor & Outdoor) | — | 6,781 | 6,781 |
| Total | 107756 | 107756 | |

*(Contd....)*

Personnel-Actual Strength
(including those on deputation)
[As on 31.03.1998]

| *Non-Gazetted* | *Non-Gazetted Group'B'* | *Group'C'* | *Group'D'* | *Total* |
|---|---|---|---|---|
| Telecom. Directorate | 387 | 980 | 840 | 2207 |
| CAO Telegraph check Office | | 112 | 41 | 153 |
| Telecommunications Factories | | 922 | 507 | 1429 |
| Telecom.Stores | | 1104 | 917 | 2021 |
| Telecom. Training Centres | | 578 | 563 | 1141 |
| Civil Engineering Wing | | 5260 | 2619 | 7879 |
| Total Non-Gazetted | 387 | 277947 | 112403 | 390737 |
| Industrial Workers (including Telecom Stores) | | | | |
| Total staff | | | | 4,25,303 |

Summary

| *Gazetted* | *Non-Gazetted* | *Industrial Workers* | *Total* |
|---|---|---|---|
| 29,395 | 3,90,737 | 5,171 | 4,25,303 |

Telegraph Traffic Armed had been merged with the Telegraph Engineering Services.

*Table*

*Number of employees-scheduled castes/tribes*
as on 31.03.1998.

| *Class* | *Total No.of* | *Scheduled Cast* | *%age to Total No.of Employees* | *Scheduled Tribe Employees* | *%age to Total No. of Employees* |
|---|---|---|---|---|---|
| Group'A' | 5,952 | 852 | 14.31 | 218 | 3.66 |
| Group'B' | 23,443 | 2,496 | 10.65 | 440 | 1.88 |
| Group'C' | 2,78,334 | 44,504 | 15.99 | 13,412 | 4.82 |
| Group'D' | 1,10,879 | 25,308 | 22.82 | 5,750 | 5.19 |
| (Excluding Sweeper & Industrial Workers) | | | | | |
| Sweeper | 1,524 | 1,479 | 97.05 | 100 | 6.56 |

*Table*

*Number of ex-servicemen as on 31-3.1998*

| *Class* | *Total Number of Emplo-yees* | *Ex-Servicemen -Abled* | *%age to total No. of Employees* | *Ex-Service-men - Disabled* | *%age to total No.of Employees* |
|---|---|---|---|---|---|
| **Group 'A'** | 5,952 | 14 | 0.23 | - | - |
| **Group'B'** | 23,443 | 47 | 0.20 | 1 | 0.00 |
| Group'C' | 2,78..334 | 2,975 | 1.07 | 59 | 0.02 |
| Group'D' | 1,12,403 | 1,651 | 1.47 | 20 | 0.02 |

*Table*

*Summary of personnel trained in various training centres during the year 1997-98*

| *Sl. No.* | | *Name of Training Centre* | *No. of Personnel Trained* Induction courses | In-service courses | *Total* |
|---|---|---|---|---|---|
| 1.A | | ALTTC Ghaziabad | | | |
| | i) | Departmental personnel trained. | 264 | 2715 | 2979 |
| | ii) | Non-departmental personnel | — | 13 | 13 |
| | iii) | Foreign personnel trained | — | 90 | 90 |
| B. | | Brbraitt Jabalpur | | | |
| | (i) | Departmental Personnel trained | 262 | 2775 | 3037 |
| | (ii) | Foreign Personnel Trained | - | 54 | 54 |
| C. | | RTTCs | | | |
| | (i) | Departmental personnel trained | 3995 | 4897 | 8892 |
| D. | | DTTCs/CTTCs Br.CTTCs | | | |
| | i) | Departmental personnel trained | 44861 | 9068 | 53929 |
| | ii) | Non-departmental personnel trained | — | 90 | 90 |
| | | GRAND TOTAL: | 49382 | 19702 | 69084 |
| 2. | | No. of DOT Officers trained abroad | — | 67 | 67 |
| 3. | | DOT Officers trained outside Institutions in India | | 52 | 52 |
| | | Total (2+3) | | 119 | 119 |

**Wireless planning and co-ordination wing**

***Performance during 1997-98***

*Radio frequency spectrum management new frequency assignments/ licences issued etc.*

Radio Frequency Spectrum Management

| | | (1.4.97 to 31.3.98) (Actual) |
|---|---|---|
| New Radio Frequency authorised to various users | — | 19125 |
| Frequency assignments intimated to Radiocommunication Bureau of the ITU for registration | — | 965 |
| No. of sites cleared for new wireless stations | — | 7764 |
| Inter-departmental meetings | — | 27 |
| No. of SACFA (Standing Advisory Committee on Frequency Allocations) meetings | — | 5 |
| Basic Services Meetings | — | 4 |
| Issues of wireless licences | | |
| Number of licences issued for new Wireless stations | — | 6711 |
| Number of old Wireless stations for which licences were renewed | — | 23422 |
| Number of Import Licence issued | — | 172 |
| Basic Services Experimental Licence | — | 1 |
| Certificate of proficiency (COP) examination/Licences | | |
| Number of COP examination conducted | — | 23 |
| Number of candidates admitted | — | 4765 |
| Number of licences issued | — | 569 |
| Number of licences renewed | — | 1984 |
| Number of new Radio Amateur licence issued | — | 530 |
| Number of Radio Amateur licence renewed | — | 785 |
| Number of certificates of importation issued | — | 58 |

**Review of National Frequency Allocation Plan (NFAP), 1981**

A meeting of Standing Committee of experts and All manufacturers of Radio equipments was called for fixing the date of issuing of frequency assignments by WPC with 12.5 KHz channel spacing in the frequency band 30-230 MHz. All the manufacturers are in a position to supply the radio equipment with channel Spacing 12.5 KHz. As such it was decided that WPC could assign frequencies with 12 KHz channel spacing to all users except DOT & Defence Services with effect from 1.4.98.

Spectrum requirements from various Major Wireless users have been received for the frequency (band 1-3GHz. A working committee has been established to harmonise the requirements of the various organisation including those of private users.

**Satellite system coordination**

***Inter-satellite system coordination***

International coordination of various satellites - GSO or Non-GSO, is required to be undertake as per the provisions of the international Radio Regulations (RR) of the ITU. The national, international activities for coordination and protection of our satellite systems vis-a-vis existing/planned systems c other countries were continued during 1997-98. Due to the increasing number of satellites in the Gec Stationary orbit of our interest, this activity is becoming extremely complex as well as important Salient aspects are given in following paragraphs.

**Insat satellite networks**

India has presently four operating INSAT Satellite networks at three GSO locations 74E, 83E and 93.5E, which are having fixed and mobile communication, Television Broadcasting an( meteorological payloads in Ku-band, C-bands and S-bands.

Additionally, a new ARABSAT-1C network carrying 24 C-band and one S-band transponder capacity, has been acquired and is presently located at 55 Deg E. This satellite has been renamed as INSAT-2DT and is the fifth operating satellite network in the INSAT series of satellite networks. This network is being treated as part of INSAT-2(55) and short-term coordination is being pursued vigorously with Administrations of USA/INTELSAT and Russia for operating this network immediately from 55E. Agreement has been successfully reached with Administrations of Singapore, Thailand and Turkey for operation of INSAT-2(55) network from the orbital location of 55E.

**INSAT-2 & 2K networks at 74, 83 and 93.5E**

Frequency assignments of INSAT-2(74), INSAT-2(83) and INSAT-2(93.5) C-band satellite networks have since been registered in the Master International Frequency Register (MIFR) of Radio Communication Bureau (BR) of ITU.

Coordination of I NSAT-2K Ku-band satellite networks at 74 Deg E and 93.5 Deg East have been completed with the Administrations of U.K., USA, INTELSAT, Japan & Thailand and frequency assignments notices have already been sent to ITU for international recognition and protection. Notices to INSAT-2K at 83E would be sent after completion of formal coordination with the Tongan Administration.

**INSAT-2 (48), INSAT-2 (55) and INSAT-2 (111-5) satellite networks**

Detailed coordination was undertaken during bilateral meetings with the Administrations of USA/INTELSAT, Singapore, Turkey, Russia, Tonga, Malaysia and Belarus. Coordination agreement was reached with the Administrations of Singapore and Turkey through bilateral satellite coordination meeting for networks at 48 and 55 E. Coordination with other concerned Administrations are being pursued.

**INSAT-2E systems at 74E, 83E, and 93.5 E**

The detailed coordination information of INSAT-2E satellite networks at orbital locations of 74E, 82E, 83E and 93.5E, sent to Radio Communication Bureau, have since been published in ITU Weekly Circular Special Sections during June 1997 and Administrations of Philippine, UAE, Australia, U.K., USA, INTELSAT, CTI, China, Singapore, Russia, and Tonga have desired detailed coordination for these networks.

Coordination has been completed with the Administrations of Malaysia, Singapore and USA. Coordination is in advanced stage with the Administrations of Russia, Thailand and Tongan Administrations. Coordination is being pursued vigorously with the Administrations of UAE, UK, Belarus, Japan, USA/NTELSAT and China.

**INSAT-2M (Mobile satellite services)/INSAT-2T (Expanded TV coverage) networks**

The detailed coordination information for INSAT-2M (Mobile Satellite services) and INSAT-2T (Expanded TV coverage) satellite networks at orbital locations of 48 Deg.E, 55 Deg.E, 74 Deg.E, 83 Deg,E and 93.5 Deg.E was published during May 1996 and the various affected Administrations viz. Saudi Arabia, U.K., Singapore, Sweden, China, Germany, New Zealand, Iran, France, Japan, INTELSAT, Tonga, Thailand, Belarus, Ukraine, Russia and Malaysia have desired detailed coordination with these networks. Coordination was pursued with these Administrations. Detailed coordination during the year was undertaken with Administrations of Tonga, Thailand, USA/NTELSAT, Turkey and Singapore.

**INSAT-13 west, 75.2 west, 108 west and INSAT-EK13W, 75.2W, EK108W satellite networks**

The detailed coordination information for INSAT-WEST satellite networks at orbital locations of 13 Deg. West,

75.2 Deg. West and 108 degree West GSO orbital locations, sent to Radio Communication Bureau, have since been published in Sept.,1997. Administrations of Canada, Germany, USA, INTELSAT, Finland, France, EUTELSAT, Brazil, Japan, U.K., INMARSAT, Spain, Sweden, Israel, Italy, Argentina, Tonga and Russia have requested for detailed coordination with these networks. Coordination needs to be taken up with these Administrations. In addition India have also started receiving coordination requests from various administrations planning satellite networks in the vicinity of INSAT west networks.

**INDAB - 51.5E, 56.5E, 71 E, 79E, 89E & 11 3.5E (digital audio broadcasting) INSAT Satellite networks**

Advance Publication Information (API) for the INDAB series of INSAT satellite networks (intended for Digital Audio Broadcasting) was published by ITU during April 1996 and request for detailed coordination were received from various Administrations viz. Korea, Ukraine, U.K. INMARSAT, USA, INTELSAT, Australia, China, Tonga, New Zealand, Russia, UAE, Japan and Singapore. Coordination information is to be published for these networks for furthering the process of orbit-frequency coordination.

**NSAT- KA50, KA54, KA63, KA67, KA74, KA76, KA78, KA83, KA87, KA93.5, KA98 & KA1 00 satellite networks**

The coordination data of the Ka band satellite networks at orbital locations of 50E, 54E, 63E, 67E, 74E, 76E, 78E, 83E, 87E, 93.5E, 98E and 1 OOE was sent to Radio Communication Bureau and the same have since been published during Sept. 1997 and request for detailed coordination have been received from Administrations of Belarus, Korea, China, Luxembourg, Italy, UAE, Russia, Germany, U.K., INMARSAT, USA, INTELSAT, Japan, France, Saudi Arabia, Malaysia, Tonga, Australia,

Bulgarian and INTELSAT etc. Coordination was taken up with the USA/Iridium and with the other Administration coordination is to be taken up at appropriate time.

**INSAT- EK & EKR Series of INSAT Satellite Networks at 48E, 55E, 74E, 83E, 93.5E, 103E & 111.5E orbital locations**

The detailed coordination information in ApS4 format for INSAT-EK series of INSAT satellite networks at orbital locations of 48E, 55E, 74E, 78E, 83E, 93.5E, 103E & 111.5E Deg. East were filed with Radio Communication Bureau (ITU). Article-XIV consultations (under INTELSAT Article XIV procedure) has also been initiated with INTELSAT. Publication of these networks in ITUAR1 VC special sections is awaited. Coordination information of INSAT-EKR networks would have to be filed at appropriate time.

**INSAT- ES48, ES55, ES74, ES83, ES93.5, ES1 00, 105E & ES1 11.5 Series of INSAT Satellite networks**

The detailed coordination information in the ApS4 format, for INSAT-ES satellite networks at GSO orbital locations of 48E and 55E, have been sent to Radio Communication Bureau in October 1997. Publication of these networks in ITU special sections is awaited. Coordination information for other networks would have to be filed as required.

**INSAT-X48, X55, X62.5, X66.5, X74, X83, X93.5, X103 & X111.5 satellite networks**

Subsequent to publication of Advance Publication Information (APIs) of these networks to operate in X-band from GSO orbital locations of 48E, 55E, 62.5E, 66.5E, 74E, 83E, 93.5E, 103E and 111.5 Deg. East, request for detailed coordination were received from various affected Administration viz. Japan, USA, Saudi Arabia, United Arab Emirates(UAE), Singapore, Ukraine, Belarus, Germany, Tonga, China and France etc. Coordination information would have to be filed at appropriate time.

**INSAT-AF48/AF55 Satellite networks**

Advance Publication Information(API) in respect of INSAT-AF48 and INSAT-AF55 satellite networks for African coverage for GSAT payload were published during June 1997. Request for detailed coordination were received from various Administrations like U.K., USA, INTELSAT, INMARSAT, Saudi Arabia, UAE, Singapore, Russia, Thailand, LAO & Australia. Coordination information is yet to be filed with ITU for publication. Article-XIV consultations (under INTELSAT Article XIV procedure) have been initiated for these networks, with INTELSAT.

**INSAT-BSS1 01 Satellite networks**

Appendix-30 information i.ro. INSAT-BSS101 pertaining to the modifications of the Region 3 BSS (Broadcasting Satellite Services) Plan has been published by ITU during July 1997 & comments/ objections have been received from various Administrations viz. Russia, Vietnam, Pakistan, Germany, Japan, Iran, Singapore, FRANCE/ EUTELSAT, Yugoslavia, UAE, Philippines, Syria, Cyprus, OMAN, Sweden, Ukraine, Malaysia, LAO Jordan, Spain and Turkey etc. However as a result of the WRC97 decisions a review of the interference calculation may drastically reduce the list of affected Administrations and therefore the coordination situation may be better in reality.

**Indian remote sensing satellite network**

*IRS-1C IRS-1E:* Coordination of IRS-1 E network is completed with Administrations of Japan, Australia, Russia and Sweden and ApS4 notices need to be sent to ITU at appropriate time. Coordination of IRS-1 C network is completed with Administrations of Russia, France and Germany and is being pursued with Sweden and Japan.

*IRS-P3:* Coordination completed with Germany & Japan and is in progress with other countries.

*IRS-113*: Advanced Publication Information for new IRS-1D Non-GSO satellite networks has been filed with ITU, for publication.

*IRS-P4*: Advanced Publication Information for IRS-P4 Non-GSO satellite networks has been published by ITU and comments have been received from the Administration of Malaysia, UAE, France, France/ EUTELSAT, Russia, Brazil, China, Japan, Germany, USA and Italy etc. coordination data to all these countries is being sent shortly.

**Stretched Rohini Satellite series network**

*SROSS-C2*: Coordination was pursued with the Administration of USA.

*Protection of INSAT space, terrestrial and radio astronomy services from the satellite networks of other countries*

A large number of new satellite networks have been planned by other countries in various frequency bands in the GSO arc of interest to India and the interference potential from these systems to INSAT Space and Terrestrial networks was assessed/evaluated on regular basis to protect our national interests.

Detailed coordination exercise for protection of Indian space & terrestrial networks and Radio Astronomy services was undertaken with other Administrations in all cases, where the potential interference exceeded the permissible limits.

**VSAT networks**

Frequency assignments for public/captive satellite communication network including that of VSAT networks were made to various service providers/users.

**Aspects relating to frequency management for terrestrial networks**

***GSM cellular***

Assignment of additional GSM mobile channels in 800/

900 MHz band has been made in four metro cities i.e. Delhi, Mumbai, Calcutta and Chennai in order to meet growth in cellular subscriber density.

**GSM cellular in circles**

Applications for frequency assignments from Cellular service providers for operation of GSM Mobile Network at various cities in all the Telecom Circles were received. Based on the requirements projected by these cellular operators, frequency assignments for GSM mobile and intra-city microwave access network have been made. In so far as inter-city microwave backbone networks are concerned, most of the assignments have been made after extremely complex task of frequency coordination with other users to ensure the electromagnetic compatibility and extensive frequency coordination process has been undertaken for the remaining.

**Radio paging service**

After successful coordination of frequencies for introduction of radio paging service, assignment of suitable frequencies, including link frequencies have been made, for operation of paging service on city wise basis as well as on circle basis, to radio paging service operators.

**Radio trunking service**

Assignment of frequencies for operation of city-wise radio trunking network in frequency bands 300 MHz, 400 MHz and 800MHz, as per channelling plans evolved for the purpose, have been made to the licenced radio trunking service operations based on their requests.

**Basic services**

Frequency sub-bands have been allocated to all Basic Service providers for their network planning. Additional spectrum requirement are being examined taking into account utilisation of spectrum by other services.

**Requests from foreign diplomatic missions**

Special requirements projected by foreign diplomatic missions for radio communications were considered and frequencies assigned.

**International conferences and meetings**

National preparations, participation and follow-up actions for the following important *international conferences and meetings were arranged by the WPC Wing.

The World Radiocommunication Conference, 1997 (WRC-97) of the ITU to consider and review the international radio regulatory processes and to provide for frequency allocation and radio regulating mechanism for various radiocommunication services within the frame work of the agenda of the conference.

The Conference Preparatory Meeting (CPM-97).

The Radiocommunication Assembly, 1997 (RA-97).

The 1997 Session of the ITU Council.

The 21st Session of the Management Committee of Asia Pacific Telecommunity (APT).

The APT Expert Group Meeting on WRC-97.

Meeting of the Radiocommunication Study Groups and their Working Parties.

**Wireless monitoring organisation**

Performance during the year 1997-98.

| | | 1.4.97 to 31.3.98 Actual |
|---|---|---|
| a) | Channel days utilised for Radio Monitoring | 6656 |
| b) | Monitoring Assignments handled. | 6499 |
| c) | No. of Wireless Stations Inspected. | 7290 |

d) No. of Radio Noise Measurements.

e) No. of Wireless Transmissions monitored. 89168

f)~ Infringements communicated to various users for remedial action. 6092

g) Technical Assistance to users to maintain their operation within specified standards. 3476

Many important Radio Surveys/Investigation assignments were carried out by way of Mobile Monitoring during the year.

Microwave Mobile Monitoring Terminals continued to monitor radio transmissions in microwave frequency bands to verify emission, characteristics and interference potential. The measurements on terrestrial microwave links viz LOS systems, Radars etc. to ensure compatibility are also being carried out regularly. Assistance was also being provided to the users by way of conducting noise surveys for wireless/earth stations and site selection. Microwave Terminals of Wireless Monitoring Organisation have earned a revenue of Rs.3.0 lakhs till 31.3.98, by way of their services to various user agencies.

Tenders for purchase of equipments/systems for establishment of specialised Monitoring Terminal at Delhi is under evaluation. The purchase order will be issued shortly.

International Satellite Monitoring Earth Station, Jalna -The International Satellite Monitoring Earth Station at Jalna is capable of monitoring of all communication satellite parked in geo-stationary orbit from 20 Deg. E to 140 Deg. E operating in "C" and "S" bands to ensure protection to Indian Space and Terrestrial Radio Communication Services against interference from space service operating by Satellites of other Administration. A number of Geo stationery Satellites (Indian Foreign) in the arc were also tracked.

The Satellite Monitoring Earth Station has actively participated in the monitoring of recently launched INSAT 2-D in coordination with the MCF Hassan of Deptt. of Space. The MCF Engineers were also present during the exercise and a close comparison of monitored results were made to establish the accuracy of the Satellite foot prints and also to ascertain the stability of the Space Craft. The monitoring mainly included the Satellite Telemetry Carriers apart from determination of EIRP levels of other communication transponders. This exercise continued for a weeks time alongwith the MCF Engineers and thereafter independently by ISMES Engineers. Necessary assignments were also issued to have a continuous monitoring of the Emissions from the INSAT 2-D Satellite to find the signal level variations. Thus the monitored data at ISMES provided vital information to compare with other monitored results and to adjudge the behaviour of the above Satellite.

Wireless Monitoring Training and Development Centre has conducted 9 Nos. inservice courses and imparted training to 89 officers/officials of the organisation in various disciplines during the period 1.4.97 to 31.3.98.

The Science and Technology Unit is in the process of development of some hardware and software required for monitoring systems and sub-systems used at various monitoring stations.

For strengthening the VHF/UHF monitoring systems 6 VHF/UHF receivers with spectrum analysers have been supplied to six monitoring stations. The systems have been installed at monitoring stations and are taking radio spectrum measurements.

VHF/UHF Direction Finding (DF) systems and one HF DF System have been purchased and its installation at the desired stations are under progress.

**Mahanagar telephone nigam limited**

Mahanagar Telephone Nigam Limited (MTNL) came into existence on 1st April 1986 as a company wholly owned by the Government of India under the Department of Telecommunications, Ministry of Communications. MTNL has been entrusted with the management, control and operations of Telecom services except telegraph services in metropolitan cities of Mumbai (including Navi Mumbai and Thane) and Delhi. At present, Govt. of India holds 56.25% of the equity of Rs.630 crores, rest of the equity is held by Fls, FIls, GDR holders and private individuals.

**Performance of the units during 1997-98**

*Tele services:* There has been all round development, growth in number of Direct Exchange Lines and improved operational efficiency. A variety of phone plus services have been made available to customers connected to electronic exchanges, computerised morning alarm, voice mail, radio paging, automatic changed number announcement etc., have been implemented. Sustained efforts have been made to maintain at high level the various operational parameters such as STD and call completion rate and manual trunk efficiency. MTNL has taken several steps to improve its interface with the customers. Telephone Adalats, Open House Sessions are being held to have effective both way communications with the customers. Quick customer service centres have been opened at all divisional offices for catering to day-to-day customers requirements for accessories, phone plus services, STD barring/restoration and local shift telephone.

**Finance**

MTNL has achieved a financial turnover of Rs.4654.59 crores, during the year under review with an increase of 15.47% over the previous year's turnover of Rs.4030.87 crores.

MTNL has registered a record profit of Rs.1 671.98 crores before tax and prior period adjustments, thus achieving a quantum leap of 18.47% over the profit of the previous year of Rs. 1411.35 crores. The net profit of the company has grown to Rs. 1130 crores thereby registering a growth of 21.37% over previous years' figure of Rs.932.78 crores.

MTNL's networth increased to Rs.5161.78 crores an increase of 45.9% over the previous years networth of Rs.3537.6 crores. This increase is on account of our asset build out and on account of accrual of funds due to our GDR issue.

During the year under review the total revenue expenditure excluding prior period adjustments was Rs.3107.35 crores registering an increase of 15.74% over the previous year's expenditure of Rs.2684.83.

*Financial results:* The financial highlights, sources and application of funds for the year under review are given hereunder:

| | 1997-98 | 1996-97 |
|---|---|---|
| | | *(Rs. in crores)* |
| Income from Services | 4654.59 | 4030.87 |
| Expenditure (excluding Interest & prior period Adjustment) | 3020.73 | 2537.21 |
| | | *(Rs. in crores)* |
| Operating Profit | 1633.86 | 1493.66 |
| Other Income | 124.74 | 65.31 |
| Interest | 86.62 | 147.62 |

| | | |
|---|---|---|
| Prior period adjustment | (-)17.18 | 70.75 |
| Profit before tax | 1654.80 | 1482.10 |
| Tax provision for the year | 524.67 | 549.32 |
| Net profit for the year | 1130.13 | 932.78 |
| Bond Redemption Reserve | | |
| Written back | 85.02 | 74.41 |
| Profit available for Appropriation | 1215.15 | 1007.19 |
| Proposed dividend | | |
| Divided Tax | 182.70 | 120.00 |
| a) Bond Redemption Reserve | 996.59 | 845.91 |
| b) General Reserve | | |
| Sources & Uses of Funds | | |
| Authorised Capital | 800.00 | 800.00 |
| Issued, Subscribed & paid up | 630.00 | 600.00 |
| Reserves & Surpluses | 4531.79 | 2937.65 |
| Secured & unsecured loan | 6549.31 | 7604.00 |
| REPRESENTED BY | | |
| Fixed Assets* (Net Block) | 4969.33 | 4605.68 |
| Net current assets | 6741.77 | 6535.97 |

* includes capital work-in-progress.

**Dividend**

MTNL paid of 30% dividend on the paid-up share capital of Rs.600 crores for the full year as against 20% for the previous year and 30% on additional paid up share capital of Rs.30 crores on prorata basis represented by GDRs issued in December'97.

**Capital expenditure on technology**

During the year under review, MTNL has spent an amount of Rs.912.54 crores as against Rs.885.27 crores in the previous year on account of capital expenditure. This was achieved entirely through internal resource generation. It has committed an amount of Rs.2772 to technology related spending in 1998-99.

**Trading of MTNL shares**

Shares of MTNL which are listed with principal stock exchanges of the country are being traded regularly in the stock exchanges of Mumbai, Calcutta, Delhi and Chennai as well as the National Stock Exchange of India.

**Global Depository Receipts (GDRS)**

MTNL has also successfully completed GDR offering of 35 million shares outside India consisting of 70 million shares. Out of this, 30 million shares were fresh issue of capital and remaining 40 million shares were divested by the Govt. of India. MTNL has also been listed on the London Stock Exchange and the GDRs issued by MTNL are being traded in London.

**Redemption of bonds**

During the year under report MTNL has redeemed bonds worth Rs.570 crores including Rs.405 crores pertaining to DOT.

*Productivity improvement:-* During the year under review, MTNL registered a significant increase in the productivity by bringing down the ratio of number of employees per thousand telephones for the two units as given below:

| *Year* | *Mumbai* | *Delhi* |
|---|---|---|
| 1992-93 | 32 | 37 |
| 1993-94 | 30 | 33 |
| 1994-95 | 23 | 28 |
| 1995-96 | 21 | 26 |
| 1996-97 | 21 | 21 |
| 1997-98 | 18 | 19 |

**Performance of the units**

Both the units at Delhi and Mumbai did exceedingly well during the year 1997-98. The details of achievements are given in next page

**Telephone systems**

| | | Achievements (Capacity in 'K' lines) Delhi | Mumbai |
|---|---|---|---|
| i. | Gross capacity additions | 159.920 | 339.106 |
| ii. | (a) Scrapping of equipment | 22.95 | 136 |
| | (b) Redeployment | — | 51.750 |
| iii. | Net capacity addition | 136.970 | 151.356 |
| iv. | DELs | 180.941 | 213.475 |
| v. | Cable laying(in LCKM) | 15.910 | 21.159 |
| vi. | Ducting (in KM) | 79.93 | 170.964 |
| vii. | Optical Fibre Cable (KMs) | 148.359 | 286.052 |
| viii. | Optical Fibre system(nos.) | 28 | 56 |
| ix. | Payphones(local & STD) (Nos.) | 2806 | 5897 |

**Quality service/operational efficiency**

Sustained efforts were made to maintain high standards of operational parameters such as fault rate, STD and local call completion rate and manual trunk efficiency.

**Fault rate**

No. of faults/100 telephones/month

| *Parameters* | *March'96* | *March'97* | *March'98* |
|---|---|---|---|
| Fault | | | |
| Mumbai | 21.20 | 13.75 | 11.72 |
| Delhi | 34.90 | 24.20 | 26.6 |

Significant improvement has been brought about in the local and STD call completion rate as is evident from the table below:-

(in percentage)

| | March 1986 | March 1997 | March 1998 |
|---|---|---|---|
| Mumbai | | | |
| Call Completion Rate (Network) | 93.00 | 91.5 | Presently fault completion rate is monitored on live Traffic basis & not On free to free Calls as in previous Years. |
| Call Completion Rate(STD) | 23.89 | 88.5 | |
| Delhi | | | |
| Call Completion Rate (Network) | 77.30 | 94.50 | 95.23 |
| Call Completion Rate(STD) | 30.00 | 90.00 | 93.80 |

**Clearance of waiting list**

With sustained efforts and timely implementation of various projects, the waiting list has a meagre figure of 1047 in Delhi whereas this is Nil in respect of Mumbai as on 31st March, 1998. MTNL is trying to provide telephone on demand.

**New services & computerisation : future projects**

***MICN : MTNL integrated computer network***

It is proposed to have a Wide Area Network (WAN) inter connecting all the computer systems of FRS, DQ & CSMS at Delhi and Mumbai. MTNL Integrated Computer Network (MICN) at Delhi and Mumbai will provide free flow of information on real time basis between systems (FRS, CSMS & DQ etc.) and will maintain integrity of data and also provide single window computer service centre.

**MTNL Delhi**

MICN is using routers interconnected through 64 kbps [eased lines to integrate the Computer systems like CSMS, FRS, Directory Enquiry, IVRS etc. During the year 1997-98,

MICN equipment was implemented to integrate CSMS in all the 8 operational areas, FRS at 13 sites & DQ systems at KBN.

**MLDN: managed leased data network**

MTNL intends to meet the requirement of 64 kbps data (and higher rate) cct. user to provide end to end manageability upto subscriber premises.

The tender for procurement of MLDN equipment for Delhi and Mumbai is already finalised. Purchase Order released, TEC approval obtained. Delivery of equipment expected by December, 1998 end.

**FRS: Fault repair/reporting system**

**MTNL Delhi** : Working in all major wire centres.

**MTNL Mumbai:** In MTNL Mumbai FRS has been computerised in all exchanges. Monsoon Cable Fault System and fault analysis system has also be implemented.

**Automatic telephone complaint booking system(2198)**

MTNL Delhi :To supplement the conventional operator booking of complaints on 198/2198 IVRS has been introduced in all the FRSs of Central area. The salient features of IVRS are:

- Booking of Telephone Complaint 198 (PSTN).
- Automatic Testing of Telephone line through FRS lost.
- Acceptance of clearance report from line man.
- Clearance of complaint after confirmation from subscriber.

**MTNL Mumbai:-** This has already been installed in 27 exchanges. It is proposed to implement this positively in other exchanges.

**DO: Directory enquiry**

**MTNL Delhi** :- Computerised Directory Enquiry:

a) Following services/systems were added/implemented during the year 1997-98. Augmentation in the Directory Enquiry Centres and operators position was done as detailed below:

| S.NO. | DO CENTRE | AUGMENTATION |
|---|---|---|
| i. | Nehru Place | 4 Operator Positions |
| ii. | Laxmi Nagar | 8 Operator Positions |
| iii. | Shakti Nagar | 8 Operator Positions |
| iv. | Janakpuri | DO centre installation under progress at KBN. |

b) Directory Enquiry updation provided at all the RSUs/RLU in MTNL through CSMS/FRS terminals on MICN during the year 1997-98. Earlier DO updation was being done through about 30 - places(Main Exch./RSU) using terminals directly connected to DO System at KBN.

c) First CD ROM for MTNL Delhi Telephone Directory with retrieval software developed by IT unit and data updated upto 6.3.97 brought out for public in July, 1997.

d) Software modifications were done for all the comments and complaints received from the first CD ROM and were incorporated in the second CD ROM with data updated upto 1 st November, 1997. The CD ROM was brought out for public on 8.1.98. The software was also developed containing STD, ISD, Mobile, home service and paging information which was distributed to the public with second CD ROM.

e) Overall position of the DO centres and the terminals (Enq./Updation) working for the centralised DQ system at KBN is as follows:

| S.NO. | DO CENTRE | ENQUIRY | UPDATION |
|---|---|---|---|
| | KBN | 60 Operator position | 33 terminals |
| | Eastern Court (Walk-in Directory) | 1 Operator position | |
| iii) | Nehru Place | 20 Operator positions | |
| iv) | R.K.Puram | 8 Operator positions | |
| v) | Karol Bagh | 24 Operator position | 50 terminals |
| vi) | Shakti Nagar | 24 Operator positions | |
| vii) | Laxmi Nagar | 34 Operator positions | |

MTNL Mumbai: The DO system has been computerised. The software has been developed by M/s National Information Centre, Pune on UNIX Platform and using Oracle.

As a first step decentralisation of computerised Directory Enquiry System commissioned in Thane - Charai and Goregaon Exchanges.

The CD-ROM second issues of the Telephone Directory has been produced.

*Change number announcement system:* A 64 port change number announcement service has been commissioned in three languages i.e. 1951 (Hindi), 1952 (English) & 1953(Marathi).

*National directory enquiry service (NDQ):* NDQ through INET is implemented between a number of cities.

*T.R.billing:* Already computerised. The printing of bar code in all the telephone bills introduced to facilitate speedy, accurate data capture of the payment details.

**CSMS (Customer Service Management System)**

A computerised CSMS at Delhi & Mumbai is being implemented to provide an Integrated Financial &

Commercial service which will enable on line updating of subscribers account and a quicker implementation of inter exchange shifts. Providing enhanced customer service etc. CSMS consists of Pre & Post connection modules, Telephone Billing, Commercial records, Telephone Revenue accounting, works accounting, Pay Bill accounting, PF Accounting and Financial accounting.

Software for an integrated on line Commercial and billing system has been implemented in South area at Mumbai.

CSMS commissioned in West-I and East-11, North, Central areas.

*TR billing:-* Already computerised. The printing of Bar Code in all the Telephone bills introduced to facilitate speedy accurate data capture of the payment details.

**Commercial service**

On line registration of new LINE APPLICATION working in eight areas in Mumbai.

*Work order compliance system:-***The** new system developed on UNIX platform using ORACL RDBIVIS has been implemented centrally for all exchanges in MTNL Mumbai.

**Inventory management system**

A LAN is working in Material Management Section in MTNL Mumbai and MTNL Corporate offices at New Delhi.

**Entry of MTNL into cellular services**

MTNL is proposing to become a Cellular Services provider in Delhi and Mumbai for establishing these services.

In this connection a tender has been floated by MTNL Corporate office and also applied to WPC for allocation of frequencies of spectrum 900/1800 Mhz GSM Cellular Band.

**Wireless in local loop**

MTNL is proposing to introduce wireless in local loop in Delhi and Mumbai. Tender floated for WIL system CDMA-IA-95 A Technology for 50K lines for MTNL Mumbai.

Applied to W. P.C. for WIL system frequency allotment 824-849Mhz/869-894Mhz band for WIL system at Delhi.

*MTNL home page in internet:-* To provide better services to the customers, application form related to various services have been made available on MTNLs Home Page in Internet.

MTNL has obtained the license to operate ISP services in Delhi and Mumbai. The equipment has already been ordered and services are targeted to be commissioned on 26th January, 1999. The initial capacity in Phase I implementation will be 9600/subscribers in Delhi and Mumbai. MTNL also plans to take these services to the common man by providing 20 Cyber Dhabas in Delhi and Mumbai each by March, 1999.

**Single window facility for customer**

*MTNL Delhi:-* CSC centres at 5 places in Central Delhi i.e. Mohan Singh Place, Jeevan Tara Building, Rajpath, Shastri Bhavan, Parliament Annexee, one place in North (Shalimar Bagh) and one place in South Delhi i.e. Panchsheel were opened during 1997-98.

**Physical achievements of MTNL at a glance**

**Development targets/achievements**

| | **Delhi** | | **Mumbai** | |
|---|---|---|---|---|
| | *Target* | *Achievements* | *Target* | *achievements* |
| | | | (Capacity in "K" Lines) | |
| 1997-98 | | | | |
| A. Switching | | | | |
| i. Gross Capacity | 319 | 159.92 | 340 | 339.106 |

| | | | | | |
|---|---|---|---|---|---|
| ii. | Scrapping | 62 | 72.95 | 60 | 187.750 |
| iii. | Withdrawn for Redeployment | | | | |
| iv. | Net Capacity | 257 | 136.97 | 280 | 151.356 |
| v. | DELs | 214 | 180.941 | 226 | 213.475 |
| vi. | TAX | 40 | 15 | 10 | - |
| B. | Subscribers External Plant | | | | |
| i. | Cable Laying (in LCKM) | 29.25 | 15.910 | - | 20.684 |
| ii. | Ducting(in Kms) | 100 | 79.93 | 100 | 170.964 |
| C. | Transmission Name of System | | | | |
| ii. | 565 Mbs OF Sys. | — | 13 | — | — |
| iii. | 34 Mbps | — | 1 | — | 1 |
| iv. | Optical Fibre cable (in Kms.) | 750 | 148.354 | — | 286.012 |

## Writing list and new registration

| | | DELHI | MUMBAI |
|---|---|---|---|
| i. | Waiting List as on 1.4.98 | 1048 | — |
| ii. | New Registration March'98 | 174562 | 229790 |
| E. | PCO's | | |
| a) | Local | 844 | 4045 |
| b) | STID | 1962 | 1852 |
| F. | DELs Provided March'98 | 180941 | 213475 |

## Financial performance (1997-98)

### *Financial indicators*

| | |
|---|---|
| Telecom. Revenue | 4654.59 |
| Other Income | 124.74 |
| Charges for National Network | 1024.00 |
| Licence Fee | 271.11 |
| Depreciation | 585.62 |

| | |
|---|---|
| Operational Expenditure | 1140.00 |
| Interest | 86.62 |
| Profit before tax | 1671.98 |
| Corporate Tax | 524.67 |
| Prior period adjustments | -17.18 |
| Net Profit | 1130.13 |

**Financial results**

***Balance sheet as on 31.03.1998***

| | *As on 31.03.1998 (Rs.)* | *As on 31.03.1997 (Rs.)* |
|---|---|---|
| **Source of funds** | | |
| Shareholder's funds : | | |
| Share Capital | 6300000000 | 6000000000 |
| Reserves & Surplus | 45317894001 | 29376456248 |
| **Loan funds:** | | |
| Secured Loans | 12582901727 | 18009092377 |
| Unsecured Loans | 52910177254 | 58030985333 |
| Total | 117110972982 | 111416533958 |
| **Application of funds** | | |
| Fixed Assets | | |
| Gross Block | 80580540699 | 69855568138 |
| Less: Depreciation | 37100044716 | 31611108522 |
| Net Block | 43480495983 | 38244459616 |
| Capital Work-i n- Progress | 6212812521 | 7812372740 |
| Current Assets, Loans & Advances | | |
| Inventories | 2558184780 | 2457084176 |
| Sundry Debtors | 6105695465 | 6222628023 |
| Cash & Bank Balances | 13284937813 | 3721217239 |
| Other Current Assets | 5392282185 | 4310001630 |
| Loans & Advances | 76269644086 | 84030798984 |
| | 103610744329 | 100741730052 |
| Less: Current Liabilities and Provisions | | |
| Current Liabilities | 23192273448 | 22186111911 |

| | | |
|---|---|---|
| Provisions | 13000806403 | 13195916539 |
| Net Current Assets | 67417664478 | 65359701602 |
| Total | 117110972982 | 111416533958 |

**Profit and loss account for the period ended on 31st March, 1998.**

| | *For the year ended 31.3.1998 Rs.* | *For the year ended 31.3.1997 Rs.* |
|---|---|---|
| INCOME | | |
| Income from services | 46545890253 | 40308746913 |
| Other Income | 1247395482 | 653050861 |
| EXPENDITURE | | |
| Employees' remuneration and Benefits | 5167019531 | 4284290098 |
| Charges for use of National Network | 10239976824 | 8822542428 |
| Licence Fee | 2711091600 | 2347015500 |
| Administrative, Operating & Other expenses | 6232962525 | 4767898217 |
| Depreciation | 5856199481 | 5150375041 |
| Interest | 866241941 | 1476160016 |
| | 31073491902 | 26848281300 |
| Profit before Tax | 16719793833 | 14113516474 |
| Provision for Taxation | 5246671000 | 5493200000 |
| Profit after Tax | 11473122833 | 8620316474 |
| Prior period adjustments | -171826550 | 707535432 |
| Profit for the year | 11301296283 | 9327851906 |
| Bond Redemption Reserve written back | 850200000 | 744136000 |
| Profit available for Appropriation | 12151496283 | 10071987906 |
| **Appropriation** | | |
| Bonds Redemption Reserve | 17588200 | 292853571 |
| Proposed Dividend | 1827041096 | 1200000000 |
| Dividend Tax | 182704110 | 120000000 |
| General Reserve | 9965869077 | 8459134335 |
| | 12151496283 | 10071987906 |

**Dividend and reserves**

The Nigam declared a dividend of Rs. 182.70 crores, on the paid up capital of Rs.630 crores.

**Capital expenditure**

The capital expenditure for the years 1987-88 onwards is as follows:

*(Rs.in crores)*

| Year | Amount |
|---|---|
| 1987-88 | 291 |
| 1988-89 | 390 |
| 1989-90 | 525 |
| 1990-91 | 558 |
| 1991-92 | 613 |
| 1992-93 | 704 |
| 1993-94 | 837 |
| 1994-95 | 998 |
| 1995-96 | 984 |
| 1996-97 | 885 |
| 1997-98 | 912 |

**Manpower**

| *Group* | *Total Staff as on 31.3.98* | *SC as on 31.3.98* | *ST as on 31.3.98* |
|---|---|---|---|
| A | 790 | 91 | 6 |
| B | 2862 | 335 | 50 |
| C | 39640 | 5914 | 1003 |
| D | 19181 | 4766 | 1101 |
| | 62473 | 11106 | 2160 |
| DRM | 793 | — | — |
| TOTAL | 63266 | 11106 | 2160 |

**Videsh sanchar nigam limited**

**Services**

*Basic services:* More than 85% of the VSNLs revenues are derived from basic services.

**Telephony**

VSNL has kept pace with the globalisation and enhanced business opportunities following the liberalisation of the economy. Its emphasis on upgrading of Answer-to-Seizure Ratios(ASR) has resulted not only in improved quality but has also served to decongest VSNL gateways leading to a substantial increase in revenue. The growth of Telephone circuits is

| | As on 31-03-1997 | As on 31-03-1998 |
|---|---|---|
| Telephone | 14184 | 15431 |

**Country direct services**

The VSNL has been enhancing basic telephony services with value added options such as the Home Country Direct Service and Toll-free calls Service.

**Telegraph service**

The International Telegraph Service is operated directly to 30 countries on 35 telegraph channels from all the four Gateway centres of VSNL.

**Specialised services**

*Leased line services*

The Leased Line Services serve as communication facilitators in an age where instant access to information is a business asset. The leased line at 64 KBPS capacity has gone up from 402 on 31.03.1997 to 603 on 31.03.1998 i.e. an increase by 50%.

**Television transmission**

VSNL handles the transmission and reception of all TV programs via satellite from India to other countries. These TV programs are currently handled by the International Television Centres (ITC) at VSNLs Mumbai and New Delhi Gateways.

**Satellite networks**

VSNL is a signatory to the INTELSAT system and operates via satellites in the Indian ocean region.

**International business services (IBS)**

International Business Services earth stations can be set up at user premises to provide fully digital streams at bit rates of 64 kbps - 2 Mbps and higher rates based upon the requirement of user.

**Inmarset services**

Inmarset Services is a global mobile satellite system providing mobile communication services to ship-based, land mobile and aeronautical terminals.

**Submarine optical fibre cables**

Submarine Cables based upon optical fibre technology are the digital highways of the Global Communications System. Compared to a satellite-based transmission where there is a delay of 250 msec., optical cables reduce transmission delays depending on the distance to 10-30 millisecs.

**Internet services**

The INTERNET Services introduced by the VSNL on a commercial scale in 1995-96 has registered a rapid increase in the number of customers. Thus where as on 31 March, 1996 the number of customers was 3932 only it increased to 28,402 on 31 March, 1997 and on 31 March, 1998 it galloped to 90,042.

**VSNLs telecommunications infrastructure**

The VSNLs Telecommunications Infrastructure today provides a comprehensive network India for high-quality and efficient international telecommunications services.

*Gateways*

VSNL has four Gateways which are located in the metropolitan cities of Mumbai, Calcutta, New Delhi and Chennai.

***Earth stations:***

VSNL has at present six Standard A Earth Stations which cater to the Gateways of Mumbai, New Delhi, Calcutta and Chennai.

***Submarine cables***

The VSNL Gateway at Mumbai is connected to the optical fibre digital highway SEA-ME-WE2 which extends from Singapore in Asia to Marseilles (France) in Europe. The submarine cable has the capability of tally digital connectivity around the globe.

***Gateway switches***

All the four Gateways of VSNL are equipped with modern digital gateways which provide facilities for international telephony. The capacity of all GDS has recently been augmented.

***Packet switches***

The VSNLs first Packet Switch has been operating at Mumbai, since 1988. The Gateway Packet Switch Services (GPSS) are the main stay of computer communications, E-mail and database access. In June, 1993, a Gateway Packet Switching Node (GPSN) was commissioned at New Delhi and Calcutta.

**Major schemes implemented in eighth five year plan**

Under the VIIIth Five Year Plan (1992-98) the following major projects are underway.

- Videsh Sanchar Bhavan at Calcutta Standard-A Earth Station at Calcutta (Completed)
- Standard-A Earth Station at Chennai (Completed) SEA-ME-WE-2Y Fibre Optic Cable (Completed)
- Mumbai-Arvi optic Fibre Link (Completed)
- Calcutta-Halisahar Digital Microwave and Optic Fibre Links (Completed) Chennai-Korattur Optic Fibre and Digital Microwave Links (Completed)

- Point to Multipoint Microwave Links at New Delhi, Mumbai, Calcutta, Chennai, Bangalore (Under Implementation). Expansion of Gateway Exchange capacities at Mumbai, New Delhi, Calcutta and Chennai (completed)
- New Gateway at Kanpur (Under Implementation)
- Packet Switches at Gateway Centres (Mumbai, New Delhi, Calcutta (completed) Restoration Earth Station facility at Dehradun (Completed)
- Participation in Global Mobile Satellite Systems e.g. ICO (INMARSET P),Iridium, Globalstar ACS Ltd. (Under Implementation).
- Value Added Services (E-Mail, EDI, Store & Forward Fax (Completed)
- Participation in Submarine Optical Fibre Systems e.g. FLAG, SEA-ME-WE-3 (Under Implementation)
- inmarsat'A, 'C', "B/M" services (Completed),
- Augmentation of Inmarsat B/M services Completed.

**Current and future plans**

***Transmission schemes***

MUMBAI (LVSB)-PUNE-ARVI MICROWAVE SYSTEM (140 MBPS 2+1 CONFIGURATION is planned to connect Mumbai gateway with Pune operating centre and Arvi earth station in order to provide diversity of transmission medium.

NEW DELHI-DEHRADUN MICROWAVE SYSTEM (140 MBPS 2+1) is planned to provide a diverse transmission medium to the Dehradun earth station.

AUGMENTATION OF CALCUTTA-HALISAHAR MICROWAVE LINK:

CAPACITY AUGMENTATION OF MUMBAI-PUNE-ARVI OPTICAL FIBRE SYSTEM (2.4 gbps 1+1):

NEW DELHI-DEHRADUN OPTICAL FIBRE SYSTEM (560 MBPS 1 +1): is planned by upgrading the existing OF systems.

AUGMENTATION OF CALCUTTA & HALISAHAR OPTICAL FIBRE SYSTEM (Scheme Cost: Rs. 800 lakhs):

SEA-ME-WE-3 SUBMARINE OPTICAL FIBRE SYSTEM is planned for connecting Singapore in the east to France in Europe.

INTELSAT STD-A EARTH STATION AT ARVI -is planned to augment the uplinking facilities in the C band for the Western region.

STANDARD A EARTH STATION AT HALISAHAR, CALCUTTA is proposed to be constructed due to the restructuring of Intelsat Satellite deployment in IOR.

STANDARD "B" EARTH STATION AT KANPUR is planned to be linked with a proposed International Gateway Switch to provide direct uplinking transmission facility. 7.1.11 STANDARD "' EARTH STATION AT ERNAKULAM is planned to cater to the large traffic requirements from the Southern Zone and Kerala region.

STANDARD "B" EARTH STATION AT BANGALORE is desired to provide direct uplinking from the Gateway Switch planned at Bangalore.

STANDARD "C" EARTH STATION AT JULLUNDUR is under the planning and implernentation phase and expected to be completed in 1998.

MODIFIED STANDARD ANTENNA FOR WORKING WITH OTHER SATELLITES is proposed to be installed during the 9th Plan.

VSNL ROOF TOP EARTH STATIONS are planned for

Calcutta and New Delhi Videsh Sanchar Bhavan which will provide diverse outlets at VSNL gateways as well as requisite additional connectivity~ for operation with new Intelset Satellite being deployed in the IOR.

TRANSPORTABLE EARTH STATIONS are proposed to be purchased at each of the four Gateways for special applications.

CUSTOMER PREMISES IBS/VSAT EARTH STATIONS

AUGMENTATION OF POINT TO MULTIPOINT SYSTEMS AT 4 GATEWAYS

AUGMENTATION OF INMARSAT MOBILE SERVICES (]INMARSAT A,C, B/M)

INMARSAT AERONAUTICAL SERVICES is proposed for the 9th Plan to enable aeronautical and airbound terminals to use the Indian LES for mobile services.

PURCHASE OF DIGITAL CIRCUIT MULTIPLICATION EQUIPMENT AT THE GATEWAY) DIGITAL SWITCHES is planned to cater to approximately 27,000 circuits as against current approximately 9,600 circuits.

CREATION OF CABLE DEPOT AND INVESTING IN CABLE SHIP are planned for the 9th Plan to provide immediate repair of cable cuts.

**Switching schemes**

GATEWAY DIGITAL SWITCH EXPANSION

ESTABLISHMENT OF INTERNATIONAL SUPER HIGHWAY GATEWAYS

PACKET SWITCHING SYSTEMS AUGMENTATION AND FRAME RELAY SERVICES

ADDITIONAL INTERNATIONAL GATEWAYS

Expansion of VIDEO SWITCHES have been planned to cater the steady rise in handling video programmes.

METRO SWITCHES (Scheme Cost: Rs. 40,000 lakhs) are planned to be augmented during the 9th Plan which will generate the base traffic through the domestic customers linkages which will flow to the international gateway switches of VSNL.

**Mobile satellite services**

GATEWAY FOR ICO SERVICES (SAN) is planned for providing uplinking of traffic to the Inmarsat -P mobile system.

GATEWAY FOR IRIDIUM MOBILE SATELLITE SYSTEM is being constructed at Dighi, Pune and the project is expected to be completed in 1998.

INVESTMENT IN DOMESTIC MOBILE SATELLITE SERVICE GATEWAYS

GATEWAYS FOR GLOBALSTAR is planned for providing mobile communications world-wide to its users.

**Management facilities**

INTEGRATED NETWORK MANAGEMENT CENTRE is proposed to beset up to provide a full fledged display of the entire network and will be capable of monitoring the status of all transmission systems as well as efficiency of traffic routing on the major routes.

INTEGRATED CUSTOMER RESPONSE SYSTEM is proposed to be established to enable the customers to access for information in respect of service features, tariffs and billing information from any centre in India.

MANAGEMENT INFORMATION SYSTEM is proposed to be further expanded during the Ninth Plan through integration of office automatic facilities to provide an integrated management information system.

CENTRALISED TRANSMISSION MANAGEMENT SYSTEM is planned to enable the VSNL to manage the Earth Stations working by extending the alarms and control of various equipments to the control location.

**Restoration schemes** are planned to provide alternative transmission media for access to international facilities.

**Technical equipments**

TEST INSTRUMENTS for various types of equipments are proposed to be procured.

PURCHASE OF EQUIPMENT FOR INTERNATIONAL TELECOM BUREAUS are proposed to further enhance the capabilities of ITBs for use by customers

MINOR EQUIPMENTS like fire control systems, in-station announcements and management, routine maintenance and other safety equipments are planned to be purchased during Ninth period for which Rs.35.00 crores have been provided.

**Value added services**

MESSAGE HANDLING SERVICES are proposed to be enhanced by upgradation of equipments and transmission facilities for high speed working.

INTERNET ACCESS SERVICES are proposed to be augmented by providing a high bandwidth bandbone net work in India linking all the nodes and providing interconnectivity services to customers and domestic service providers.

VSAT SERVICES -An investment of Rs.40 crores is envisaged for this project and it is to be carried out in phases by June,2001.

MANAGED DATA NETWORK SERVICES are proposed to be expanded by enhancing the circuit capacities and the node locations.

VIDEO CONFERENCE FACILITIES are proposed to be upgraded and also extended to other locations not currently covered by this service.

TELECOMMUNICATIONS FACILITY PROVISION- A provision of Rs.20 crores has been kept for the purchase of equipment and placement at customers premises as turn key contracts in international telecom facilities.

INVESTMENT IN JOINT VENTURES -During the 8th Plan VSNL had taken steps to form joint ventures with TELSTRA AUSTRALIA for VSAT and value added services. For 9th Plan also provision has been made under this.

**Replacement schemes**

POWER PLANTS-10 Power Plants are planned to be replaced.

AC PLANTS-20 AC Plants are planned to be replaced.

VEHICLES-40 vehicles are planned to be replaced.

REPLACEMENT OF MICROWAVE SYSTEM AT DELHI DEHRADUN AND MUMBAI-ARVI is planned by superior updated systems during the next five years.

REPLACEMENT OF STANDARD A ANTENNA AT ARVI is planned by a new Standard A Antenna by 2001-02 to ensure reliable operation and maintainability.

**Video facilities**

VIDEO UPLINKING FACILITIES- The VSNL proposes to provide these facilities in view of frequent requirements of up-linking TV Programmes from India for the purpose of satellite broadcasting.

MODIFIED STANDARD A ANTENNA FOR UPLINKING is planned for Arvi by June, 1 998 with the purpose of commencing operations with the Panamsat Satellite systems for video up-linking and distributions.

DTH SATELLITE SYSTEMS FACILITIES- The VSNL is contemplating an investment of Rs.1 00 crores to form a Joint Venture company with INTELSAT in introducing this service.

**General**

OFFICE AUTOMATION SCHEME which was implemented in VSNL covering senior officers is proposed to be extended fully to all operating sections/Divisions during the 9th Plan.

COMPUTER FOR FINANCE AND ACCOUNTS- An integrated computer system with OA network is proposed to be provided for the management of the finance and accounts in VSNL.

**Research and development**

ESTABLISHMENT OF STANDARDISATION FACILITY to test prototypes by June,2001.

OTHER ACTIVITIES-it is proposed to take up R & D activities on a large scale from Mumbai and Bangalore during the 9th Five Year Plan.

**Training programmes to upgrade employee skills**

The training facilities at training institute, Pune are proposed to be expanded and developed in line with the requirements of VSNL in terms of staff, training and operational support.

TELECOM MANAGEMENT SCHOOL- Upgradation of Pune training facility to provide a management course with special emphasis on telecom management is also being planned in the 9th Five Year Plan.

Balance sheet as on 31.03.1998

| *Particulars* | | *As on 31/03/98 (Rupees in Millions)* | *As on 31/03/97 (Rupees in Millions)* |
|---|---|---|---|
| 1. | SOURCES OF FUNDS | | |
| 1. | Shareholders' Funds | | |
| (a) | Share Capital | 950.00 | 921.65 |
| (b) | Reserves and Surplus | 40,853.09 | 28,857.18 |
| 2. | Loan Funds | | |
| (a) | Secured Loans | 1,562.31 | 2,502.77 |
| | TOTAL | 43,365.40 | 32,281.60 |
| 11. | APPLICATIONS OF FUNDS | | |
| 1. | Fixed Assets | | |
| (a) | Gross Block | 15,215.69 | 12,345.20 |
| (b) | Less : Depreciation | (4,631.53) | (3,960.64) |
| (c) | Net Block | 10,584.15 | 8,384.56 |
| (d) | Investments in Communications Satellites | 2,250.20 | 1,617.86 |
| (e) | Capital Work-in Progress | 1,669.34 | 1,309.79 |
| 2. | Investments | 3,735.54 | 3,137.73 |
| 3. | Current Assets, Loans & Advances | | |
| (a) | Inventories | 10.49 | 11.66 |
| (b) | Sundry Debtors | 16,816.71 | 15,298.52 |
| (c) | Cash and Bank Balance | 25,137.62 | 14,593.59 |
| (d) | Other Current Assets | 206.26 | 58.52 |
| (e) | Loans and Advance | 6,406.31 | 7,540.98 |
| | TOTAL (A) | 48,577.40 | 37,503.2 |

| | | | |
|---|---|---|---|
| | Less: Current Liabilities & Provisions | | |
| (a) | Current Liabilities | 18,042.87 | 13,072.84 |
| (b) | Provisions | 5,399.37 | 6,598.77 |
| | TOTAL (B) | 23,442.24 | 19,671.61 |
| | Net Current Assets | | |
| | (A-B) | 25,135.16 | 17,831.66 |
| | TOTAL | 43,365.40 | 32,281.60 |

**Profit and loss account for the year ended 31.03.1998**

| *Particulars* | *As on 31/03/98 (Rupees in Millions) (Audited)* | *As on 31/03/97 (Rupees in Millions) (Audited)* |
|---|---|---|
| INCOME | | |
| Traffic Revenue | 60,749.84 | 51,730.21 |
| Revenue from Intelsat/ Inmarsat | 501.28 | 375.59 |
| Other Income | 3,110.21 | 747.24 |
| TOTAL (A) | 64,361.33 | 52,853.04 |
| **Expenditure** | | |
| Payment to & Provision for Employees | 804.18 | 566.46 |
| Network Cost | 47,121.59 | 42,413.02 |
| Operating & other expenses | 417.67 | 470.37 |
| Administrative expenses | 1,066.55 | 305.22 |
| Interest | 12.31 | 44.27 |
| Depreciation | 659.14 | 581.18 |
| Less : Transferred from Capital reserve | (4.26) | (4.85) |
| | | 576.33 |
| TOTAL(B) | 50,077.19 | 44,375.67 |

| | | |
|---|---|---|
| Profit before tax(A-B) | 14,284.14 | 8,477.37 |
| Prior Year Adjustments | (294.85) | (214.69) |
| Provision for Taxation | (4,310.12) | (3,220.10) |
| Excess Tax Provision written back | 0 | 4.85 |
| Profit After Taxes | 9,679.16 | 5,047.43 |
| Surplus brought forward | 32.62 | 193.18 |
| Amount available for Appropriations | 9,711.77 | 5,240.61 |
| Appropriations | | |
| Proposed Dividend | 380.00 | 280.00 |
| Tax on Proposed Dividend | 38.00 | 28.00 |
| Transferred to General Reserve | 9,200.00 | 4,900.00 |
| Surplus carried to Balance Sheet | 93.77 | 32.61 |

**Personnel**

Statement showing the table number of Employees and the number of Scheduled Castes and Scheduled Tribe as on 31/03/1998.

| | TOTAL | | SC | | ST | |
|---|---|---|---|---|---|---|
| | Mar'97 | Mar'98 | Mar'97 | Mar'98 | Mar'97 | Mar'98 |
| Group A | 634 | 635 | 96 | 102 | 18 | 15 |
| Group B | 295 | 312 | 46 | 45 | 24 | 26 |
| Group C | 1335 | 1344 | 287 | 280 | 88 | 86 |
| Group D (Excluding Safai Karmachari) | 555 | 516 | 166 | 164 | 47 | 45 |
| Group D Safai Karmachari) | 54 | 54 | 45 | 44 | 02 | 02 |
| Total | 2873 | 2861 | 640 | 635 | 179 | 174 |

**Indian telephone industries limited**

ITI Limited, Bangalore was established in July 1948 as a Departmental Undertaking of the Government of India and was converted into a Company in January 1950. It was the first Public Sector Undertaking to be established in the Country. The Company is the largest Public Sector Undertaking in the field of Telecommunication. It is a Total Solution Company. Eversince its inception, it has been a profit making Company till the year 1993-94. ITI has seven manufacturing units, out of which, three are in the south and four are in the north. In the south, the units are located at Bangalore, Palakkad and EC Unit on Hosur Road. In the north, they are located at Naini, Rae Bareli, Mankapur and Srinagar.

The Company manufactures almost the entire range of Telecom equipment and has been responsible for building around 70% to 80% of the country's existing Telecom Infrastructure. This has been possible through its countrywide service network and state-of-the-art technology. In addition, ITI has expertise in Defence Telecom, being the provider of nearly the entire static network of the Army. The other major customers of the Company are Railways, Industrial Organisations, Electricity Boards etc. The thrust of the Company is to enlarge the customer base including exports.

**Financial review**

The company has shown a marked improvement in its performance during 1997-98 as compared to 1996-97. The highlights of the performance for the year 1997-98 are as follows :

Increase in Sales by 24% with respect to 1996-97 and by 61 % with respect to 1995-96.

Increase in production value by 24% with respect to 1996-97 and by 81% with respect to 1995-96.

Interest cost (Net) as percentage to production value has come down to 11.66% from 18.04% for 1996-97 and 21.13% for 1995-96.

Profit before tax is Rs.11.26 Crores during the year as against the loss of Rs.87.66 Crores in 1996-97 and loss of Rs.283.96 Crores in 1995-96. After taking into account the provision for tax of earlier years which is no longer required, the profit stood at Rs. 15.26 Crores.

Increase in positive networth from Rs.58 Crores to Rs.83 Crores.

Saving of Rs.36 Crores by the way of interest cost by better working capital management.

Reduction in material consumption by 5% w.r.t. production value.

Reduction in inventory from 6.50 months to 4.90 months of production value.

Working capital brought down from 8.48 months to 7.44 months of production.

Decrease in borrowings by Rs.50.67 Crores in spite of increase in production.

During the year 1997-98, several actions has been taken by the company for building up a competitive edge. The actions initiated are:

Reduction of Manpower through VRS, Lien etc. to an extent of 902 employees.

Increase in the volume of production through competitive bidding.

Activation of Regional Offices for Non-DOT business.

The summarised profit and loss account for the year 1997-98 and Balance Sheet as on 31 st March 1998 are furnished below:

**Profit and loss account for the year ended 31st March 1998**

*(Rs. in Crores)*

| *Particulars* | *Amount* |
|---|---|
| INCOME | |
| Sales & services | 1263.05 |
| Accretion/(Decretion) to Work-in-Process and Stock-in-Trade & Manufactured Components | 3.89 |
| Value of Production | 1266.94 |
| Other Income | 152.16 |
| Total | 1419.10 |
| EXPENDITURE | |
| Material Cost | 677.58 |
| Employees Cost | 321.68 |
| Depreciation | 27.31 |
| Interest (Net) | 147.73 |
| Others | 227.83 |
| Total | 1402.13 |
| Profit before Tax for the year | 16.97 |
| Prior Period Adjustments(net) | (-) 5.71 |
| Profit before Tax | 11.26 |
| Less: Provision for Tax | — |
| Add : Provision for Tax of earlier years no longer required | 4.00 |
| Profit after Tax | 15.26 |
| Own Funds | |
| Share Capital | 88.00 |
| Reserve and Surplus (including Grant-in-Aid) | 158.20 |
| Loan Funds | |
| Cash Credit and Secured Loans | 677.28 |
| Bonds and Secured Loans | 177.85 |
| Unsecured Loans | 51.83 |
| Total | 1153.16 |

| | |
|---|---|
| Application of funds | |
| Fixed Assets | |
| Net Fixed Assets including | |
| Capital Work-in-progress | 306.96 |
| Current Assets, Loans and Advances | 1501.53 |
| Less : Current Liabilities | |
| and Provisions | 785.93 |
| Investments | 34.95 |
| Miscellaneous Expenditure | |
| not written off | 1.17 |
| Profit and Loss Account | 24.15 |
| Total | 1153.16 |

**Physical performance**

The production performance in physical units for the years 1996-97 and 1997-98 areas indicated below:

| *Description* | *Accounting Unit* | *1997-98 Actuals* | *1996-97 Actuals* |
|---|---|---|---|
| *Switching Equipments* | | | |
| Small Switches | KL | 15.70 | 2.70 |
| E1013 Local | KL | 893.70 | 1035.60 |
| El 013 DTAX | KC | 18.00 | 36.50 |
| OCB 283 Local | KL | 950.30 | 513.50 |
| OCB TAX | KC | 364.00 | 223.00 |
| C-DOT Exchanges | KL | 801.70 | 563.80 |
| *Transmission equipments* | | | |
| OPEN WIRE SYSTEM | Nos | 263 | 2014 |
| MARR | Nos | 355 | 50 |
| DIG RADIO TX/RX (2/6/7/11/13 GHZ) | Nos | 1240 | 995 |
| OPTIC FIBRE PDH | Nos | 1938 | 671 |
| OPTIC FIBRE SDH | Nos | 116 | NIL |
| MCPC VSAT | Nos | 67 | 25 |
| *Terminal equipments* | | | |
| Telephones | Nos | 1.03 | 0.840 |
| Solar Panels | Nos | 18000 | 26125 |

It maybe noticed that during the year 1997-98, the Company has shown a marked improvement in its physical performance.

### Manpower

The manpower employed by the Company as on 31st March 1998 stood at 24552 as against 25915 employees as on 31st March 1997. During the year 902 employees opted for the Voluntary Retirement Scheme. The manpower as on 31 st March 1998 included the following:-

i) Scheduled Caste - 4,623 Nos.
ii) Scheduled Tribe - 169 Nos.
iii) Physically Handicapped - 262 Nos.
iv) Ex-servicemen - 420 Nos.

### Hindustan teleprinters limited

HTL Ltd. was established in December 1960 at Chennal for manufacture of teleprinters and ancillary equipments. The Company has diversified into various fields, after phasing out the manufacture of teleprinters, so as to meet the various requirements of Department of Telecommunications.

### Share capital

The Paid Up Capital of the Company is Rs. 15 crores and the Authorised Capital Rs.20 crores. The entire shares as on 31.3.1998 are held by the Government of India.

### Performance

The overall performance of the company as compared to previous two years is summarised below:

*(Rs. In lakhs)*

| | | 1997-98 | 1996-97 | 1995-96** |
|---|---|---|---|---|
| (i) | Gross revenue | 29261.15 | 12524.32 | 16677.84 |
| (il) | Sales & Services | 27709.13 | 11156.97 | 15697.43 |
| (iii) | Profit before tax, Depreciation & Interest | | | |
| | (a) Profit before tax | 677.10 | (-)809.63 | 76.89 |

| | | | |
|---|---|---|---|
| (b) Depreciation | 283.60 | 208.87 | 197.74 |
| (c) Interest | 565.42 | 747.48 | 670.92 |
| (d) Provision for tax | 111.11 | 3.80 | 30.00 |
| (e) Profit after tax | 565.99 | (-)813.43 | 46.89 |

**Review of operations**

The target for equipment sales as per RE 1997-98 was Rs.25813 lakhs while the achievement amounted to Rs.27458 lakhs (Rs.10922 lakhs in the previous year). The value of sale of different products for the year under review with comparative figures for the previous two years is as follows :

*(Rs. In Lakhs)*

| Product | 1997-98 | 1996-97 | 1995-96* |
|---|---|---|---|
| 1. Switching Equipments | 23634 | 6041 | 10813 |
| 2. Main Distribution Frames | 1522 | 2031 | 2287 |
| 3. Data Modems, transmission equipments, PC based products | 971 | 2080 | 1458 |
| 4. Other equipments, fax machines, accessories & spares | 1331 | 770 | 992 |

**Financial review**

The Paid Up Capital of the company remained at Rs.15 crores as on 31.3.1998 as against the authorised capital of Rs.20 crores. Borrowings amounted to Rs.29.71 crores compared to previous year of Rs.39.04 crores on account of (i) repayment of Rs.12 crores to Unit Trust of India and (ii) increase in the interest accrued and due on Government of India loans from Rs.5.37 crores to Rs.6.12 crores. The company also received a loan of Rs.2 crores from the Government of India. The financial position as on 31.3.1998 as compared to the previous two years is as follows:

*(Rs. in lakhs)*

| | 1997-98 | 1996-97 | 1995-96 |
|---|---|---|---|
| (i) Capital employed | 6040 | 6209 | 7819 |
| (ii) Gross fixed assets including capital work in progress | 3904 | 3422 | 2882 |
| (iii) Net fixed assets including work in progress | 1688 | 1476 | 1132 |
| (iv) Working capital | 4523 | 5194 | 6813 |
| (v) Net worth (paid up capital plus reserves) | 3932 | 3410 | 4162 |
| (vi) Reserves & surplus | 2432 | 1910 | 2662 |

**Production performance:** The Production Performance during the year under review is as follows:

| ITEMS | 1997-98 | 1996-97 | 1995-96 |
|---|---|---|---|
| (i) Switching equipments (LINES) | 677 K | 282 K | 352 K |
| (ii) MAIN DISTRIBUTION FRAMES: (LINES) | 964 K | 724 K | 812 K |
| (iii) TRANSMISSION EQUIPMENT: | | | |
| 6 RU 10 Channel (No. of systems) | 78 | 71 | 80 |
| 2\15 MARR Nos. | 60 | - | |
| 4\36 MARR Nos. | - | 131 | |
| (iv) Data & Networking Products (Nos.) | 3931 | 6636 | 6398 |
| (v) Line Jack Unit\ DP Box | 1018344 | 123467 | 61131 |

*Export:-* The company bagged an order from Ethiopian Telecom Authority for US $ 1.88 Million (Rs.71 0 lakhs) against stiff global competition and executed the order.

The company also signed an agreement for supply of 300 nos. PCO monitors for Rs.57 lakhs during 1998-99.

Implementation of new projects research and development (Position as on 31.3.1998)

*V25 BIS command*: Command set has been introduced in V32 Bis Modem. TEC approval is awaited.

*KBPS modem (interface approval)*: Development work has been completed and offered to TEC for approval.

*High density sub-rack*: Development work was over and is under process for TEC approval.

*V34 modem for internet purposes:* Proto type has been made and 2 nos. had been given for evaluation. TEC has to firm up final specifications.

*64 KBPS line driver*: (Improved version): Type approval has been obtained.

*2\34 skip mux* : Proto Unit is ready and will be offered to TEC shortly

*8Mbit OLTE (indigenous design) :* Development work is in progress.

*EKB & EKBC :* Based on field reports, upgradation of software has been implemented.

*Biscriptual telegraphic equipment:* Development work has been completed and field trial is in progress.

*Biscriptual VDU terminal:* Development work has been completed and the field trial is in progress.

*10 channel digital radio:* Design improvement has been done on MAS card and Channel & Signalling Card. A repeater version has also been developed.

*Manpower:* The total no. of employees on the rolls of the company as on 31.3.1998 was 1314 including 298 Officers as against 1487 employees including 317 Officers at the end of the previous year. The company during the year under review implemented the Voluntary Retirement Scheme under which 120 employees proceeded on retirement and to this extent, there is reduction in the staff strength.

*Employment of SC/ST, Ex-servicemen, women and minorities:* 286 employees belonging to SC\ST were on the rolls as on 31.3.1998 as against 313 employees as on 31.3.1997. The total strength of employees in different groups and the group wise distribution of SC\ST are furnished below:

No. of employees as on 31.3.1998

| | *Total* | *SC* | *ST* |
|---|---|---|---|
| Group "A" | 120 | 10 | 02 |
| Group "B" | 178 | 29 | 06 |
| Group "C" | 930 | 169 | 12 |
| Group "D" (Excluding sweepers) | 63 | 35 | 02 |
| Group "D" (Cleaners & Sanitary Services) | 03 | 01 | nil |
| Total | 1314 | 264 | 22 |

The comparative figures for 1996-97 and 1995-96 are as follows :

| *Year* | *Total strength* | *SC* | *ST* |
|---|---|---|---|
| 1997-98 | 1314 | 264 | 22 |
| 1996-97 | 1487 | 290 | 23 |
| 1995-96 | 1548 | 303 | 24 |

The company also employed In suitable positions women, ex-servicemen, minorities and physically handicapped persons. The details as at the end of the last 3 years are as follows :

| *Year* | *Women* | *Ex-servicemen* | *Physically Handicapped* | *Minorities recruited to group c&D* |
|---|---|---|---|---|
| 1997-98 | 143 | 51 | 16 | NIL |
| 1998-97 | 140 | 62 | 17 | NIL |
| 1995-96 | 137 | 63 | 18 | NIL |

*Industrial relations* : The Industrial relations during the year under review remained cordial.

*Implementation official language policy*: The company continued Its efforts to promote the progressive use of Hindi for official purposes by organising training classes In Hindi as well as Hindi Typewriting during the year under review. As In the past, Hindi elocution contest, Hindi essay competition and Workshop were organised and Hindi Day was celebrated during the year.

*Contribution to the exchequer:* The company during 1997-98 contributed a sum of Rs.6,700 lakhs to the Exchequer amounting to 24.4% on sales as follows:

(Rs. in lakhs)

| | | |
|---|---|---|
| 1. | Excise duty | 2599 |
| 2. | Customs duty | 3120 |
| 3. | Sales tax | 981 |
| | | 6700 |

*ISO 9001 quality system certification:* The Bureau of Indian Standards, has accredited Quality System Certification as per IS\ISO:9001 to HTL for design, Development, Manufacture and supply of Switching Systems and their spares and components; Manufacture and Supply of Transmission Products and their spares and components, Manufacture and supply of data network products and their spares and components.

*Excellence rating for HTL:* The company's performance for 1996-97 and 1997-98 has been rated "Excellent' under the

MOU Scheme by the Government of India. The company's rating has been Excellent every year since inception of the scheme in 1991-92.

*Outlook for the future:* With the increased requirement of interaction via Internet, HTL is planning to provide internet solutions\services. Another area of thrust is on Access Products both wireless as well as wire line. HTL is also looking seriously to expand its foray into the export market and to enter Into non-DOT telecom areas.

**Telecommunications consultants India limited**

Telecommunications Consultants India Ltd. (TCIL) was set up as a Public Sector Undertaking under the Deptt. of Telecommunications in August, 1978 for providing globally know-how in all the fields of telecommunications and to acquire the state-of-art technology on continuing basis.

**Mission**

The mission statement of the Company is to "To excel in providing Communication Solutions globally by anticipating opportunities in Technology".

Starting with an initial Paid-up Capital of Rs.10 lakhs in 1977-78, the Paid-up Capital of the Company was increased to Rs.30 lakhs in 1982-83. The Paid-up Capital of the Company after Bonus Issues of 1:1 in 1987-88,1992-93,1993-94 and 2 share for 1 held in 1996-97 now stands at Rs.7.2 crores.

**Financial performance : 1997-98**

Company achieved all-round growth in its operations. The turnover of the Company increased to Rs.622.28 crores as against previous year's figure of Rs.471.25 crores. The profit before tax in 1997-98 was Rs.46.67 crores as against the previous year's figure of Rs.43.6 crores. The turnover of the Company includes Rs.355.91 crores from foreign projects which is over 57% of the total turnover of the Company. Company declared dividend of 120% on the Paid-up Capital of the Company. This is 4th consecutive year when the Company has given dividend of 100% or more even after tape, Bonus Issue in the ratio of 2:1 in the year 1996-97. For the 7th consecutive year, Company's performance has been adjudged "Excellent" under MOU Evaluation Criteria. Company has also been given status of RATNA by the Govt. of India. Company is ISO-9001 and holding Export House status also.

**Highlights of performance : 1997-98**

Following are the highlights of performance in the year 1997-98 :

(i) Foreign exchange earning of Rs.332 crores as against Rs.244 crores in 1996-97.

(ii) For 7th consecutive year, Company's performance has been "Excellent" under MOU evaluation Criteria.

(iii) Record order booking abroad of over Rs.300 crores.

(iv) Entry in new market areas of Madagascar, Malawi, Palestine and Comoros.

Core competence of TCIL is in Network projects, Software Support, Switching and Transmission Systems. Cellular Services, Rural Telecommunications, Optical Fibre based backbone network. Company is considering to enter into Satellite based Networks and Multi-media services using state Of art technology by participating in global tenders in India and abroad.

*Future strategy* : As per Corporate Plan, Company is to achieve a turnover of Rs. 1250 crores by the year 2005. It intends to achieve this growth by developing strategic alliances with world leaders in technology and also to enter into new business areas like Intelligent Buildings, GPS (Global Positioning Systems) based automatic vehicle location and Traffic Management System, Highway Communication Systems and Direct to home (DTH) TV Services. TCIL is also planning to enter into the field of Technical and Management Consultancy Services by joining hands with a world leader in this field.

**Joint ventures of TCIL**

***Existing joint ventures***

*HEXACOM India Ltd:* TCIL is operating Cellular Telephones through HEXACOM INDIA LTD., a joint venture promoted by TCIL with Shyam telecom and foreign partners. An investment of Rs.53.77 crore in equity has been approved by the Govt. TCIL has already made an investment of Rs.28.53 crores till 31.03.1998 in this company. Provision of Rs.15.24 Crore for 1998-99 and Rs.10 Crore for 1999-2000 have been kept.

*Joint venture for cable manufacturing and optic fibre cables:* Tamilnadu Telecommunications Ltd. (TTL) was promoted with Tamilnadu Industrial Development Corp.(TIDCO). Govt. of India has recently approved expansion of capacity of Jelly Filled Cables manufacturing plant from 6.25 LCKM to 9 LCKM and diversification to manufacturing of Optical Fibre Cables with a further equity of Rs.3.9 crores by TCIL which has already been subscribed by the Company. With additional investment, the equity of TCIL in TTL stands at Rs.6.95 crores.

*TCIL bellsouth Ltd.:-* TCIL had promoted alongwith BELLSOUTH of USA a company in India viz. TCIL BELLSOUTH LTD. TCIL's share in the equity of this company is 40% which is Rs.78 lakhs.

*TCIL Saudi Co. Ltd.(TSCL):-* TCIL had promoted a company with National Telecommunications Ltd. (NATEL) of Saudi Arabia to undertake Access Network and other projects in that country as there is restrictions on foreign companies to participate in such works. TCIL has deputed over 200 experts to Saudi Arabia for execution of the projects. TCIL has a share-holding of 40% in TSCL which is Rs.66.84 lakhs.

Other Joint Venture Companies of the Company where Company has equity participation of less than Rs.50 lakhs are orange telecom software in Netherlands. Telecommunications Consultants Nigeria Ltd. in Nigeria and intelligent communications systems India Ltd. in New Delhi.

**Proposed joint venture**

Company has proposed equity participation in following Joint Venture Companies:-

*Hybrid mail system:* Company is setting up a Joint Venture in collaboration with Dept. of Posts and ELSAG BAILEY of Italy for Hybrid Mail Systems. The equity of the new JVC shall be Rs.55 crores. TCIL's share in the equity has been proposed at about Rs.22 crores. Company has made a provision of Rs.5 crores for the year 1998-99 and Rs. 17 crores for the year 1999-2000.

*Joint venture with rail India technical and economic services:* Railways have allowed RITES to establish OFC Network along railway routes from Mumbai to Chennai by giving certain capacity to railways for their use and remaining capacity can be commercially utilised. RITES have proposed TCIL to be a joint partner for the new company which will construct and operate the services in this area. TCIL has made a provision for equity in this company for Rs.5 crores in 199899 and Rs. 10 crores in the year 1999-2000-

*Joint venture with MTNL:-* Company has proposed to Telecom Commission for setting up a Joint Venture Company with MTNL and other foreign collaborators for operation of Basic Services in India and abroad. The initial plan is to set up Basic Services in 2 Circles (WEST

BENGAL and JAMMU & KASHMIR). TCIL has proposed equity participation of 25% in this company

TCIL's equity requirement in this Company has been proposed at Rs.375 crores by the 5th year of its incorporation. For the year 1998-99, a token provision of Rs.2 crores has been. kept and for 1999-2000, a provision of Rs.25 crores; has been kept.

**Services directly under telecom commission**

***Telephone service***

*Local switching*

Local switching: 232 nos. of new Telephone Exchanges have been added till November, 1998 bringing the total to 23624 exchanges.

The Switching Capacity and Direct Exchange Lines have increased by 17.2 lakh lines and 16.5 lakh lines respectively. The total exchange equipped capacity as on 31.12.98 is 229.8 lakh lines and the total number of working connections is 194.5 lakh.

Commissioning of large telephone exchanges

MAX-1 achievements from 1.4.98 to 31.12.98

| *S.No.* | *Type Gross* | *Achievements* | *Anticipated Achievements* |
|---|---|---|---|
| 1 ~ | E-10B4,96,515 | 4,13,536 | |
| 2. | Ex.Large(NT) | 11,18,105 | 10,79,413 |
| 3. | C-DOT XL | 73,404 | 2,02,596 |
| 4. | C-DOT L | 3,17,462 | 3,58,254 |
| 5. | PRX 1,000 | | |
| | TOTAL | 20,06,486 | 20,53,799 |

However, Net anticipated from MAX-1 switches from 1-1-99 to 31-3-99 would be 18,50,000 and Actual Net achievements so far made (from 1.4.98 to 31.12.98) from MAX-1 Switches is 13,87,122.

**Communications of rural exchanges**

Gross lines achievement in respect of small & medium capacity exchanges during 1.4.98 to 31.12.98 was 496068.

**Public telephones**

The number of Public Telephones added during 1.4.98 to 30.11.98 are 47,396, thereby raising the total No. of Public Telephones as on 30.11.98 to 475336.

**Long distance service**

957 new stations have been connected to TAX network bringing the total no. of stations connected on STD to 16976 as on 31.12.98.

**The number of approved NSD/STD stations**

| | | |
|---|---|---|
| a) | As on 31.3.1998 | : 11157 |
| b) | Number of new stations approved from 1.4.98 to 31.12.1998 | : 1632 |
| c) | As on 31.12.1998 | : 12789 |
| d) | No. of New Stations likely to be approved from 1.1.99 to 31.3.99 | : 500 |

**Transmission system**

5748 Route KMs of Microwave Systems have been pressed into service by 31.12.98. The status of Microwave as on 31.12.98 is 78340 Route KMs.

940 open wire carrier channels have been added in the network during this period. A total of 91868 carrier channels are working as on 31.12.1998.

7856 Route KMs of Optical Fibre Systems have been added during the period bringing the total to 84117 Route KMs.

**Trunk automatic exchanges (Tax)**

47500 lines have been added to the TAX network raising the TAX switching capacity to 1309000 lines. A total of 374 TAXs are working as on 31.12.1998.

**Trunk services**

The number of Trunk Circuits that has been added in the National Network from 1.4.98 to 30.9.98 is 39351 bringing the total number of Trunk Circuits in the country to 3,51,981.

**National sanchar doot awards**

National Sanchar Doot Awards for the year 1997-98 were presented to the meritorious employees of the Department of Telecom by Hon'ble Minister for Communication on 17.5.98, the World Telecommunication Day. The amount of cash award for Sanchar Shree given to meritorious employees at circle level has been enhanced w.e.f. 1998 from Rs.5000/- to Rs.1 0000/- for each category.

**Computerisation of trunk manual exchanges**

Three(3) CTMX systems have been commissioned at the following places on the dates shown against each:-

| | Date of Commissioning |
|---|---|
| a. Salem | 21.8.98 |
| b. Thanjavur | 15.8.98 |
| c. Madurai | 7.8.98 |

**Home country direct service**

In the year 1991, in association with Videsh Sanchar Nigam Ltd. (VSNL), Home Country Direct Service was first introduced to eight countries. As on 31.12.98, the service is available to 31 countries. It is anticipated that with the commissioning of the services to Sri Lanka probably in the period 1.1.99 to 31.3.99 the total number of countries where the service is available shall become 32.

**India direct service i.e. Home country direct service from other countries**

In June 1998, DOT conveyed its approval to VSNL for the

introduction of India Direct Service from all countries where outbound service has been commissioned for 23 countries of the world.-With the commissioning of the service to Sri Lanka the number would become 24 in the period 1.1.99 to 31.3.99.

**Private sector participation in basic services**

On the basis of three rounds of tenders for entry of private sector into Basic Telephone Service, 9 bidders were selected for 13 Telecom Circles. Six companies have so far signed the Licence Agreements for providing Basic Telephone Service in Madhya Pradesh, Andhra Pradesh, Gujarat, Maharashtra, Punjab and Rajasthan Circles.

**Events from April 1998 to December 1998**

Basic Services have been started by M/s Bharti Telenet Ltd. and Mls Hughes Ispat Ltd. in MP Circle (Indore and Bhopal Cities) and Maharashtra Circle (Navi Mumbai) respectively.

A high level Group on Telecommunications (GOT) has been constituted by the Government in Nov.98 to give recommendations in respect of the New Telecom Policy as also on the issues relating to the existing licensees of Basic & Cellular Services and suggest appropriate remedial measures within the framework of the New Telecom Policy.

**Anticipated developments from January '99 to March '99**

M/s Techno Telecom is likely to sign the Licence Agreement for Bihar Circle.

**Private sector participation in value added services**

The Department of Telecommunication has franchised various Value Added Telecom Services like Radio Paging, Cellular Mobile Telephone Service, Public Mobile Radio Trunked Service, Electronic Mail, Voice Mail/Audiotex, Closed User Group Domestic 64 kbps Data Network via INSAT Satellite, Internet and Global Mobile Personal

Communication Service by Satellite to the Indian Registered Companies on a non-exclusive basis. The companies can also submit their proposal for any other Value Added Service giving complete details of the same.

**Status of licensing of these value added services is**

(i) *Cellular mobile telephone service :* The Cellular Mobile Telephone Service is available in four metro cities of the country i.e. Delhi, Mumbai, Calcutta and Chennai by two operators in each city. In addition, 34 licences have also been issued to 14 Indian companies covering 18 Territorial Tetscl= Circles for operation of this service. The service is already operational in select cities in all the 18 Circles. The total number of cellular customers in the country are approximately 10 lakhs.

(ii) *Public mobile radio trunked service:* 103 License Agreements signed with 22 companies for operation of PMRTS in 47 cities are current. The service has already started in 29 cities by 21 companies.

(iii) *Voice mail/audiotex service:* 11 licences issued to five companies for operation of this service in eight cities are current. The Service has already started in seven cities.

*(iv)* *Global mobile personal communication by satellite service:* One licence has-been issued to M/s. Irldium India Telecom Limited for operation of the service in the country.

*(v)* *Internet service provider (ISP):* The new ISP policy was announced on 6th Nov., 1998. Under this policy 76 licences have been issued on date to Companies for providing Internet Services.

*(vi)* *Vsat closed user group domestic 64 kbps data network:* 12 licences issued to Companies for operation of

this service In the Country.

**Mission better communication**

| Parameter | Achievements as on 30.9.98 |
|---|---|
| a) Fault/100stn/month | 18.2 |
| b) Trunk Efficiency(%) | 81.4 |

**Public grievance redressal machinery**

There are several means for redressing public grievances, including Public Grievances Cells, Telephone Adalats, Open House Sessions and Customer Service Centres.

During 1.4.98 to 31.12.98,5813 complaints were received by PG Cell of TCHQ, 5479 complaints were disposed off and balance are vigorously perused for their redressal.

**Public telegraph service**

Modernisation of telegraph services

32 L SFMS system installed at Shillong and kept on Traffic trials.

Two F.T.Cs have been commissioned at Gorakhpur & Sultanpur T.Os. in Eastern U.P. on 4.6.98 & 13.1.99 respectively.

**Quality of service**

96% of the telegrams were delivered within 12 day light hours during the period from April, 98 to Nov., 98 against the yearly target of 94%.

**Developmental activities**

One Telegraph Off ice & seven Telecom Centres were opened upto Sept., 98.

**Customers facilities**

Express Money Transfer Service is working well in Andhra Pradesh and Tamilnadu circles and now introduced in Maharashtra and Kerala Circles with limited transactions within the state.

Particulars of EMTs. ) No. of EMTs booked:

| | | |
|---|---|---|
| (a) | Andhra Pradesh (upto Nov.,98) | 1,34,201 |
| (b) | Tamilnadu(upto Dec.,98) | 66,524 |

| | | |
|---|---|---|
| EMT Transaction : | | |
| | Andhra Pradesh (upto Nov.,98) | 12,26,85,379 |
| | Tamilnadu (upto Dec.,98) | 5,59,46,937 |
| EMT Revenue (commission): | | |
| (a) | Andhra Pradesh (upto Nov.,98) | |
| (b) | Tamilnadu (upto Dec.,98) | 32,49,737 |
| Particulars of B-fax messages | | 15,86,650 |
| | Total no. of B-fax centres upto Nov.,98 | |
| | Total no. of B-fax messages booked upto Sept.,98 | 1,359 |
| | No. of incoming fax messages delivered upto Sept.,98 | 10,41,001 |
| | Total revenue earned from booked fax message upto Sept.,98 | 1,37,603 |
| (e) | Total revenue earned from delivery of incoming fax messages upto Sept.,98 | 4,11,05,911 |

Note:- (b) to (e) excludes the information from Assam, Bihar, Delhi, Gujarat, Tamilnadu, Karnataka UP(West).

**Policy matters**

The proposal of franchising of Telegraph services through franchised PCO holders stands approved by Telecom. Commission in principle.

**New technologies and projects of special significance**

*Installation of multichannel per carrier very small aperture terminals (MCPC-VSATs):*

36 number of MCPC-VSATs were made operational from 1.4.98 to 31.12.1998 at various place in the country. Under this scheme, the stations which cannot be provided long distance media through terrestrial system, are provided STD facility through INSAT system. Such stations are mostly locate at remote, hilly and inaccessible places including islands having small telephone exchanges with low traffic areas.

**Installation of remote area business message network-VSATs.**

Additional 3 (Three) numbers of RABMN-VSATs were commissioned during the period 1.4.98 to( 31.12.1998. These VSATs are low speed terminals and with availability of High Speed Terminals there is not much demand for RABMN-VSATs. These VSATs are directly purchased by the customers from suppliers. These terminals are also able to switch on to the Telex network of the country, [-NET (Le terrestrial packet switched public data network) and to GPSS (i.e. Gateway Packet Switching System: for international connectivity.

**Installation of high speed VSAT network**

A satellite based network using Very Small Aperture Terminals (VSATs) to provide high speed 64 Kbps switched data service known as HVNET was made operational by the Deptt. 41 nos. of HVNETVSATs were made operational till 31.12.1998 alongwith 8 nos. of VSATs provided temporarily for Amarnath Yatra. The network has access to DOT's Packet Switched Public Data Networks (INET/ RABMN·) and International data networks through the Gateway Packet Switching System of VSNL. The Network envisages voice facility amongst VSATs including connectivity to Public Switched Telephone Network (PSTN). The Hub station is co-located with satellite earth station at Mumbai.

**Ku-Band facility**

8.1 M Antenna has been successfully tested and commissioned at NOCC Sikandrabad. KuBand antennae at Karolbagh TAX New Delhi and Jayanagar TAX Bangalore are being tested for commissioning. Ku-Band equipments with provision for 2 Nos. of 34 Mb Streams between Delhi and Bangalore have been installed and tested.

**Anticipated from 1.1.99 to 31.3.99**

About 48 nos. of MCPC-VSATs are expected to be made operational from 1.1.99 to 31.3.99 in various parts of the country.

Digital connectivity utilising 2 Mb (30 Chl.) IDR equipments is expected to be commissioned between Car-Nicobar, Port-Blair and Calcutta.

Digital connectivity utilising 34 Mb equipments in KU-Band is expected to be commissioned between Delhi and Bangalore.

**Integrated services digital network (ISDN)**

The Integrated Services Digital Network (ISDN) Services have been provided in 24 stations during 1.4.98 to 31.12.98 and 2375 connections have been extended. Thus the total number of ISDN stations and the customer base have gone up to 43 and 3748 respectively as on 31.12.98.

It is anticipated that during 1 st Jan. 1999 to 31 st March 1999 another 10 stations shall be brought on ISDN map with about 250 additional connections.

**Appointment of marketing agents**

A pilot scheme for marketing of Value Added /New Telecom Services viz. INET, HVNET, RABMN, ISDN and Intemet(TCP/IP) through Department appointed marketing agents in Maharashtra, Tamilnadu, Madhya Pradesh, Andhra Pradesh, Gujarat, Rajasthan, Punjab Telecom. Circles & Delhi, Mumbai and Calcutta

Telephone Distts. have been introduced.

**Internet access through local calls**

As per the Gazette Notification No. 160 of 25th July, 1998 it has been decided that Internet access nodes will be opened by DOT and authorised ISPs at all District Hqrs. and local charging areas by 26th Jan. 2000. As an interim measure and till nodes are provided in all local charging areas, orders to allow access to the nearest Internet node on local call rates progressively w.e.f. 15.08.98 have been issued for implementation by Telecom circles.

*Inet :* Inet Phase-11 Network has been commissioned for providing the Data services in 101 cities. These cities have been classified into three categories depending upon the business activities and demand. Type-I nodes have been commissioned in 10 Group "A" cities, 34 Type-11 nodes have been commissioned in Group "B" cities and 57 Type-I 11 nodes have been commissioned in Group "C" cities.

The Network provides following types of services:

i) X.25 leased access at 2400bps, 9600bps, 19200bps*, 64000bps.

ii) X.28 leased access at 2400bps, 9600bps.

iii) X.28 dial up 2400bps and 9600bps.

iv) X.32 dial up access at 2400bps, 9600bps as back up to X.25 leased access.

v) Frame Relay in Group "A" and Group "B" cities for high speed (64Kbps) connectivity between LANS in different cities.

The Network provides several user facilities which enables the Network to be used in different applications effectively. Some of these facilities are :

- Reverse charging
- Closed user group

- Fast select
- Charging information indication
- Call redirection
- Call deflection
- Abbreviated address calling
- Hunt Group
- Multiple packet sizes
- Network user identification

Actual Achievements for the period 1 st April '98 to 31 st December '98

Frame Relay Services at 64 Kbps has been commissioned at all Type-I and Type-II locations. 10 numbers of Frame Relay Connections have been provided at 64Kbps at Mumbai, Calcutta and Chennai.

During the period 3 Inet nodes were commissioned. One at Hosur by deploying Inet Phase-11 equipment and two nodes at Mahad and Asansol by redeploying Inet Phased equipment.

Alternate routing have been provided for 8 type-II locations in order to have better reliability of the Inet node.

Upgradation of 11 Nos. trunk routes from 9.6 Kbps to 64 Kbps for increased data transportation speed from Type-III and Type-II nodes to Typed nodes.

Tender for a new Billing Software for Inet Phase-II was floated.

Back up VIP was commissioned in order to further improve the reliability of the dial up facility available to Inet customers.

Anticipated Achievements for the period 1st Jan '99 to 31st March '99.

Alternate routing is to be provided for 6 type-II

locations during the period.

Upgradation of 5 Nos. trunk routes from 9.6 Kbps to 64 Kbps for increased data transportation speed from Type-III and Type-II nodes to Typed nodes.

Installation of Inet Phase-II node at 3 more locations by redeployment of Inet Phase-I equipment.

Purchase order for procurement of Billing software will be placed on successful bidder during the period.

Annual Maintenance Contract for Inet is likely to be finalised.

**Internet services**

Department of Telecommunications has drawn up plans to provide range of Internet services (DOT's Internet Access Services (DIAS) on all India basis by using VSNL's gateways at Bangalore, Calcutta, Chennai, Delhi, Mumbai and Pune. Both the Shell account and TCP&IP dial up access are being provided at these nodes. In addition to the leased access at 64 Kbps is also being provided.

The various services which are available on Internet are: E-mail, USENET, Telnet, FTP, Archie, Veronica, World wide web, Mosaic, Wais.

**Actual achievements for the period 1st April '98 to 31st December '98**

DOT's Internet nodes have been commissioned at 31 locations during the period.

DOT has drawn a plan for multi-tier National Internet Backbone to provide convenient and easily accessible Internet access points for DOT's Internet nodes as well as for the private ISPs. Tender for procurement of NIB equipment has been opened and evaluation is under process.

**Anticipated achievements for the period 1st Jan. '99 to 31st March '99.**

Installed and Commissioning of DoT web site on Internet.

DoT's Internet nodes to be commissioned at 5 locations during the period.

**Telecom accounts**

The Department had introduced a new system of monitoring bank transactions, called "Focal Point Branch System", in 1993-94 to minimise unlinked items. A meeting of the Standing Committee dealing with the subject was called by the Ministry of Finance in November 1998 to review the handling of Govt. transactions by various banks credited to Civil Ministries/Departments. The Department's representative also attended the same to present difficulties of the Deptt. in the matter.

During 1997-98 it was decided to computerise the telecom accounting function in all primary accounting units in the Circles. For this, the "Cash Account Current (CAC)" software package developed by Trivandrum SSA of Kerala Telecorn Circle had been provisionally approved and TA-II Section asked to monitor the progress. Upto 31 st December 1998, about 66% of the over 680 SSAs/Divisions/other Primary Accounts Units stand computerised.

The Telecom Accounting (TACT) software, which was developed by NIC and introduced in the department in 1992-93 for computerising the compilation of telecom accounts in Circle headquarters and at Directorate, was extended to five more Circles, viz., Task Force (Guwahati), Uttar Pradesh (West), Telecom Engineering Centre, Himachal Pradesh and Assam during 1998-99 (upto 31.12.98). For this the TA-II Section organised hands-on training at Guwahati and Shimla in coordination with Assam and Himachal Pradesh Circles respectively.

After finalising the Annual Accounts for 1997-98, the TA-I I Section sent the Statement of Central Transactions to the Controller General of Accounts, Ministry of Finance on 27.7.98 and the Union Finance Accounts (DOT) to Controller General of Accounts and Audit on 28.9.98. The Detailed and Condensed Appropriation Accounts were furnished by the Section to Additional Dy. Controller and Auditor General of India (P&T) on 5th and 26th October, 1998 respectively. The Section also prepared and placed printed Commercial Accounts of the Department, in an improved format, in Lok Sabha and Rajya Sabha on 9.12.98 and 10. 12.98 respectively.

In a major breakthrough, the Section effected a reduction of over Rs. 6884 crores in the balances of the department under Major Head 8782-Remittances. These stood at about Rs.10,129 crores on 31.3.97 and were reduced through Prior Period Adjustment, duly approved by the Controller General of Accounts, Ministry of Finance, to give an opening balances of Rs.3245 crores on 1.4.97.

**Major achievements in computerisation**

An integrated Commercial, Directory Enquiry (DQ) &TR billing & accounting package has been in house developed by Andhra Pradesh Telecom Circle. This package consists of modules which take care of following customer needs:

- Commercial
- TR billing & accounting activities
- Directory Enquiry

Second version of this S/W package will consist of FRS module also. The system is designed to have an integrated data base for all these applications & the transactions & updation are automatic.

It is decided to implement DOT SOFT in atleast one SSA in each circle for start.

**C-DOT**

**Major achievements/projections during 1998-99**

Achievements for the period April '98 - Dec. '98 Projects Completed/In-field)

*Integrated service digital network (ISDN) and 800K BHCA:-* C-DOT has developed Integrated Services Digital Network (ISDN) capability for its exchanges. The ISDN interfaces, bearer services and supplementary services have been developed according to ITU-T and national standards. The TEC testing of ISDN, 800K BHCA handling capability and environmental testing of ISDN hardware with high performance processor (for 800K BHCA capability) card successfully completed at ITI Bangalore. A MAX-XL exchange with the ISDN and 800K BCHA capabilities has been installed in the field trial site at Yelahanka, Bangalore. TEC testing completed at the field trial site and the exchange is ready for commissioning. The ISDN software release (Rel.X2-1 -1 -1) had also been installed at some of the working sites in different configurations e.g. SMB-L, SBM-XL, MAX-L, MAX-XL.

*Intelligent network(IN) services:-* Intelligent Services provide immense value-addition and revenue earning potential for service providers and services to the subscribers get improved flexibly and economically. Some of the IN services are Freephone, Virtual Card Calling (VCC), Virtual Private Network (VPN), Premium Rate Services, Televoting and Universal Access Number. C-DOT has developed very cost effective total solution viz. Service Switching Point (SSP) and Service Control Point (SCP) functionality for provisioning of IN services.

The TEC evaluation for IN services (SSP and SCP) have been successfully completed. The IN services have also been commissioned in MTNL-Delhi and Mumbai and Indore(M.P.). The SCP has been installed at Bhikaji Cama Place in Delhi while SSPs are located at Bhikaji Cama Place (Delhi), Prabhadevi (Mumbai) and Inclore.

The IN solution based on C-DOT technology shall be deployed nation-wide during this financial year at Jaipur, Ahmedabad, Pune, Bangalore, Chennai, Hyderabad, Lucknow, Patna. C-DOT has already installed a SSP at Calcutta. All the SSPs in DOT network will be connected to the SCP at Calcutta via CCS#7 signalling network.

*CCS#7 signalling system:* CCS #7 (SS7) signalling has been awarded technology approval after successful completion of its field trials in C-DOT SBM, MAX-L, and MAX-XL exchanges. CCS#7 signalling can be implemented in the existing MAX-UMAX-XL exchanges by suitable hardware and software enhancements.

**Technology Deployment in the Field**

*Max-XL:-* Fifteen MAX-XL exchanges have already been commissioned in the network and some are under installation. Department of Telecom (DOT) has placed an order for 207.5K lines of MAX-XL exchanges on ITI, Bangalore. Besides, educational orders on C-DOT MAX-XL manufacturers (other than M/S ITI, Bangalore) for 5K lines each have also been placed.

*Tax-XL:-* TEC awarded technology approval for TAX-XL after successful field trials. Dispatch of equipment for 45K TAX-XL lines (in addition to 207.5K lines of MAX-XL orders placed on M/s ITI as indicated above) is also in the pipeline.

Number of C-DOT Switching Systems commissioned in the network

**Switching systems**

| | Operational | |
|---|---|---|
| | *Exchanges* | *Lines (Lakhs)* |
| 128 RAX | 13500 | 12.00 |
| 256 RAX | 8555 | 15.85 |
| SBIVI RAX | 2452 | 22.20 |
| SBIVI TAX | 200 | 1.40 |
| MAX-L | 338 | 13.77 |
| MAX-XL | 11 | 1.30 |
| MAX-XL TAX | 1 | 0.01 |
| Expansion | | |
| 128 RAX | - | 1.25 |
| SBM RAX/MAX | - | 2.82 |
| TOTAL | 25057 | 70.60 |

*TDMA PMP system:-* All the pending point related to software have been incorporated and upgraded software has been offered to TEC for revalidation. Department of Telecom (DOT) has placed an order on M/s ITI for supply of 2.5 systems.

*VSAT systems:-* Department of Science and Technology (DST) so far has placed an order for supply of 87 VSAT 16 Kbps systems and out of this order, 67 systems have been dispatched till date.

*Field and manufacturing support:-* C-DOT continued to provide product support to 25,057 switches with 7.0 million lines of C-DOT technology in the network in terms of upgradation, retrofitting and training to field staff. C-DOT continued its interaction with the manufacturers and field installations for providing all types of maintenance support. C-DOT in co-ordination with TEC conducted a seminar on TDMA-PM P to familiarise DOT officers with TDMA-PM P product so that first twenty-five systems being procured from M/S ITI can be installed and commissioned in a smooth manner. The seminar was followed by a visit to field trial site - Mysore where C-DOTTDMA-PMP equipment has successfully completed the field trial.

Projection for the period Jan'99 - March'99 (On-going Projects under Completion Stage)

*V5.1/5.2 interface for C-DOT switches:-* C-DOT worked on V5.2 interface, which is an emerging concept for connecting Access Network Product (ANP)to the main exchange. This interface can serve different type of interfaces including radio system of the "Wireless In Local Loop (WILL)".

C-DOT has implemented the standardized protocols related to V 5.1 / V 5.2 to interface access network with C-DOT switches. This will help in interconnecting various access technologies to C-DOT exchanges. TEC has successfully completed its validation. The field trial for V5 interface shall commence shortly.

*Composite MUX (remote line concentrator):-* A 120 line unit which will serve both analog and ISDN subscribers is under lab. Testing /development. The Composite MUX (C-MUX) is an Access Network (AN) product. As a Remote Line Concentrator (RLC)for as AN], it is connected to LE-Local Exchange (e.g. C-DOT DSS) using V 5.2 interface. The V5.2 interface consists of a single 2.048 Mbps link supporting 120 subscribers.

*Synchronous digital hierarchy (SDH) systems:-* These projects constitute a series of products namely, STM-1, STM-4, Digital Access Cross-connect (DACCS) and Network Management System. The development of these products are in different stages of product cycle. The STM-1 is in the internal validation stage and it is scheduled for offer to TEC/QA evaluation during end of this financial year, whereas STM-4 and DACCS are in the lab. realization stage.

*Digital enhanced cordless technology (DECT) system:-* This system provides Wireless In the Local Loop (WILL) solutions both in the urban and in the rural scenarios. While one solution uses Base Station Controller (BSC), Base Station Units (BSU) and remote radio units, the other uses an interface card in the remote line of the TDMA system. The later can serve wireless subscribers instead of wired subscribers usually supported by TDMA. Both these systems are in the validation stage and scheduled for offer to TEC/QA evaluation during end of this financial year.

*VSAT system:-* In the field of satellite communication, C-DOT had already developed technology for C and Extended-C band. The products-MCPC and ISD 64 based on these technologies have been already evaluated and field tried by TEC. The technology for Ku-band is under validation/& advance phase of development and the products - MCPC and ISD 64 kbps VSATs in. Ku-band are expected to be available for TEC/QA evaluation during end of this financial year.

**Standards and specifications**

***Generic requirements***

*GRs finalised*

Optical Time Domain Reflectometer (Full feature& Mini); Optical power meter (Type A& B); Stabilised Light Source at 1310 nm and 1550 nm; 1.5 GHz Yagi Antenna; 7 GHz Sub-STM-11 microwave equipment; Voice Mail Service; PABX with wireless extensions; DID-PABX with wireless extensions; "U" Interface for ISDN; Requirements for Computerised Material Procurement Information system of CGMTS, Calcutta; V.34 voice band data modem; Interface for High speed Line Driver; Interface for Remote access Server; Hardware requirements for DoTSOFT, Store and Forward Fax service; Indian Script Code for Language Paging for

Hindi/Marathi; Indian Script Code for Language Paging for Gujrati; Digital Wireless Local Loop system for Rural Areas; TDMA PMP system of C-DOT; Electronic Locator System; 5 Pair/0.50 mm PIJF Under Ground Telecom Cables.

**GRs revised/amended**

Digital Mux Channel Systems for 2/8, 8/34, 2/34 and 34/140 Mbps; Digital Distribution Frame; 30 Channel PCM Mux; Uninterrupted Power Supply 1-7.5 KVA; Optical Attenuator; Optical telephone; Optical Splicing Machine; Single Mode Optical Fibre Jumper (Patch cord and Pig Tails); Optical Spectrum Analyzer; Single Mode Optical Fibre (raw material); 40m Narrow Base Tower; 15m Self Supporting Mast; Multi Channel Per Carrier Very Small Aperture Satellite Terminal; SDH microwave equipment in 4,6,11 GHz band; 2 GHz Grid paraboloid Antenna; 2 GHz Feeder Cable; 6 GHz, 7 GHz, 11 GHz and 13 GHz High performance Antenna; 6 GHz, 7 GHz, 11 GHz and 13 GHz Wave guide; Interface requirement of Primary rate Digital Signal at 2.048 Mbps between DOT and Licensed Service Providers; :Large size Local-cum-Tandern Digital Exchanges; Interface requirement of ISDN CPE; Service description for Analog Subscriber; Requirements for Computerised Material Procurement Information system of MM cell of DOT, National Internet Backbone; Interactive Voice Response System; Line Jack Unit; Electronic Telephone Instrument (TPS); Subscriber Service Unit for Calling Line Identification

Presentation; Formatted Terminal and Line Concentrator regarding bilingual/multilingual working; Boss-Secretary system; DIP Box for Internal and External use; Thermoweld Sleeves; Aluminium Canister for Thermoweld Joint; Cable Duct Sealing system; Aluminium Canister for TSF Joint; Adhesive PVC Tape,

Cleaning Tissue, Adhesive Ployster; Tape, Silica Gel, and Microcrystalline wax; GD Tubes for Internal and External use; MDF and protection arrangement for Rural Automatic Exchanges.

GRs withdrawn

Optical Time Domain Reflectometer (Old Issue, Jan. '94); Power Meter (Precision); Power Meter (Handy); Light Source; Multi Channel Per Carrier Very Small Aperture Terminal (issue Feb. '95); 7 GHz 34 Mbps Digital M/W equipment (Old Issue, Mar'92); 11 GHz 140 Mbps Digital M/W equipment (Old Issue, Jan'93); 140 Mbps M/W equipment in 6 GHz (extended C band) (Old issue, Jan'94); STD Coin Collection Box (Old issue); Quarter Modular Line Cord; Electronic Telephone Instrument (Decadia/ DTMF)); Add-on unit to Coin Box Telephone (CBT-80); Card Vending Machine (Old issue); Disposable Smart Card (Old issue); Monitoring and Control system for Direct Exchange Line; PIJF Quad Trunk/ Carrier Cables.

**Engineering guidelines issued for**

SMPS Power Plant; Infrastructure Assessment of Traders for VRLA battery; Storage/Transportation of VRLA batteries; 10 Channel Digital UHF equipment; IS GHz 8 Mbps microwave equipment; Technical instructions for testing GMPCS services at Pune; Technical details and acceptance testing procedure for parenting of CSED rack of El O-B switches to OCB switches; Synchronisation of exchanges in the Indian Telecom network; Use of C-DOT Network Synchronisation equipment 2.0 in C-DOT and E10-B exchanges; Use of STP in local CCS7 Network; PSTN Access from Inet. -

**Testing field trial and evaluation of products**

Managed Leased Data Network of M/S HTL; STM-1 PDH/SDH Analyser of M/s W & G Pvt. Ltd.; Bench and Chamber testing of ADM-1 of M/s ITI Naini, Allahabad;

Bench testing of ADM-1 6 of M/S ITI Naini, Allahabad; Assisted M/s UPTRON Powertronics Sahibabad in testing of 100A SMPS Power Plant; Testing of software for traffic analysis of EWSDTAX/Local exchanges; Wind Tunnel test for 15m mast; Evaluation of a 40m Narrow Base Tower (first product); Evaluation of Circular Polariser retrofit Wits for use with 2.4m VSAT antenna; Post field trial Test of MCPC VSAT, Testing of INSAT MSS System at Jayanagar Earth Station, Bangalore; Evaluation of DCME-500 system; Evaluation of 18 GHz 8 Mbps microwave equipment of Mls HFCL; XIPC tests of 11 GHz, 140 Mbps microwave equipment of Mls Natelco; S/W version 2-1-1 -1 of C-DOT in Lab; V5.1 Protocol system for C-DOT; V5.2 Protocol in S/W 1-5-1-2 for C-DOT system; 800K BHCA for C-DOT MAX-XL with software version 2-1 -1 -11; 1200K BHCA overload in MAX-XL for C-DOT, C-DOT ISP-SO2 Card in 256 Port RAX; Protocol test of Intelligent Network Application Part (INAP) for C-DOT SSP; Protocol test of SCCP for C-DOT SSP; Protocol test of Transaction Capability Application Part for C-DOT SSP; lab. testing of C-DOT SCP; Interworking tests of NEAX 61 E with OCB-283 TAX on CCS7 for national and International calls; Testing of ISDN features in NEAX61 E exchange; Lab testing of Analog- and ISDN supplementary Services in C-DOT switch; Testing of Patch in AXE- 10 system regarding implementation of 10 digits uniform CLI; Validation of ISDN V5.1 in new technology exchange; Testing of pending problems of EWSD system Gurgaon; Validation testing of ISDN features in C-DOT MAX-XL exchange at Yelhanka, Bangalore; Signalling connection and control Part (SCCP) test for SSP Functionality of AXE-10 Switch at Malleswaram Exchange, Bangalore; Technology approval of C-DOT Network Synchronisation Equipment for use in C-DOT MAX-L and C-DOT SBM exchanges and E10B exchanges; Interactive voice response system at

Alwar; DOT SOFT package for customer's application; Management of Lease, Line Data Network; Testing of X.25 PVC between ACX and PSX; Testing of Frame Relay Over lrioi, Low Bit rate Data Analyser; Data Terminal Test set; Testing for Internet Telephony; TDMA PMP system of C-DOT, DECT system of M/s Siemens at Noida; Electronic Locator System; Preliminary evaluation of permanently Lubricated HDPE pipes.

**Synchronisation**

Fundamental and Planning guidelines of Synchronisation for Transmission Network; Refurbishment of Cesium Clocks at Backup National Reference Clock Centre;

**Field support/software development**

SMPS Power Plant of M/s ITI installed at Telephone Exch. Saharanpur; SMPS Power plant at CIDCO and Up nagar Telephone Exch. Nasik of M/s RBDC; Software solutions for Y2K issues in El O-B system; Software patches for ND-NE correspondence, CLIP-A in El O-B system; Software developed for revenue leakage issues in El O-B exchanges; Software package developed for subscriber management in E10B and OCB-283 exchanges; Suppression of LAC in the meter reading TAXIL tape consequent on the implementation of 10 digit CLI; Implementation of 10 digits uniform CLI in El 0-13, AXE-1 0, OCB-283; A report prepared of misuse of Call forwarding facility by mobile operator; Copies of Commandir and Ell O-B maintenance advisor supplied to field units; Training given to the staff of DTTC, Hyderabad in installation of New Type of Drop Wire Accessories and termination of 0.5 mm SS Drop Wire.

**Field problems solved**

SDH microwave Link on Lucknow-Sitapur route; Conversion of 34 Mbps Radio system from Analog Wideband 6 GHz to Digital in Jamnagar-Rajkot section; The interlinking of Indo-Bangladesh; Point of Inter connect functionality in respect of detail billing on calling line identification and level 1 services; Implementation of IMA software in Ell O-B exchanges; No Dial Tone during night peak hours in Arnbala Cantt. Ell O-B exch.; Interworking of OCB-283 and FETEX-1 50; Technical assistance provided to solve the problem of the following exchanges; OCHLA report in Bhopal and Allahabad; TAXIL in Arnbala; Wakeup service in Jhansi; Saturation of ROU file in Varanasi; Detailed Billing in Cuttak and Pune; Local Cum TAX functionality in Janpath E10-B TAX; Failures of calls to malicious number in E10-B exch. Bikaner, Amritsar and Jullandhar; Implementation of 10 digit CLI in Guwahati E10B exch.; Restoration of Akola E10-B Exch.; Introduction of Internet Service from Hisar to Ambala; FRCT file saturation in Kanpur El 0-13 TAX; Dynamic STD locking facility at Surat.

**Networking planning engineering**

Inter-TAX circuit requirements for the year 1998-99 as part of National TAX Traffic study; Calculation of traffic data for dependent stations of TAXs for the purposes of National TAX Traffic study; Calculation of traffic data for dependent stations of TAXs for the purposes of National TAX Study; Participation of Interference coordination meeting between:-(a) INSAT Satellite System with Russian Satellite System and INTELSAT, USA, (b) INSAT and Indonesian Network in WPC, (c) INSAT and JAPAN Network in Japan, (d)Australia and India in WPC, (e) India Administration and representative of EMARSAT Satellite Networks in WPC; Appraisal of the validation report of testing of 8 Mbps, 18 GHz equipment of M/s HFCL; Advice to Telecom. Commission regarding special conditions for tender for procurement of 13 GHz microwave equipment; Report submitted to TCHQ for Call completion Rate and technical instruction for level 1 TAX overflow Traffic Management in the Network; Prepared status of Synchronisation of Indian Telecom.

Network; Prepared proposal on Internet Numbering.

**Type approval issued**

| | | |
|---|---|---|
| Type Approval | : | 384 |
| Interface Approval | : | 234 |
| Service Test Certificate | : | 227 |
| Source Compatibility | : | 49 |

**Anticipated achievements**

***Generic requirements***

*GRs to be finalised*

Pasive Optical Network; Global Positioning Satellite Primary Reference Source Receiver; 100m Tower; Distance Learning Equipment via Satellite; Interface requirements of Closed Group KU band VSAT Networks; SDH Analyser; Accessories and Components for Antenna, Waveguides and feeder cables; 13 GHz SDH equipment; Extra Large Local Cum Tandem Cum Transit Switch; Gateway Switch; National Synchronisation Plan; Primary reference Clock Cesium Frequency Standards; Interface requirements of Router with TCPAP; ISCLAP for Regional Language; Telecom. Aids for disabled persons; PVC Insulated Copper Clad Steel Drop Wire.

**Test schedule/test procedure**

GPS Receiver; High Bit Rate Digital Subscriber Line; Conventional Power Plants; 13 GHz SDH equipment of HFCL; 10 Channel digital UHF equipment; 8 Mbps 18 GHz PDH equipment; Antenna, Waveguides and feeder cables; Radio instruments; Accessories and components of Antennas, waveguides and feeder cables; SDH Analyser; Digital Cable Fault Locator for Low Insulation Faults; Resistance and Insulation Resistance Tester; Electronic Locator System; TWF Sleeves and TW Canister; Sheath Connector Assembly; Splice Filling Compound; Cable Cleaning Liquid; Emery Strip; Water Blocking

Powder; Adhesive Aluminium Foil; Sealant Tape.

**Test schedule/test procedure**

GPS Receiver; High Bit Rate Digital Subscriber Line; Conventional Power Plants; 13 GHz SDH equipment of HFCL; 10 Channel digital UHF equipment; 8 Mbps 18 GHz PDH equipment; Antenna; Waveguides and feeder cables; Radio instruments; Accessories and components of Antennas, waveguides and feeder cables; SDH Analyser; Digital Cable Fault Locator for Low Insulation Faults; Resistance and Insulation Resistance Tester; Electronic Locator System; TWF Sleeves and TW Canister; Sheath Connector Assembly; Splice Filling Compound Cable Cleaning Liquid; Emery Strip; Water Blocking Powder; Adhesive Aluminium Foil; Sealant Tape.

**Testing/field trial and evaluation**

ADM 4 M/s ITI, Naini; ADM-1 /4/16 PDH/SDH Analyser of M/s W & G Pvt. Ltd.; Passive Optical Network system at Ludhiana; Evaluation of 40m Narrow Base Tower; 6 GHz SDH equipment of HFCL; 11 GHz SDH equipment; 7 GHz 34 Mbps of PCL; Multipath fade simulator; DCME System of M/s HTL; Validation of switching equipment for 1.3m, 1.69m lines; C-DOT Internet; Equipment for APT - Multimedia Project; Irnplementation of Synchronisation as per national Plan; CDMA system of M/s Qualcom; First product testing of Boss Secretary System; Technology approval of subscriber Service Unit for Calling Line Identification Presentation of C-DOT; Permanently Lubricated HDPE pipes.

**Field support**

Compliance of Y2K issues of E10-13, C-DOT and New Technology switches; Over Load control for CSE of E10-13; Storage and retrieval of OMC log of E10-13.

**Network planning engineering**

Inter-satellite Interference Coordination.

**Tender evaluation**

High Voltage Lab; Mechanical Testing Lab; Cable testing Lab.

**Other activities**

Forecast of TAX circuit requirements (Capacity) for the year 2002 as a part of National Tax Stud, Release of software for traffic analysis of EWSD switches for field units; External Plant simulate Network; Spectrum management: Future requirements of frequencies by Telecom Operators.

**Studies made**

Propagation studies; EMC Studies; Radio Modem; Infra red links; LMDS; HDFS; High Altitude Platform Station; Cross Polar Interference Calculation; Number Portability; Fraud management in Telecom; Internet Traffic bypass; Call Centre; Call Completion rate.

**Tyre approval to be issued**

| | | |
|---|---|---|
| Type Approval | : | 128 |
| Interface Approval | : | 78 |
| Service Test Certificate | : | 76 |
| Source Compatibility | : | 16 |

**Manpower development**

About 40,000 persons are proposed to be trained during 1998-99. Details of the personnel trained during April 1998 to December, 1 998 and the number of persons likely to be trained between January, 1999 to March, 1999 are as under:-

| *Courses* | *No. of persons trained during April'98- Dec.'98* | *No. of persons anticipated to be trained during Jan.-March 1999* | *Total* |
|---|---|---|---|
| i) Induction Courses | 10651 | 2000 | 12651 |
| ii) Inservice Courses | 23578 | 4000 | 27578 |
| iii) Courses for | | | |

| | | | |
|---|---|---|---|
| (a) Non-Departmental persons | 50 | 30 | 80 |
| (b) Foreigners | 34 | 5 | 39 |
| Total trained in departmental Training Centres | 34313 | 6035 | 40348 |
| iv) Trained abroad | 53 | 20 | 73 |
| v) Trained in India in various other institutions | 36 | 15 | 51 |

**Rural development**

During the year 1998-99, 10,941 new villages have been covered for the period from 1.4.98 to 31,12.98 against a target of 45,000 villages. It is hoped that further achievement will be made in the remaining three months to achieve the target.

New Technologies such as Wireless in Local Loop (WILL), Macro Cellular, C-DOT TDMA PMP (after successful completion of the trial of 25 systems ordered on M/s ITI), satellite based VPTs will be introduced from the year 1999-2000. Tenders have been floated for the procurement of WLL system.

**Tribal Sub-Plan and N.E. Region**

***Tribal Sub-Plan Under 20 Points Programme***

Important achievement during the period from 1st April,1998 to 31st December, 98 under Tribal Sub Plan are:

- Commissioning of 35 New Telephone Exchanges.
- Addition of 84076 Lines of Switching Capacity.
- Addition of 76101 Lines of Direct Exchange Lines.
- Commissioning of 1339 Village Telephones.

- Commissioning of 86 STD Stations.
- Commissioning of 31 UHF/Microwave/OFC schemes with 480.95 RKMs.

**Development of telecom in N.E. region**

Important achievements in N.E. Region during the period from 1st April, 1998 to 31st December, 98.

- Addition of 26,812 lines of switching capacity.
- Addition of 30,115 Direct Exchange lines.
- Opening of 480 Telephones in Villages.
- Opening of 14 Nos. of New Exchanges.

**International co-operations/seminars/meetings**

***Bilateral cooperation meetings***

Joint Working Group/Joint Working Commission & Inter-Ministerial Meetings.

Bilateral Co-operation meetings held in various Ministries were attended during lst April to 31 st December, 98 as detailed below:-

Meeting with H. E. H RISTO MI HAI LOVSKI the Bulgarian Deputy Minister of Trade and Tourism alongwith on official and business delegation on 28.4.98 to discuss the issues of Bilateral Co-operation.

Inter-Ministerial Meeting in connection with preliminary round of talks preceding to the next session of the Indo-Libyan Joint Commission held on 28.5.98.

Inter-Ministerial Meeting in connection with 1st Meeting of the Indo-Belarus Inter Govt. Commission on Economic, Trade, Industrial, Scientific, Technological and Cultural Co-operation held on 10.6.98.

Inter-Ministerial Meeting in connection with the next session of Indo-Belgium Joint Commission held on

11.6.98.

Inter-Ministerial Meeting in connection with 1st meeting of Joint Trade committee between India & Zimbabwe held on 17.7.98.

Indo-Zimbabwe Joint Trade Committee Meeting held in Harare on 18th & 19th August 1998 with DOT participation of a business delegation.

Inter-Ministerial Meeting in connection with the third session of the Indo-Czech Joint Committee on Trade & Economic Co-operation and third session of Indo-Slovak Joint Committee on Trade & Economic Co-operation held on 25.8.98.

Inter-Ministerial meeting held in MEA on 26.8.98 to consider the Agenda items for 12th session of the Indo-Iraq Joint Commission meeting.

Inter Ministerial meeting in connection with third meeting of Indo-Cyprus Joint Economic Meeting held on 31.8.98.

XIth Indo-Bhutan Telecom operational co-ordination meeting held on 14th & 15th September, 1998 in Thimpu (Bhutan).

Indo-Nepal Telecom operational co-ordination meeting held on 24th & 25th September, 1998 in New Delhi.

Inter-Ministerial Meeting to finalise the Agenda for discussion with the New-Zealand side for the review Meeting of India & New-Zealand JTC held on 6.10.98.

A preparatory meeting to discuss the Agenda for the first meeting of the India-Korea Joint Commission held on 6.10.98.

A preparatory meeting held on 7.10.98 to finalise the

Agenda for the Joint Trade Committee (JTC) meeting between India & Kenya.

A Mid-Term review meeting of the India & New-Zealand Joint Trade Committee was held on 13.10.98.

An Inter-Ministerial preparatory meeting for the second session of Indo-Israel Joint Trade & Economic Committee was held on 16.10.98.

An Inter-Ministerial Meeting for finalisation of brief for the Indian delegation to Indo-EC Sub-Commission was held on 16.10.98.

A preparatory meeting in connection with the forthcoming visit of official delegation led by Commerce Secretary to Yangon(Myanmar) to discuss the present status was held on 23.10.98.

The Second meeting of the Indo-Israel Joint Trade and Economic Committee was held in New Delhi on 27.10.98.

An Inter-Ministerial preparatory meeting in connection with Fourth session of the Indo Croatia Joint Committee on Trade & Economic Cooperation was held on 2.11.98.

An Inter-Ministerial meeting to finalise the Agenda for the session of Indo-French Joint Committee was held on 2.11.98.

An Inter-Ministerial meeting in connection with Fourth session of the Indo-Greek Joint Economic Committee was held on 3.11.98.

An Inter-Ministerial preparatory meeting in connection with the Commerce Secretary level discussions between India and Pakistan on "Economic Cooperation" was held on 2.11.98.

A meeting on Economic and Commercial

Cooperation between India and Pakistan at Commerce Secretary level was held on 10.11.98.

First meeting on Joint Project Steering Group in connection with CIDA assisted Telecom. Frame work project was held on 11.11.98.

The third meeting of the Indo-Kenya Joint Trade Committee was held at New Delhi on 11.11.98.

An Inter-Ministerial meeting on account of the third meeting of the Indo-South African Joint Commission was held on 13.11.98.

An inter-Ministerial meeting in connection with XIIIth session of Indo-italian Joint Commission was held on 18.11.98.

9th session of Indo-French Joint Committee held in New Delhi on 23-24th November, 1998.

An Inter-Ministerial meeting to finalise the issues to be taken up during XIIIth session of the Indo-Romania Joint Commission meeting was held on 26.11.98.

An Inter-Ministerial preparatory meeting was held on 1.12.98 in connection with 10th session of the Indo-Iran Joint Commission.

Meeting on CIDA Assisted Telecom. Operation Project was held on 4.12.98.

A meeting to review the implementation of decisions taken during 9th session of Indo-fran Joint Commission by the Committee on Transport and Communication was held on 10. 12.98.

An Inter-Ministerial meeting was held on 16.12.98 in connection with Commerce Minister visit to Tanzania.

An Inter-Ministerial meeting in connection with the first meeting of Joint Trade Committee(JTC) between

India & Zambia held on 16.12.98.

An Inter-Ministerial meeting held on 23.12.98 to finalise the Agenda for the Indo-EC Joint Commission.

Visit of Foreign Ministries and other dignitaries to Department of Telecom.

Mr. NORIMASA HOUSE GAWA, Vice-Minister for International Affairs. Ministry of Posts & Telecommunications, Japan called on Chairman (TC) & Hon'ble Minister of State for Communications on 24.9.98.

H.E. Mr. AHMET DENIZON GUN, Minister of Transport Communications, Turkey, alongwith Mr. YUSUF BULG, Ambassador of Turkey in New Delhi, called on Hon'ble Minister of State for Communications on 10. 12.98.

H.E. Mr. JAY NAIDOO, Minister for Posts & Telecommunications & Broadcasting South Africa called Hon'ble Minister of State for Communications on 9.12.98.

Russian Ambassador, Embassy of Russia, New Delhi made a courtesy call on Hon'ble Minister of Communication on 18.12.98.

**MOU signed**

An MOU between India & South Africa in the field of Telecommunications was signed on 9.12.98.

Agreement between the Govt. of the Republic of India & the Govt. of the Russian Federation on Co-operation in the field of Communications was signed on 21.12.98.

Joint Working Committee/Working Group constituted for the implementation of following MOUs between India and the following countries:-

i) Tanzabua ii) Belarus iii) Germany iv) France v) Canada, CIDA assisted projects i.e. Framework &

operation.

**Seminars/workshops/Meeting**

The event was organised by International Telecom Union (ITU) in Johannesburg, South Africa during May 4-9,1998. Telecom: units from India, namely, MTNL, VSNL, ITI, HTL,TCIL, Telecom Factories, C-DOT in public sector and Tata Telecom. from private sector as well as Department of Electronics participated alongwith Department of Telecommunications under the banner of India Pavilion. The pavilion was visited by large number of businessmen and official visitors including many important dignatories; Minister of Communications, South Africa, Ethiopia and Mauritius as well as Secretary General of ITU. Number of important meetings were also arranged between Indian companies and South African businessmen community.

A delegation of senior officials from DOT visited the exhibition and participated in the Seminar organised by ITU. Chairman(TC), Mr. A.V.Gokak, had a meeting with Mr.J.Naidoo, Minister of Posts & Telecommunications, South Africa.

India Tech '98 at Nairobi, Kenya during 1-4 Sept., 1998: DOT, MTNL, HTL, ITI, C-DOT and Telecom Factories participated successfully under the banner of "Telecommunications". The participation in the exhibition over four days was quite successful. The response was overwhelming from visitors, government functionaries and businessmen and in all, approximately 1200-1400 visitors came to various booths set up by telecom. units.

The dignitaries who visited are as under:

i) Hon'ble Minister of Transport & Telecommunications, Mr. Nitimama.

ii) Deputy Minister of Transport & Telecommunications, Mr.Obure.

iii) Hon'ble Minister of Industrial Development, Mr. Masakhalia.

iv) Hon'ble Asstt. Minister of Finance, Mr. Muathaias Keah.

v) Executive Chairman of Investment Promotion Centre, Dr.N.Gok.

vi) Senior Government officials/officials of Ministry of Defence & Industry Chambers.

vii) Number of Ambassadors and High Commissioners.

viii) Representative of Banking Institutions.

Second SAARC Trade Fair in Colombo (Sri Lanka) from 8-15 September, 1 998 organised by India Trade Promotion Organisation (ITPO). M/s. HTL Ltd. and M/s. TCIL participated.

**National**

IITF '98:- It was held during 14-27, November, 1998. Department of Telecommunications,

Department of Posts, MTNL, VSNL, TCIL, HTL, C-DOT and HCL participated successfully under the banner of "Communications". The pavilion received award for excellence.

**International Relations**

Deputation of officers to foreign countries for the period April'98 to December, 1998 is as follows:

i) Deputation of 21 officers to Geneva, Jersey (U.K.), Johannesburg (S.A.) and Maldives for attending meetings on different study Groups of ITU-T, ITU-R, WTO India's Trade Policy review, African Telecom. '98. Radio Communication Bureau and Regional Tariff Groups.

ii) Deputation of 16 officers to Washington, Minneapolis(USA), Manila and Bangkok for attending meetings on different study groups of APT, Business colloquium, Plenipotentiary, Inter-Active medical curriculum, Development Information Infrastructure in Rural Areas & World Economic Development Congress.

iii) Deputation of 8 officers to Tampere (Finland), Manila, Tunisjunisia), Netherland and Pretoria (South Africa) for attending different meetings/ conference on ICET'98, user supplier EWSD switch, Africa one, improving electricity efficiency in commercial buildings and Regional workshop on year 2000 (Problems on Telecommunications).

iv) Deputation of 22 officers to Seoul (Korea), Bhutan, Paris (France) & Kansai (Japan) for attending meetings of APSCC, CDMA Training programme, APII, Indo-Bangladesh link & infrastructure conference.

v) The 15th Plenipotentiary Conference of the International Telecommunication Union (ITU) was held at Minneapolis (USA) from 12 October to 6 November 1998. A high level inter-departmental Indian delegation, led by the Hon'ble MOS(C) participated in the Conference. The Conference was attended by more than 1600 delegates and participants from 170 countries and 98 from International Telecom Organisation.

**Anticipated achievements**

***Bilateral cooperation***

Joint Working Group is to be constituted for the implementation of MOU signed between India & South Africa.

***Exhibition & seminar***

a) International:- CEBIT '98 at Hanover, 18-24 March, 1999. Participation of M/s. VSNL has been approved. A delegation from Deptt. of Telecom. is also likely to participate.

b) National:- Sunderban Mela'99 at Canning Town, South 24 Parganas, West Bengal from 3rd January to 12th January,1999 organised by Bandhu Mahal. Chief General Manager, West Bengal Telecom Circle, Calcutta has been requested to participate.

**International relations**

About 37 officers are expected for attending different seminars/conferences etc. abroad from January'99 to March'99 as mentioned below:

| *Activity* | *No. of Officers* | |
|---|---|---|
| ITU-T/ITU-R/ITU-D | 20 | |
| APT Meetings/Seminars | 4 | |
| APSCC Meetings/Seminars/Workshop | | 1 |
| INTELSAVINMARSAT Meetings 1 | | |
| Meetings/Workshop/Consultancies with UNDP/ITU Projects | 3 | |
| Other misc. International Activities | | 8 |
| | Total : | 37 |

Meeting and Seminar of Telecommunication Management Network (TMN), Expert Group of ITU, held on 6-15 January'99 at Bangalore.

**Telecom Factories**

Department of Telecommunication has seven Departmental Telecom. Factories.

Total turn over of Telecom. Factories during the year 1997-98 was 188.49 Crores against the target of Rs.198 Crores. The Financial and Quatitative achievement upto

December 1998 and expected achievement upto March 1999 during the current year is indicated as under:

**Financial**

*(Rs. in Crore)*

| *S.N.* | *Telecom Factory 1998-99* | *Target* | *Achievement from April-Dec'98* | *Expected achievement upto March'99* |
|---|---|---|---|---|
| i. | Mumbai | 55.00 | 30.95 | 48.00 |
| ii. | Calcutta & Gopalpur | 70.00 | 48.34 | 70.00 |
| iii. | Kharagpur | 5.00 | 1.82 | 3.00 |
| iv. | Jabalpur | 65.00 | 45.21 | 65.00 |
| v. | Richhai | 35.00 | 15.38 | 25.00 |
| vi. | Bhilai | 12.00 | 8.03 | 12.00 |
| | Total | 242.00 | 149.73 | 223.00 |

**Physical**

| *S.N.* | *Item* | *Annual target 98-99* | *Achievement from April-Dec'98* | *Expected achievement upto March'99* |
|---|---|---|---|---|
| i. | Bkt Ch.Ir4W | 1300000 | 863500 | 1300000 |
| ii. | Buttenski Telephone | 10000 | 2800 | 4600 |
| iii. | CBT-95 | 12000 | 4043 | 7000 |
| iv. | CD Cabinets | 16500 | 11064 | 15900 |
| V. | CT Box 100 pair | 150000 | 99470 | 150000 |
| vi. | DP Boxes | 500000 | 205627 | 358037 |
| vii. | Line Jack Unit | 2400000 | 1389700 | 2000000 |
| viii. | Mast 15M | 12000 | 5917 | 10000 |
| ix. | Mast 40M | 300 | 131 | 200 |
| X. | MDF C-DOT | 3500 | 2229 | 3500 |
| xi. | Modems | 1500 | 460 | 700 |
| xii. | MW Tower (in MT) | 8000 | 4620 | 8000 |
| xiii. | Saddles | 1000000 | 37275 | 40000 |
| xiv. | Socket B | 40000 | 25000 | 40000 |
| xv. | Sole Plate | 200000 | 85 | 500 |
| xvi. | Stalks | 800000 | 330000 | 550000 |
| xvii. | Support Bkt. | 1500000 | 563000 | 800000 |
| xviii. | Tube B-8 | 785000 | 492385 | 800000 |
| xix. | U-Back | 1750000 | 703000 | 1200000 |

**Telecom factories also participated in following major exhibition during the Year 1998-99**

Africa Telecom'98 from 4th to 10th May,1998 in Johannesburg, South Africa.

India Industrial & Electronics Technology Exposition 1998 from 1st to 4th September 1998 in Nairobi, Kenya.

India International Trade Fair 1998 from 14-27 November 1998 at Pragariti Maidan, New Delhi.

**Status of cag paras**

During the year 1998-99 (upto 15.1.99) the Budget-II Section of DOT(HQ) attended to various coordination activities relating to Draft Audit Paragraphs, Audit Reports and PAC/COPU cases pertaining to the Department, besides other works indicated below.

Draft Audit Paragraphs covering P&T as well as Commercial Audit.

157 C&AG's (Union Govt.) Report on DOT for 1996-97, containing 40 paragraphs involving 163 Action Taken Notes and C&AG's (Commercial) Reports for 1996-97 containing 3 paragraphs involving 21 Action Taken Notes.

Lists of Questions on seven paragraphs selected by the PAC of Lok Sabha from C&AG's (Union Govt.) Reports on DOT for detailed examination during 1998-99. In three of these, oral evidence of the Secretary, DOT was also taken by the PAC.

Sitting of Lok Sabha's Committee on Public Sector Undertakings (COPU) on 21.12.98 for discussing with the Secretary, DOT. The follow up action taken by the department on C&AG's (Commercial) Reports.

Visits of the PAC on 9.11.98 to Patna and on 16.1.99 to Cochin for on the spot study of paragraphs of C&AG's Report (P&T) No. 6 of 1998 relating to Bihar and Kerala Telecom. Circles respectively

Review of IFAs Quarterly Reports received from field units.

Review of Quarterly statements of Audit Inspection Reports and Audit Objections received from field units.

**Industrial assistance and export promotion group**

During the new Industrial Policy period(01 .08.91 to 31.08.98) 452 Foreign Collaborations (106 technical and 346 financial) have been approved. During this period a total of Rs. 31466.12 crores of Foreign Direct Investment (FDI) has been approved for Telecom. sector which accounts for 18.15% of FDI approved by the Government of India.

Total production of telecom equipment and cables during 1997-98 was Rs.9960 crores. It is estimated the production would register healthy growth this year.

Private Investment Promotion Cell has been created to encourage, stimulate and facilitate private investment in telecom. sector and to smoothen the implementation of these projects.

**Activities of industrial assistance and export promotion group**

The Industrial Assistance and Export Promotion Group of Production Wing of DoT is responsible for the development and regulation of the Telecom Industry in the country. The main activities of the Group are:

Providing assistance in formulation of Import and Export policies for the Telecom Sector.

Providing assistance in formulation of foreign investment policies and procedures for the Telecom Sector.

Processing of applications for foreign investment and foreign technology in Telecom. Sector.

Matters relating to promotion of Telecom Exports

including sponsoring of trade delegation, setting up of Indian pavilions in international Exhibition and Organisation of Seminars etc.

Assistance in matters relating to Customs and Excise duties and other Direct and Indirect Taxes for the Telecom Sector.

Assistance in matters relating to Trade and Industrial policies for the Telecom Sector.

Assistance to various industrial units in the Telecom Sector for implementation of their projects.

**Activities of private investment promotion cell**

This group has been created to encourage, stimulate and facilitate private investment in telecom sector and to smoothen the implementation of these projects. Main activities of this group are:

**Promotional activities**

Interaction with Business Councils/industry Associations.

Interaction with Indian Investment Centre and other Govern me nt/Sem i-Government bodies concerned with investment promotion.

To recommend formation of policies to catalyse and stimulate private investment in Telecom. Sector.

Printing of Promotional Literature and their distribution.

Organisation of Investment Conferences/Seminars/ Exhibitions and dissemination of information, arrange publicity about avenues/scopes of private investment in telecom sector.

Deputation of officers from DoT for attending the National/International Conferences/ Seminars/ Exhibitions concerned with investment promotion.

**Follows up action on the following issues relating to project implementation**

Issues which are to be resolved within Telecom. Commission.

Issues to be resolved with other Government, Ministries, State Governments and other concerned agencies.

Issues related to VSNL/MTNL/DOT connectivity to be provided to private operators.

Issues related to foreign collaborations and other concerned approvals.

Any other problem coming in way of implementation of private telecom projects.

**Financial review**

***The budget and revised estimate for 1998-99 and the budget estimates for the year 1999-2000 are as follows:***

(Rs.in Crores)

| | B. E. 1998-1999 | R.E. 1998-1999 | B.E. 1999-2000 |
|---|---|---|---|
| Revenue Receipts | 17142.13 | 17508.42 | 19788.20 |
| Working Expenses (net) | 10369.45 | 10256.59 | 10656.87 |
| Net Receipts | 6772.68 | 7251.83 | 9131.33 |
| Divided to General Revenue | 286.50 | 211.88 | 291.11 |
| Surplus | 6486.18 | 6969.45 | 8840.22 |
| Appropriation of Surplus | | | |
| Capital Reserve Fund | 6398.68 | 6854.50 | 8735.22 |
| Revenue Reserve Fund | 87.50 | 115.40 | 105.00 |

**Tariffs**

Introduction of Clip Facility and fixation of Tariff there of issued vide order No. 3-2/98-R&C dated 11.8.98.

Rebate in installation charges in respect of new telephone connections issued vide order No. 320/98-R&C dated 11. 12.98.

**General**

***The composition of telecom commission (full time members) during 1998-99 is as follows:***

| | | |
|---|---|---|
| Chairman | Shri A.V.Gokak | W.E.F. 4.11.96 to 28.8.98 |
| | Shri Anil Kumar | |
| Member(Finance) | Shri A.Prasad | W. E. F. 31.7.97 |
| Member(Production) | Shri R.R.N.Prasad | W.E.F. 1.10.97 to 14.1.99 (Vacant W. E. F. 15.1-99) |
| Member(Services) | Shri P.S.Saran | W.E.F. 11.1.95 |
| Member(Technology) | Shri N.K.Sinha | W.E.F. 15.11.95 |

**Use of Hindi**

Acquainted all the Telecom. Circles/Administrative Offices/Undertakings with the O.L. Act, Rules and instructions issued thereunder for their compliance for achieving the targets fixed by O.L. Department in their Annual Programme for the year under report.

Reviewed the Quarterly Progress Report regarding progressive use of Hindi received from all the Sections of DOT(Hq.) and all the Telecom. Circles/other Administrative Offices/Undertakings etc. and took necessary corrective measures in respect of those wherein defects were noticed.

Provided Hindi information through Hindi Vishesh Seva (177) and monitored thereof. This service has been extended by the Department in 30 cities.

Arranged nomination for Hindi training for those officers/officials who had not acquired working knowledge of Hindi. Similarly, Stenographers/Typists who had not undergone training in Hindi Stenography/ Typing were nominated for the above respective training courses.

Carried out inspections of Telecom. Circles/ Administrative Offices/Undertakings to ensure as to what extent the provisions of O.L. Act/Rules and instructions issued thereunder are adhered to. About 7 inspections were carried out during the year under review.

As usual Hindi Fortnight was organised from 01.09.98 to 15.09.98 which is a regular activity of every year prescribed by Deptt. of Official Language.

O.L. Branch works as a Co-ordinator from D.O.T. (Hq.) during the course of inspection of circles etc. by Committees of Parliament on Official Language which is also a regular feature every year. About 4 inspections were carried out by Committee of Parliament on Official Language during 199798. Parliamentary Committee also inspected D.O.T(H.Q) during the year under report.

Translated all the documents in Hindi/English specified in section 3 (3) of Official Language Act 1963 and Official Language Rule 1976, all the papers/reports to be laid by DOT on the table in both the Houses of Parliament.

Quarterly meetings of the Departmental Official Language Implementation Committee were held at regular interval during the period under review.

Two days Hindi Workshop was conducted in D.O.T. (H.Q) to remove the hesitation of officials in doing their daily official work in Hindi.

Akhil Bhartiya Rajbhasha Sammelan were organised in various Circle offices.

Out of minimum 10 inspection prescribed by the Department of Official Language during the year 7 inspections have been made so far remaining three inspections are to be carried out during this period.

As per programme received so far, the Committee of Parliament on Official Language is expected to carry out 4 inspections of field offices of D.O.T. during this period.

Arranged nomination for Hindi Stenography/ Typing training of those Stenographers/Typists who had not acquired working knowledge of Hindi Stenography/ Typing for the Session starting from February, 1999.

**Deputations/delegations abroad**

| I. No. of deputations/delegations of Govt. Officers abroad approved for attending conferences,Seminars, Inspections and Trainings etc. (excluding deputations/delegations sponsored under Colombo Plan UNDP Technical Assistance Programme for the year 1998-99 (upto 31.12.98). | No. of Officials included in deputation/ delegations | Estimated expenditure sanctioned (Rs. in lakhs) |
|---|---|---|
| 96 | 155 | 170.95 |

| II. No. of projects estimates/ Expenditure Finance Committee Memo. for construction of Telephone Exchange Buildings Installation of Telephone Exchange/ Satellite Earth/ Co-axial/MW/UHF-VFT/ Railway Electrification Scheme etc. sanctioned during the period from 1.4.98 to 31.12.98 | No. of PEs | Total estimated capital expenditure. (Rs. in Crores) | Remarks (2) CTB under consider-tion |
|---|---|---|---|
| Remunerative PEs | — | — | — |
| Anticipated achievement & developments for the period ending 1.1.99 to 31.3.99 | 5 | 80 | CTB |

**Work study and EB and inspection**

***Actual Achievements (from 1.4.98 to 31.12.98)***

52 Norms Studies in respect of STS cadre in Telecom. Wing have been completed.

5 Work Measurement studies of the Headquarters have been completed.

Administrative Inspection of 5 circle offices have been completed and 1 Heads of Telecom. Circles conference was convened on 17.9.98 and minutes issued on 27th Oct. 98.

***Anticipated achievements and developments (from 1.1.99 to 31.3.99):***

Norms Studies in respect of STS Cadre in Telecom. Wing and 1 Norms Study in respect of Accounts personnel in SSAs is expected to be completed.

3 Work Measurement Studies in Headquarters are expected to be completed.

**Welfare and sports**

An amount of about Rs 4 crores has been provided to the Welfare and Sports activities to the Department of Telecommunications during the year 1998. An amount of Rs.3,26,64,982/- has been disbursed to different circles/ units for meeting their Welfare and Sports expenditure from 1st April, 1998 to 31 st December, 1998.

The following important schemes for grant of financial assistance from Welfare fund to the Telecom. employees or their dependents have been formulated and are being enjoyed by our employees and their dependents as the case may be.

(a) Financial assistance to the dependents of deceased employees.

(b) Supply of sewing machines to the families of deceased employees.

(c) Financial assistance in cases of death of casual labourers (temporary status mazdoor); in cases of death of retired employees; in prolonged illness cases of employees; in serious illness/major operations etc; on account of prolonged illness of the dependents of employees; for nutritive diet for TB patients; by way of loans in emergency cases; to victims of natural calamities; to handicapped for purchase of artificial limb centre; to handicapped children on account of transport/hostel/mess charges; towards railway fares from headquarters to Artificial limb centre.

(d) Scholarships and awards.

(e) Book awards and incentives to meritorious childrens.

(f) Grant-in-aid to Recreation/sports club.

(q) Holiday excursion trips.

There is Telecom. Women's Central Organisation (TWCO) for undertaking Welfare activities for Telecom. Women and their children which includes opening of creches, tailoring centres, nursery school and arts and crafts classes. The annual grant to TWCO is Rs.2 lakhs (and for its branches located in circles is to Rs. 15,000/-). Creches can now be opened in both office buildings or in Colonies depending upon the consensus and convenience of the user employees. In any cases building would not be rented specifically for this purposes.

Out of 36 holiday homes at present functioning in the important hill stations/health resorts, 14 are under administrative control of Department of Telecom. These are utilised by the employees of Department for holidaying purpose.

To develop Sports among Sportsmen, tournaments in 17 disciplines were conducted at different places on all India basis. An amount of Rs.83,52,500/- was spent for Sports and Cultural activities upto December 1998.

P&T Sports Control Board has sent combined P&T teams for Nationals in the Power lifting, Weightlifting, Chess, Wrestling and kabaddi tournaments upto 31st

Dec.,1998. We have spent Rs.76,482/- for sending teams for National tournaments. For improving standard of Sports in the Department, 4 sports have been selected for special development and achieving excellences.

**Vigilance**

***Highlights of important vigilance activities during the period (1.4.98 - 31.12.98)***

| | | | |
|---|---|---|---|
| (i) No. of vigilance complaints on which action completed | | : | 2883 |
| (ii) No. of Officers suspended | | | |
| | G.O. | : | 14 |
| | N.G.O. | : | 48 |
| (iii) No. of Officers charge sheeted for | | | |
| (a) Major penalty | | | |
| | G.O. | : | 110 |
| | N.G.O. | : | 116 |
| (b) Minor penalty | | | |
| | G.O. | : | 85 |
| | N.G.O. | : | 186 |
| (iv) No. of Officers punished with | | | |
| (a) Major penalty | | | |
| | G.O. | : | 50 |
| | N.G.O. | : | 42 |
| (b) Minor penalty | | | |
| | G.O. | : | 81 |
| | N.G.O. | : | 85 |
| (v) No. of Officers prosecuted | | | |
| | G.O. | : | 11 |
| | N.G.O. | : | 36 |

**Training**

Vigilance Officers' Conference at ALTTC, Ghaziabad was organised in December,1998 in which 60 Officers from all the telecom circles participated. The participants were informed about techniques of investigation, framing of chargesheets, store management and avoidance of frauds in high tech areas. Two more vigilance courses are proposed to be organised at Hyderabad and Chennai in March, 1999.

**Other training**

***Other activities***

Special CBI Cells set up in metro cities to prevent leakage of telecom revenue continued to perform well and gave encouraging results. Though it is not possible to quantify their gains in concrete financial terms, these cells have registered 140 cases involving 157 Departmental officials and 35 outsiders.

*Special squads*

Special Squads were formed in the year 1995 for surprise visits to the subscribers' premises and Telephone exchanges. The main job of these squads is random checking of equipments, telephone lines etc. to find out tampering, if any, with the equipments or lines in the switch room/external plant. Follow up action was taken on various irregularities/omissions found by the special squads. This has resulted in considerable improvement in the services and preventing misuse of lines.

***Technical solutions***

A committee of technical experts was constituted to examine the technical aspects involved in the matter of revenue loss caused by long duration ISD unbilled calls. The committee has made various valuable recommendations like uniformly sending CLI alongwith station code from exchanges, no access for ISD from analogue exchanges, serving ISD subscribers from CLI supporting exchanges, use of CCS #7 signalling for preventing sample monitoring of ISD calls from VSNL, spare NEND checking, taking threshold printouts and making sample checks and investigation of long duration ISD calls. Instructions to the field units for implementation of these recommendations are being issued by the concerned authorities in the DoT headquarters.

Further, a core group of experts under the chairmanship of DDG(SW), TEC has been constituted vide order dated 30.10.98 to examine and identify the areas in the new technology systems (both switching and transmission) having scope for possible frauds leading to loss of revenue and to suggest remedial measures to prevent possibility of such incidences. The report since submitted by the Committee is under examination.

A Committee was set up under the Chairmanship of GM(Vig.), MTNL, New Delhi to study the proposal for establishment of a Fraud Management & Control Centre on experimental basis. The report submitted by the Committee is under examination.

**Economic Research Unit & Statistical Section**

The following studies/exercises have been undertaken/completed during the year 1998-99:-

Impact of Group Dialling Scheme on Revenue.

Operating Ratio and rate of Return in Telecom distt.

Traffic Pattern of STID PCOs.

Economics Viability of VPTs.

Telephone Revenue - An Analysis of Trends and An Examination of Determinants for 199596 and 1996-97.

Call Slab Wise Distribution Pattern of Subscribe rs/ Calls - A case study of 8/28 Telecom, District: 1995-96 and 1996-97.

Downfall in Average Revenue per DEL in Tamil Nadu Telecom. Circle.

Indian Telecommunication Statistics - 1997.

Impact of Rural Tariff on Calling Pattern, Demand Sensitivity and the loss due to subsidy.

Reduction in Average Revenue per DEL and its correlation with Metered Call Unit per DEL.

Impact of the present Four-tier tariff structure and policy of dimensioning of long distance circuits on Revenue per DEL.

Composite publication of DOT for wider circulation amongst public/consumer business.

Telephone Demand Projections - Towns having exchanges with 200 lines and above 1999 -2009.

Survey to ascertain the social background and income strata of PCOs/telephone users.

**Electrical Wing**

The Electrical Wing of the Department of Telecom. is providing supporting services to the Telecom Network and is mainly responsible for providing all the Electrical and Electromechanical Services like Building Electrification, A.C. Plants, stand by Generating Sets, Sub Stations, Fire Fighting and Fire Detection systems etc. in the Telecom. Technical and Administrative buildings and Staff Quarters of the Department of Telecom.

In physical terms our contribution for the year 1998-99 is as under:

| Year | Air Conditioning | Sub Stations | Stand by Gen. Sets |
|---|---|---|---|
| From 1.4.98 to 31.12.98 | 17,943 TR | 61,015 KVA | 1,25,690 KVA |
| Proposed from 1.1.99 to 31.3.99 | 19,000 TR | 83,000 KVA | 1,28,000 KVA |

In financial terms our budget for the year 1998-99 is Rs.400 crores.

**Review of rules and procedures**

An expert group under the Chairmanship of Shri R.N.Goyal, Advisor(HRD) reviewed the telecom. service procedures governing the customer services to make them more customer friendly.

Indian Telegraph Rules 1951 have been updated till August 1998.

Indian Telegraph Act 1885, Indian Telegraph Rules 1951, TRAI Act 1997 and Indian Wireless Telegraphy Act 1933 have been documented in the form of a compendium in billingual form. The document is awaiting printing.

**Telecom Quality Assurance**

Value of stores accepted upto December 1998 : Rs.3501 Crores.

(a) No. of QA Centres Opened: One at the premises of M/s. Fine Cable Industries, Madurai,

(b) No. of QA Centres closed : Four located at M/s. L&T, Mysore, M/s. Udaya Semiconductors, Coimbatore, M/s. KTL, Bangalore, M/s. Amco, Bangalore; depending upon the shift in DoTs ROs,

No. of Infrastructure Assessments carried out: 136.

(a) Conventional Products - 50

(b) TEC Products - 86

(c) No. of Type Approval Certificates issued: 304

(d) No. of Type Approval Certificates withdrawn : Nil.

No. of important meetings held: 25

(a) User's Meet: 17

(b) Others : 8

No. of First Product Qualification Cases

No. of Major Quality Problems settled

a) No. of AIS accorded : 5 including 4 extensions

(b) No. of DIS accorded: 7 including 6 extensions

Total working strength of QA Circle is reduced to 743.

Component Approval Centre for Telecommunications (CACT):

*(a) Augmentation of test facility*

- An instrument CAVIDERM Model CD 8 was procured from M/s UPA Technology, USA and installed in PCB lab. of CACT, Bangalore for measurement of plated through hole of copper plating thickness of double sided & multilayer PCBs.
- Test Programmes were developed for testing 22 new components viz., (a) 4-ICs (b) 9-Transistors & (c) 9-Diodes.
- Solvent Resistance Test Machine, Accelerated Ageing machine have been procured and installed in PCB Lab.
- Three Terminal Test Cell with heater has been procured in FA Lab. to test Cable Filling Compound.
- Bulk Density Apparatus for testing PVC Resin addle d in FA Lab.
- UV light source is installed to verify uniformity of conformal coating.

*(b) Activity:*

- No. of Components Type Approved: 358
- No. of components manufacturer's infrastructure assessed : 25
- No. of components tested in various laboratories : 14198
- No. of products subjected to climatic and environmental tests

  (i) Equipments 1884

(ii) Components 290

(iii) Others 58

- Total climatic chamber hours utilised : 20819
- No. of devices subjected to Failure Analysis : 511
- Failure Analysis reports will be released progressively.
- No. of reports generated by SCRAM : 26

***Important feedback cases settled***

- There was a complaint from OTC, Lucknow, OTC Project, Allahabad and OTC (Installed), Hyderabad on 8 Mbps OLTE of M/s. MAC, Bangalore supplied by M/s. Natelco, Nasik.
- The system failed in stability test after installation and even in local loop test also. The failures were noticed at different time intervals in different systems.
- The problem was analysed by M/s. MAC, Bangalore (technology provider) and finally software was modified for E-2 supervisory card. The manufacturer has changed all EPROM with modified software in all existing system (258 Nos.) which were already supplied and installed. All systems with modified EPROM are performing well and no further complaints.
- There was a feed back report from Gujarat, Karnataka besides one or two other circles on EPBT instruments supplied by M/s. Webel, Calcutta.
- The instruments failed in field during warranty in the range of 0.5 to 1.5% of the total numbers supplied. The problem was noticed in earlier batches supplied.
- Proper investigations were carried out and necessary corrective and preventive actions were taken besides

attending to the field problems by M/s. Webel for repair or replacement of the instruments.

- There was a feed back case from CTS Lucknow and CTS Bhopal on 2/15 MARR Systems supplied by M/s. HTL, Chennai-32.
- Packing cases damaged and packing note not tallying with the ICs at Lucknow and packing cases damaged at Bhopal.
- It was observed by the field unit at Lucknow that there was no damage to the equipments even though almost all packing cases containing BSU, BSUs and feeder cables were damaged. Further the packing note was not tallying with the ICs due to inadvertent despatch of the system by M/s., HTL. The firm was advised to be more careful in future to avoid such discrepancies.
- M/s. HTL visited the site at Bhopal during August 1998 and observed that there was no damage to the equipment.
- However the firm was advised to improve the packing. Accordingly M/s. HTL has improved packing by reinforcing the packing boxes by providing three steel bands over the shook boxes. Also the RP cables for RSUs are being packed separately in wooden boxes to avoid damages. Further the thickness of ply is increased from 3mm to 6mm.
- OPC Project, Hyderabad has made a complaint on 12P OP Cable supplied by M/s. Sterlite Industries, Aurangabad.
- Field units encountered some difficulty in removing the outer jacket of the cable as the jelly content is found to be very less comparatively.

- It is clarified by the manufacturer that the difficulty expressed by the field units in removal of the outer jacket is due to the fact that while removing the outer jacket and sheath the polyster tape is not being cut and that for smooth and easy removal of outer jacket it is essential that the polyster tape should be cut.
- This procedure was demonstrated by the firm successfully and to the satisfaction of the field staff as per the joint inspection report.

*Major Quality Problems*

In C-DOT switches, 96 & 64 pins female euro connectors of ESSEN make were giving problem after 72 hours burn in test at 50 degree Centigrate some pins were coming out resulting in improper connection. The problem was set right by certain modification in manufacturing process.

- The EPBT instruments supplied by M/s. ITI encountered moisture and low insulation problem in coastal areas.
- Conformal coating on PCB has been implemented by EPBT manufacturers to overcome the above problem.
- The fault of voltage appearing on edge strip of some XEJ cards of M/s. ITI, Mankapur were rectified by modification in PCB circuit.
- There was a field complaint on 140 Mb/s OLTE and 2/34 skip mux of M/s. HPCL that the jack in & jack out problems were existing in the racks. This has been solved by re-engineering the mechanical design of rack.

*Quality Control at major factories*

The fault rate in C-DOT switches of M/s. HTL were observed to be more in earlier. To minimise the faults and shorten the testing time, M/s. HTL was advised to involve the same team of engineers, technical assistants right from the first stage of production till integration/ testing of the complete equipment. This was implemented by M/s. HTL in addition to performing comparative study on the four teams set up for this purpose. After the introduction of this procedure, the faults of QA testing stage have come down.

- The QA systems at M/s. ITI, Palakkad, M/s. BPL, Palakkad, M/s. Tata Telecom, Palakkad, M/s. Trace Cables, Cochin & M/s. Keltron, Trivandrum are satisfactory.
- In view of the feedback complaints from field about the self supporting drop wire as poor in quality the following steps were taken by the manufacturers.

(a) Printing the identity of the manufacturer is introduced instead of embossing and 100% inspection on pirating is carried out.

(b) The PVC should be from CACT approved sources.

(c) Tight inspection is being followed.

*Important Events*

Member (Tech), Telecom. Commission, New Delhi had visited Bangalore on 7.9.98 and 8.9.98. He has visited CACT lab. and had an interaction with Sr. Officers of TQA Circle and RTEC, Bangalore.

The "Sanchar Shree" award function was held in association with Karnataka Telecom Circle on 17.5.98.

The "Sanchar Sarathi" award function for southern region of Telecom Quality Assurance Circle was held at Bangalore on 20.7.98 and for northern & eastern region it was held at M/s. ITI, Naini on 24.7.98.

*Seminars/training*

- 19 seminars/workshops on various subjects were

conducted by Telecom. QA Circle for the benefit of its personnel.

- QA Circle also participated in Seminars/training programmes conducted by outside agencies.

***UNDP project activities***

- Three DoT QA Officers were deputed abroad for training in the field of software QA and Digital Transmission Equipment.
- UNDP, New Delhi authorised chartered accountant, conducted audit on the on going UNDP project at CACT, Bangalore.

***World telecom day celebration***

World Telecom Day was celebrated. On this occasion, GM (PIg), Calcutta Telephones delivered a lecture on Technologies Driving Telecommunications in the office of Director (QA), Calcutta.

Representatives from various industries in Calcutta and DoT (QA) officials attended the lecture. CACT Building at Bangalore was illuminated on this occasion.

Value of stores anticipated for the period from 1.1.99 to 31.3.99 : Around Rs.1500 Crores.

(a) No. of QA Centres likely to be opened : One at Jamshedpur.

(b) No. of QA Centres likely to be closed : Two located at M/s. BPL, Palakkad and M/s Keltron Communications, Mudadi (Kozhidone Dt. Kerala)

No. of infrastructure assessments likely to be carried out : 42

(a) Conventional Products - 15

(b) TEC Products - 27

No. of type approval certificates likely to be issued : 75

No. of important meeting likely to be held : 5

(a) User's Meet:4

(b) Others : 1

No. of First Production Qualification cases likely to be completed 4

No. of major quality problems likely to be settled : 2

(a) No. of AIS likely to be accorded 5

(b) No. of DIS likely to be accorded 2

Component Approval Centre for Telecommunications (CACT)

(a) Augmentation of Test Facility :

Peel pull tester is likely to be installed.

(b) Activities :

- No. of components likely to be type approved : 98
- No. of components manufacturer's infrastructure likely to be assessed 19
- No. of components likely to be tested in various laboratories : 4300
- No. of products likely to be subjected to climate and environmental tests : 165
- Total climatic chamber hours likely to be utilised : 6600
- No. of devices likely to be subjected to failure analysis : 150
- No. of failure analysis reports likely to be released : NIL
- No. of reports likely to be generated at SCRAM : 15

**Wireless planning and coordination wing**

**Performance during 1998-99**

***Radio frequency spectrum management new frequency assignments/licenses issued etc.***

*Radio frequency spectrum management*

| | *01.04.98 to 31.12.98 (Actual)* | *01.01.99 to 31.03.99 (Anticipated)* |
|---|---|---|
| New Radio Frequency authorised to various users | 10543 | 6346 |
| Frequency assignments intimated to Radiocommunication Bureau of the ITU for registration | 395 | 228 |
| No. of sites cleared for new wireless stations | 5604 | 2132 |
| Inter-departmental meetings | 133 | 40 |
| No. of SACFA (Standing Advisory Committee on Frequency Allocations) meetings | 5 | 3 |
| **Issue of wireless licences** | | |
| Number of licences issued for new Wireless stations | 7800 | 1000 |
| Number of old Wireless stations for which licences were renewed | 22700 | 18500 |
| Number of Import Licence issued | 493 | 150 |
| **Certificate of proficiency (COP) examination/licences** | | |
| Number of COP examination conducted | 16 | 10 |
| Number of candidates admitted | 3620 | 3000 |
| Number of licences issued | 407 | 120 |
| Number of licences renewed | 1432 | 500 |

| | | |
|---|---|---|
| Number of new Radio Amateur licence issued | 448 | 402 |
| Number of Radio Amateur licence renewed | 462 | 340 |

**Review of national frequency allocation plan (NFAP), 1981**

Review of NFAP upto 40 GHz is in progress. Besides formal meetings of the Review Committee, several bilateral discussions have been held with several departments and organisations. Further, with several technologies emerging on the scene and with more and more privatisation several modifications are required to be carried out. With this in view, various private agencies like TEMA, TISA, CII, GOAI, ABTO FICCI, Technical Group of Experts comprising manufactures etc. have been requested for giving their inputs. Review Committee is examining these inputs along with the inputs from Govt. Sector to finalise the revised plan.

**Satellite system coordination**

***INSAT satellite networks***

India has a large and ambitious space communication programme having four operating INSAT Satellite networks at three GSO locations (55E, 83E and 93.5E), which are having communication, TV Broadcasting and meteorological payloads in S, C, Upper extended C and Ku bands.

The ITU Radio Regulatory process for various payloads of INSAT system filed with ITU in L,S,C,X,Ku and Ka bands in the INSAT series from different GSO locations are being pursued as requested from time to time by the Department of Space which is the only agency to build and operate satellites in India.

**INSAT- 2K satellite networks at 74,83 and 93.5 E**

Coordination of INSAT 2-K Ku-band satellite networks at 74 Deg E and 93.5 Deg East have been completed and notices have been sent to ITU for recording in the MIFR for international protection. Coordination of INSAT-2K at 83 E with Tonga was pursued during the year and notices could be sent to ITU on completion of the same.

**INSAT-2 (48), INSAT-2 (55) and INSAT-2 (111.5) (C/KU band) satellite networks**

Detailed coordination was undertaken during bilateral meetings with the Administration 0' Russia, INTELSAT, Inmarsat, Thailand, Indonesia, Germany, UAE and Japan during the year. Coordination was also pursued with the Administrations of Belarus and Singapore. It has been possible to get the coordination of Singapore, Russia, INTELSAT and Turkish Administrations for short term operation of INSAT-213T network from 55 E location and the same is being operated from this location.

**INSAT-2E systems at 74 E, 82 E, 83 E and 93.5 E**

Coordination of INSAT-2E series of networks were pursued during the year with various Administrations. With Philippines, Ivory Coast, Singapore and Australia coordination was pursued by correspondence. Bilateral coordination meetings were held to achieve or improve the provisions of coordination agreement with the Administrations of Russia, INTELSAT, UAE, Indonesia, Thailand, UK/Inmarsat and Japan. Coordination is planned with Administrations of China, UK and Belarus. Notices for recording the frequency assignments in MIFR for INSAT-2E 83 network is submitted to ITU.

**INSAT-2M (mobile satellite services INSAT-2T (expanded TV coverage) networks**

Bilateral coordination for these networks was continued with various affected Administrations alongwith other networks during the year. The countries which requested for coordination for these networks are Singapore, U.K., Sweden, China, Germany, Netherland, France, Japan, INTELSAT, Tonga, Belarus, Malaysia and Russia. Coordination was pursued during the year with the countries have objected for these networks. Coordination was pursued with the Administrations of Japan, Russia, UAE, Germany, Thailand, Indonesia and INTELSAT.

**INSAT- 72.5 DEG west, 108 DEG west and INSAT-EK75.2W, EK1 08 DEG W satellite networks**

In response to our coordination data for these networks Administrations which requested for detailed coordination are Canada, Germany, USA, France, Brazil, Japan, Inmarsat, UK, Argentina, and Tonga. Coordination was completed/pursued with the Administrations of Japan and Indonesia for some of the networks.

**INDAB - 51.5 Deg E, 56.5 Deg E, 71 Deg E, 79 Deg E, 89 Deg E & 113.5 Deg E (digital audio broadcasting) series of INSAT satellite networks**

Detailed coordination information for the INDAB series of INSAT satellite networks (intended for digital audio broadcasting) have been sent to ITU. Coordination was pursued with the Administrations of Japan, Australia and Indonesia for these networks.

**3.1.7 INSAT- KA50, KA54, KA63, KA67, KA74, KA78, KA87, KA93.5, KA98 & KA100 satellite networks**

Coordination information for these networks have already been published by the ITU. The Administrations which requested for coordination are Germany, UK, France, Japan, USA, Singapore, Malaysia, UK/Inmarsat, Tonga, Russia, Belarus, Italy, UAE, China and Korea. During the year coordination was undertaken with the Administrations of Japan, Russia and Indonesia.

**INSAT-EK & EKR series of INSAT satellite networks at 48E, 55E, 74E, 83E, 93.5E, 103E & 11 1.5E orbital locations**

The detailed Appendix-3 coordination information for INSAT-EK series of INSAT satellite networks at 48E, 55E, 74E, 78E, 83E, 93.5E, 103E and 11 1.5E was published by the ITU and the countries who have requested for coordination are China, UK, Russia, Singapore, Tonga,

USA, Saudi Arabia, Belarus, France, Indonesia, Japan, Korea, Laos, Pakistan, Philippines, Penang, Thailand, Turkey, UAE. Bilateral coordination for these networks were taken up during the coordination meetings with the Administrations of Russia, INTELSAT, Japan, Indonesia, UAE, Germany and UK during the year. Coordination information for additional carriers in C band and Ku band have been sent to ITU for publication under INSAT EK and EKR series.

**NSAT- ES48, ES55, ES74, ES83, ES93.5, ES100, ES105E & ES111.5 series of INSAT satellite networks**

The detailed coordination information sent to ITU for publication was pursued for early publication of Special Section in ITU weekly circulars.

**INSAT- X48, X55, X62.5, X66.5, X74, X83, X93.5, X1 03 & X1 11.5 (X-band series) satellite networks**

Detailed coordination information of INSAT-SX series satellite networks is to be sent to ITU at appropriate time as per the planning requirement of the Department of Space. Bilateral coordination was continued with the Administrations of Thailand and Indonesia during the year.

**INSAT-AF48/AF55 satellite networks**

Detailed coordination information for these satellite networks were filed with ITU for publication and international circulation.

**INSAT-BSS101 satellite networks**

Coordination for the network was concluded the Administration of Indonesia during the year. ITU published revised appendix information pertaining to the modifications of the region 3 BSS (Broadcasting satellite service) plan and fores comments/objections are awaited from various affected Administrations.

**Indian Remote Sensing Satellite Network (IRS)**

*IRS-1 Cars-1 E* : Coordination was achieved with all affected Administrations and action for registration of frequency assignments with ITU is in progress.

*IRS-P3:* Coordination data was provided to the Administrations of U.K., USA, Canada, Spain, Germany, France, Russia, Japan and Malaysia, for coordination of IRS-P3 satellite network. Coordination agreement was reached with Germany & Japan and is in progress with UAE and USA.

*IRS-P4:* Request for coordination was received from the Administrations of Brazil, China, Germany, France, Italy, Japan, Malaysia, Russia, UAE and USA in response to Advanced Publication Information for this network. Coordination was completed with the Administrations of Japan and coordination with other Administrations is pursued.

*IRS-1D:* Advanced Publication of Information for this network has been published by ITU and request for coordination has been received from Italy, Saudi Arabia, Indonesia and USA.

**Protection of INSAT space, terrestrial and radio astronomy services from the satellite networks of other countries**

The interference potential to INSAT Space and Terrestrial networks, from various new satellite systems, planned by other countries, was assessed/evaluated on regular basis to protect our national interests. Many of our new INSAT satellite networks in various frequency bands, cover other parts of the world. Protection from interference for these networks is also being taken into account, increasing the complexity of analysis/evaluation immensely.

Detailed coordination exercise for protection of Indian space & terrestrial networks and Radio Astronomy Services was undertaken with other

Administrations in all cases, where the potential interference exceeded the permissible limits.

**VSAT Networks**

Frequency assignments for public/captive satellite communication network including that of VSAT networks were made to various service providers/users.

**Aspects relating to frequency management for terrestrial networks**

***GSM cellular***

*GSM cellular in metro areas*

Based on detailed technical presentation made by private cellular operators for Calcutta and Chennai service areas, assignment of appropriate additional GSM mobile channels in 800/900 MHz band has been made.

**GSM cellular in circles**

Applications for frequency assignments from private cellular service providers for operation of GSM Mobile Network at various cities in all the Telecom. Circles were received. Based on the requirements projected by these cellular operators, frequency assignments for GSM mobile and intercity microwave access network have been made. In so far as inter-city microwave backbone networks are concerned, most of the assignments have been made after extremely complex task of frequency coordination with other wireless networks to ensure the electromagnetic compatibility and intensive frequency coordination process has been undertaken for the remaining.

**Radio paging service**

After successful coordination of frequencies for introduction of radio paging service, assignment of suitable frequencies, including link frequencies have been made, for operation of paging service on city wise basis as well as on circle basis, to all Radio Paging Service operators. Assignment of suitable frequencies owing to expansion of paging networks is being undertaken based on the requests of paging operators.

**Radio trunking services**

Assignment of frequencies for operation of city-wise radio trunking network in frequency bands 300 MHz, 400 MHz and 800 MHz, as per channelling Plans evolved for the purpose, have been made to all the licensed radio trunking service operators based on their requests. Assignment of suitable frequencies owing to expansion of radio trunking networks is being undertaken based on the requests of radio trunking operators.

**Basic services**

Assignments of frequencies for operators of Basic Telephone Services using Wireless in Local Loop have been made. The frequency requirement of MW Access & backbone networks are being met. Coordination are also initiated on special requests of the service providers as and when required.

**Requests from foreign diplomatic missions**

Special requirements projected by foreign diplomatic missions for radio communications were considered and frequencies assigned.

**International conferences and meetings**

National preparations, participation and follow-up actions for the following important international conferences and meetings were arranged by the WPC Wing.

The Pleniopotentiary Conference, 1998 (PP-98) of the ITU to determine the policies for fulfilling the purposes of Union as prescribed in the constitution of ITU. Plenipotentiary Conference is the supreme organ of the ITU and meets once in a 4 year.

One of the important task before Plenipotentiary Conference is to hold the elections for various posts.

India was re-elected in the ITU Council also. Shri R.N.Agarwal, Wireless Adviser to the Govt. of India was elected for the post of Member Radio Regulation Board securing the highest number of votes among the candidates from the Asia & Australia region.

The Conference decided upon the policies for important function of ITU especially for the period 1999-2003.

The 1998 Session of the Council of the ITU which acts as the governing body of the ITU in the intervals between Plenipotentiary Conferences.

Regional meeting on HF Interference in Aeronautical and maritime services and replanning of Broadcasting Satellite Service including steering committee meeting was held during 5-8 May 1998 at Bangkok Thailand and Shri R.N.Agarwal, Wireless Adviser to GOI was unanimously elected as Chairman of the meeting.

The 22nd Session of the Management Committee of Asia Pacific Telecommunity (APT). The Management Committee is the governing body which meets annually to consider, review and approve the various programme of the APT India was re-elected as Chairman of the Management Committee. Shri A. Narayan of India was elected as Dy.Executive Director for 3 years.

Meeting of the Radio communication Study Groups and their Working Parties to study the technical, operational questions pertaining to different type of radio communication services with a view to adopting recommendations with focus on standardising performance characteristics and planning operation of radio systems on world-wide basis for ensuring, efficient use of the Radio Frequency Spectrum (RFS) and Geo-stationary Satellite Orbit (GSO) and appropriate interaction with Telecommunication Standardisation Sector through Intersector Coordination Group (ICG).

First annual review meeting of GMPCS MoU Group to review and evaluate the effectiveness of the procedure established and to make any necessary changes.

**Wireless monitoring organisation**

*Performance during year 1998-99*

| | | *01.04.98 to 31.12.98 (Actual)* | *01.01.99 to 31.03.99 (Anticipated)* |
|---|---|---|---|
| a) | Channel days utilised for Radio Monitoring. | 5118 | 2000 |
| b) | Monitoring Assignments handled. | 8957 | 2750 |
| c) | No. of Wireless Station Inspected. | 2138 | 1000 |
| d) | No. of Radio Noise Measurements. | 35956 | 7000 |
| e) | No. of Wireless Transmissions monitored. | 81303 | 2700 |
| f) | Infringements communicated to various users for remedial action. | 5448 | 1650 |
| g) | Technical Assistance to users to maintain their operation within specified standards. | 1996 | 750 |

Many important Radio Surveys/Investigation assignments were carried out by way of Mobile Monitoring during the year.

Microwave Mobile Monitoring Terminals continued to monitor radio transmissions in microwave frequency bands to verify emission, characteristics and interference potential. The measurements on terrestrial microwave links viz LOS systems, Radars etc. to ensure compatibility are also being carried out regularly. Assistance was also being provided to the users by way of conducting noise surveys for wireless/earth stations and site selection. Microwave Terminals of Wireless Monitoring Organisation have earned a revenue of Rs.2.0 lakhs till 31.12.98, by way of their services to various user agencies.

For establishment of Specialised Monitoring Terminal, purchase order for Integrated Mobile Monitoring Terminal has been issued. The system is likely to be delivered by March, 1999 and will be made fully operational during 1999.

The Satellite Monitoring Earth Station at Jalna is capable of monitoring of all communication satellite parked in geo-stationary orbit from 20 Deg. E to 140 Deg. E operating in "C" and "S" bands to ensure protection to Indian Space and Terrestrial Radio Communication Services against interference from space service operating by Satellites of other administrations. A number of Geo-Stationary Satellites (Indian and Foreign) in the arc were also tracked.

ISMES Jalna in co-ordination with Master Control Facility (MCF) Hassan, ISRO carried out signal level measurement during INSAT-2D transponders characterisation.

Wireless Monitoring Training and Development Centre has conducted 5 Nos. in service courses and imparted training to 49 officers/officials of the organisation in various disciplines upto December 1998. It is expected that at least 20 more officers and technical staff will also get training prior to 31.3.1999.

The Science and Technology Unit is in the process of development of some hardware and software required for monitoring systems and sub-systems used at various monitoring stations.

VHF/UHF Direction Finding (DF) systems and one HF DF System have been purchased and installed at the desired stations. The proposal for augmentation of existing DIF systems are under consideration.

# 3

# Future Prospects

With the number of telephones in India aggregating to a mere 5.8 million to service a population of over 850 million people, telecommunications is an industry of tremendous growth potential. It is also one of the most profitable business areas in India today with the pay back on a line being only two years.

The new Ministry of Communication has drawn up a very ambitious 26 point program for this Industry. Some of the highlights are that private participation has been invited for building and operation of telecom networks in 'growth centres and satellite towns'.

In the new Industrial Policy, telecom equipment was delicenced and thrown open to foreign investment. Several joint ventures came up- GPI and K.K. Birla, Ericcson with their long term collaborators the Jiwarajkars, AT&T with Tata Telecom, Fujitsu with the Punjab State Electronic Production and Development Corporation and Alcatel with B.K. Modi. Of these companies gearing up to meet the indigenous requirements, the last two are near ready to commence production of equipment to meet the specifications set out by the Department of Telecommunications.

The Ministry of Communication has in October this year allowed eight private companies to establish cellular telephone systems in the four metropolitan cities kof Delhi, Bombay, Calcutta and Madras. In each of the four metros, the two private companies would operate the system along with their two foreign partners. Tenders are expected to be floated soon inviting private manufacturers to set up value-added celluler telephone systems in other secondary cities in the country. Mobile telephones will be made available against foreign exchange payment. Video conferencing, Email, Radio Paging and other value added services and manufacturing of ten thousand line exchanges, will be available to joint/private sector without licensing (capacity) regulation.

Until now only terminal equipment and PABX manufacturing was permitted in private sector subject to lecensing.

**New Import Export Policy**

A new Import-Export Policy was announced on 1st April, 1992. The policy statement eliminated a number of import categories, exceptions and exemptions, special lists, open lists etc. The new 5 year exim policy makes trade "free" subject to a small negative list. Even the short negative list which prohibits import of certain items is likely to be curtailed further during the year.

The Finance Minister, Dr. Manmohan Singh, while inaugurating the International Asia Pacific Conference on private sector has stated that "bureaucratic controls would be fully dismantled, quantitative import restrictions phased out and customs tariff reduced to international levels to make the private sector vibrant."

Collaboration by non-Small Scale Industrial units for items reserved for the SSI sector is allowed subject to the condition that the firms concerned would undertake to export at least 75% of its output. Applications for 100% EOUs are cleared by the SIA and those for 100% Export Processing Zone (EPZ) units are cleared by the

Development Commissioner of the particular EPZ, subject to the guidelines aplicable to such units.

Export obligations are no longer imposed in other cases of collaboration. Instead, the export offers made by the applicants are taken note of as being in the nature of a gentlemen's agreement, and are not linked to legal or bank guarantees. Their fulfilment is a matter of trust, and not compulsion.

The Government has liberalised the guidelines for * automatic approval in 30 days for all cases involving an equity of upto US $ two million.

The Government has initiated steps to deregulate the domestic civil aviation industry and bring an end to the public sector monopoly in domestic civil aviation. The Ministry of Civil Aviation has proposed to withdraw the three major constraints on private taxi operators namely:

- Restriction on level of fare.
- Route restriction.
- Flight time restriction.

The ministry has given support to the 'open sky policy' for air taxi licenses in India. Selling Indian airlines or Air India is however not on the immediate agenda.

Liberalisation and 'open sky policy' has opened the vast domestic market to new scheduled airlines in India. There are 22 registered private airlines of which a few are already operational. The most notable being East West Airlines which has already acquired 3% of the total domestic market, that was till now monopolised by Indian Airlines.

The ministry of Civil Aviation and Tourism has recently invited foreign capital and technology for 'collaborative partnership' for an "integrated development of the Indian aviation industry".

'Liberalisation window to opportunities was the theme of the 41st annual convention of the Travel Agents' Association of Inida, held at Hydrabad recently.

Many interesting facts emerged during the convention. Partial convertibility has made visiting India and even shopping an inexpensive proposition. For example, there is a charactered flight every day from Uzbekistan carrying 240 passengers stopping at New Delhi for a day of shopping!

In a radical departure form the Industrial Policy of 1956, the Union Government has announced that it will allow 100% foreign equity participation for setting up of power plants in India. It has also permitted substantial modification in the Electricity (Supply) Act 1948 to hasten the private sector's participation in the ailing power sector.

These two decisions have been taken by the cabinet and the bill containing the amendments in the Electricity (Supply) Act and the 100% foreign equity participation proposals will be tabled soon before the Parliament.

The 100% foreign equity participation proposals allows free repatriation of profits and other incentives. Besides, it will facilitate foreign parties to set up power plants without time delays, which are solely responsible for the cost escalation in the power projects.

Proposals from foreign investors for new power units are expected to be cleared through a high powered committee. The domestic private company's proposals will be cleared through a single window to minimise bureaucratic and other delays. The Government is likely to invite various foreign consortia including non-resident Indians (NRI's), particularly those in Japan and the UK to come forward.

Since the 1960's, the two public sector companies, Oil & Natural Gas Commission (ONGC) and Oil India Limited have held a monopoly over oil exploration in India. ONGC is seeking a change of its status to an autonomous corporation with the freedom to raise its resources directly from markets in India and overseas. It is prepared to enter into new projects such as country wide gas grid in collaboration with the private sector. It is understood that 73 drilling and exploratory blocks have been offered to international oil companies through international tendering. The Government has invited offers for joint ventures to develop designated medium-sized as also small sized oil and gas fields offering a range of incentives. Companies may singly or as a consortium bid by the 31st December 1992. Major tax concessions are made both for Indian and foreign companies engaged in oil exploitation. Income Tax will be levied at a flat rate of 50% without surcharge as against 65% now applicable to foreign companies in other businesses.

The Government has accorded status of importance to the Bombay High oil producing belt in the Arabian Sea and initiated highly sophisticated defence procedures for safeguarding the rigs from aggression.

Potential estimates claim that India should produce 70 metric tonnes of crude per annum by 1999 and will be considered a major economic power of the next century.

The rate of tax applicable to foreign companies continue to be 65%. Surcharge is not levied in the case of non-resident assessees.

Section 80 HHC of Income Tax Act 1961 provides for 100% exemption from income tax if the entire business income is generated from exports. The deductions available to an assessee involved in exports in now to be calculated on a new formula. The formula makes a distinction between a manufacturer exporter and a trading exporter. The actual deduction is calculated taking into consideration the FOB value of the exports as against the turnover and profits/gains of the business.

Under the provisions of Section 80-0, 50% of technical services fees, royalties etc derived under an approved agreement are deductible from income. This concession which was available to Indian corporate bodies has now been extended to non corporate bodies. This concession has been granted with the prupose of encouraging professionals such as architects, accountants etc to earn foreign exchange for the country. Further clarifications are expected from the Government on how this scheme would be applied to professionals as prior approval of agreements may be very difficult to administer.

Some immediate effects of the changes outlined above can be seen from the following events:

— As early as April 1992, a 1243% increase in foreign investment has been registered in India since the announcement of the liberalised industrial policy in July 1991.

— Foreign Collaborations in India recently approved by the Indian Government include companies like General Motors, General Electric, Coca Cola, Suzuki, Leasaffre (French), GERB (German), Buhler (Swiss), IBM, BMW, Ford etc. In the communication sector, AT&T, Siemens, France and British Telecom have shown keen interest in bidding for setting up cellular phone networks in India.

— 100 senior Japanese business executives spent a week in India in February 1992 and Nomura Securities Company has established a presence in

Delhi. The opening of a trading office of a securities house in known to be a major jumping off point for further investment in India.

— 200 foreign participants attended the Euromoney conference in Delhi on "Business, Finance and Investment in India" in the last week of March, 1992.

**New Horizons**

In the recent few months, with the Bombay Stock Market Scandal in which banks and financial institutions stand to lose upto Rs. 30 billion, inflation running upto 13% on occasions and other regional and national political problems, the feeling has been that the Government is now in the danger of letting opportunities slip away. The Government did announce de-licensing of the electronic industry, liberalisation which would permit foreign financial institutions to invest in India and permission to open branch offices by foreign companies in the last few months to counter the allegations that there has been a slow down in the economic reform process. Although there may be some truth in this allegation the process of liberalisation has certainly not stopped. The Government has given an assurance that it will endeavour to proceed with the intended further liberalisation as promised.

On the whole, along with devaluation of the rupee in June 1991, the new trade policy and the further reforms promised includding full convertibility of the rupee, if the new Industrial Policy and its effect does turn out to what it promises to be, new horizons will open. This should lead to faster growth of industries in India. Indian industries would be open and accessible to the world. The opening up of new areas such as air transportation and power generation for private sector participation will result in opportunities for contractors and financial institutions to bid for project and asset work. The feeling in India is that a clear signal has been sent to industrialists, both local and foreing, that the government really means business. The radical nature of the industrial policy has met and continues to meet some resistance from the bureaucratic machinery which it seeks to dismantle. Its fine print still requires further clarifications. But more important than the fine print is the inescapable fact the political power has finally recognised that it is time for a new order to emerge. For some, their efforts may have fallen short of expectations, but the Government has acted, at last.

This update has been prepared by Thakker & Thakker Solicitors & Advocates, Bombay, for the AIJA 1992 conference in Bombay on "Emerging Investment Opportunities in India". The Update is necessarily of general nature and seeks to provide information only on some of the major changes announced by the Government and cannot be regarded as legal advice.

**Status of the Indian Telecom Network**

India today operates one of the largest telecom networks in Asia comprising

— Over 20 172 telephone exchanges;

— About 118 400 route kms of coaxial terrestrial UHF/ microwave radio relay systems up to 140 Mbit/s apart from analogue systems;

— 23 300 kilometres of optical fibre systems comprising of systems up to 565Mb/s;

— 50 per cent of Transmission network is digitalised.

About 7 700 cities and towns are connected to the National Subscriber Dialling (NSD) network and the Department of Telecommunications (DOT) plans to extend the facility to all automatic exchanges by 1997.

Fully automatic International Subscriber Diallilng

(ISD) service is available to 237 countries through two international earth stations and submarine cable systems. Trunk manual service is also available to all countries.

To meet the low speed data communication needs of Business/industrial units in Remote and far flung areas, a Business. Message Network (RABMN) with a hub-station near Delhi, having a capacity of 1000 subscribers has been commissioned. About 456 Very Small Aperture Terminals (VSAT) are deployed in this network for providing data service at maximum speeds up to 9.6kbits.

A dedicated Packet Switched Public Data Network (PSPDN), with international access for computer communication services is available in the country with speeds up to 2Mbit/s.

For providing international connectivity, a Gateway Packet Switching System (GPSS), is available which offers the capability of sophisticated telecommunication networking terminals and computers internationally.

INSAT satellite systems are being used to provide over 4126 two-way speech circuits through 165 earth stations across the length and breadth of the country. In 1975, the government of India took a decision to have its system for meeting domestic communication needs of the country and approved the scheme in 1977 for the multi purpose Indian National Satellite System (INSAT).

The INSAT-I series of satellites, comprising four satellites were launched in 1982, 1983, 1988 and 1990 respectively. INSAT-II series of the satellites comprising four satellites in orbit and one ground spare, are being manufactured indigenously. Under this series, INSAT-IIA was launched in July 1992 and INSAT-IIB Satellite was launched in July 1993.

The present space segment comprises of * INSAT IIA

and IIB Satellites in orbit. The ground segment of INSAT-ID & INSAT-IIA, IIB comprises of 82 fixed Satellite earth stations. In addition to the above, 29 satellite earth stations have been commissioned as captive networks to meet the telecommunication needs of Government undertakings.

Besides above fixed satellite earth stations the ground segment also comprises 23 mobile terminals including three Flyaway Terminals. These terminals are capable of being transported to different parts of the country by road/air to restore the telecommunication services as well as to meet an urgent telecommunication need from any part of the country. There are also nine special routes/networks.

About 185000 villages out of 604 734 villages are provided with telecommunications facililties;

There were 2.5 telephones per 1000 population in the rural areas at the end of march 1995, as against the figure of 107 in the country as a whole. These figures are expected to become 3.00 and 15.00 respectively by the year 1997 as per the modest government investment. Private sector participation, which is expected shortly, will raise telephone density considerably.

The total equipped capacity of the Indian local network is 12 million with over 10 million main lines. There has been a rise of 25 per cent in telephone traffic in 1991-1992 and 35 per cent in 1992-1993 as compared to the previous year.

The pending demand however is 215 million and is growing at over 20 per cent per annum. In the past the registered demand has grown at a rate of 10 to 13 per cent per annum while the supply remained between 9 to 10.5 per cent. As a consequence the waiting list has grown. Over the last two years, we have stepped up the growth rate to 15 per cent per annum to see a slight dip in the demand.

The Indian Telecommuinications network provides nearly 400 000 Long Distance Switching Circuits with 94 per cent digitization.

A number of state-of-the-art switching technologies have been inducted in Indian network, ie FETEX 150, EWSD, AXE 10, No.5 ESS, OCB 283, System X, NEAX 61E and the indigenous CDoT.

Enhancement of capacity and digitalization of the transmission network is being carried out with optical fibre, digital microwaves and satellite.

A great emphasis is being laid on R&D of sophisticated digital switching and transmission equipment to meet india's urban and rural needs. The Centre for Development of Telematics (C-DoT) has successfully designed a family of digital-SPC switching systems from small to large main automatic exchanges.

Technology for several transmission products such as 10 channel UHF-600 MHz, 2/8 and 8/34 Digital mux, Satellite Based Rural Telegraph Network (SBRTN) Single Channel VHF and 2/8 Mbit/s OLTE has also been indigenously developed by CDoT and technology successfully transferred to a large number of local manufacturers. CDoT technology has also been offered to other countries as well.

Value added services are being indigenously developed exchanges through introduction of better signalling features such as Common Channel Signalling No. 7 and through ISDN.

The ultimate goal of R&D units is however to lead to the development of an Intergrated Services Digital Network (ISDN) and eventually to Broadband ISDN (B-

ISDN) through Synchronous Digital Hierachy (SDH). Digital Access Cross Connect System (DACCS), Asynchronous Transport Module (ATM) etc.

There is a Telecommunications Engineering Centre (TEC) for issuing of specifications, type approvals, interface approvals and evaluation of new telecom products and for standardisation.

Over the years, the Department of Telecom, have built up extensive training facilities starting at the apex with Advanced Level Telecommunications Training Centre, near Delhi, set up with the systems and support of the UNDP and ITU.

The Telecommunications Training Centre at Jabalpur and 11 Regional and 25 State and District Level Training Centres also provides extensive training facilities. India has been extending assistance to Asia and Pacific countries too in meeting their training needs in the high tech areas of telecommunications.

Through DOT's consultancy group known as Telecommunication Consultancy India Limited (TCIL), India has been offering a wide spectrum of consultancy services in the international arena.

These include technical and management support, training, inspection, rehabilitation, modernization of existing systems, techno-economic studies in the core sectors of engineering and design studies, besides construction management and electronic data processing etc.

The consultancy services, include feasibility studies, network design studies, software support, installation, testing and commissioning of switching systems and transmission systems, operation and maintenance of networks.

TCIL has executed various contracts abroad and has been operating in about 28 countries.

**The Indian Telegraph (Amendment) Bill, 1995**

The National Telecom Policy 1994, has inter-alia laid emphasis on achieving the universal service, bringing the quality of Telecom service to world standard, provision of the widest permissible range of services to meet the customer's demand at reasonable price and participation of the companies registered in India in the area of basic telecom services as also making arrangements for protection and promotion of consumers' interest and ensuring fair competition. The Department of Telecomomunications feel that to achieve these objectives, there is need to separate regulatory functions from service providing functions which will be in keeping with the prevailing general trend in the world. It has, therefore, proposed to set up an independent Telecom Regulatory Authority to be called 'Telecom Regulatory Authority of India' which, to begin with, will be non-statutory in character but will have well defined functions and responsibilities and powers to play the role of a watch-dog body for the Telecom sector in an effective manner.

The Indian Telegraph Act, 1885 regulates the functioning of Telecommunications services in the country. Under Section 4 of the Indian Telegraph Act, 1885, the Central Government has the exclusive right of establishing, maintaining and working telegraphs and under the first provision of this section, it may grant a licence on such conditions and in consideration of such payment as it thinks fit to any persons to establish, maintain or work a telegraph within any part of the country. Under Section 4(2) of the Act, the Central Government may by notification in the Official Gazette delegate to the Telegraph Authority all or any of its powers under the first proviso to subsection (1). Section 3(6) of the Indian Telegraph Act, 1885 describes Director General (Posts and Telegraphs) as the Telegraph Authority and includes any officer empowered by him to perform all or any of the functions of the Telegraph Authority under the Act. Presently, the Secretary, Department of Telecommunications who has been notified as the Director General Telecommunications in his capacity as a Telegraph Authority exercises regulatory powers and performs regulatory functions as delegated by the Central Government under the Indian Telegraph Act, 1885. In order to vest the powers of the Telegraph Authority with the proposed Regulatory Authority in respect of certain assigned functional areas. It has become necessary to amend Section 3(6) of the Indian Telegraph Act, 1885 by including "any statutory or non-statutory authority".

The secretary, Department of Telecommunications stated in evidence that at present all the regulatory authority under the Indian Telegraph Act is exercised by the Secretary, Department of Telecommunications. This power of the telegraph authority can be further delegated by him to another officer of the Government. It cannot be delegated to a statutory or a non-statutory authority as such. So, the basic purpose of the proposed amendment of Section3(6) of the Indian Telegraph Act, 1885 is to delegate certain regulatory powers of the Telegraph authority to the proposed Telecom Regulatory Authority.

The Secretary, Department of Telecommunications further clarified that the reasons for not coming up with a comprehensive Bill to setup a statutory with independent powers at this stage, are that the Government would like to watch the working of such an authority for a year or two and learn from such an experience. After getting the feed-back from the

Chairman and Members of the authority and various interest groups viz, operators and subscribers etc., it would frame a comprehensive law to make it a statutory authority. Then the authority will derive its powers directly from an Act of Parliament.

The witness further told the Committee that "the need for amendment is based not only on Government perceptions of the local market but also arises from the international experience that wherever there has been a situation of more than one player in the market scene, a need has been felt for an independent umpire. The current trend in the telecommunication sector the world-over is to distance policy making functions, operational functions and regulatory functions from each other and to entrust regulatory functions to an independent Regulatory Authority for regulating Telecom services".

The Secretary, Department of Telecommunications informed the Committee that in due course the proposed authority would be independent and autonomous; it would operate outside the Government, at arm's length from the Government so that it could inspire the confidence of various operators as well as the subscribers. He further added that for this purposes the intention of the Government is to ensure that it is manned by people of eminence and independent views. Therefore, the Cabinet has decided that it would be chaired by a retired or a serving Chief Justice of a High Court or a retired or a serving Judge of the Supreme Court and it will have two members who should have worked in the State Government or the Central Government in a position not lower than the position of an additional Secretary to Government of India for a period of three years. These Members would enjoy the status of Secretary to Govt. of India. It was further stated that the tenure of the Chairman and the Members would be secure and protected. Their removal will require the same safeguards as are available to Judges of the Supreme Court. Similarly their emoluments and other terms and conditions of service would not be changed to their disadvantage. The Secretary Department of Telecommunications stated that the apparent idea was to send across a strong signal that there would be an authority who would act independently, impartially, in an objective manner to protect the interests of the operators as also of the subscribers.

Clarifying the position further in reply to a query by the Committee, the Secretary, Deptt. of Telecommunications stated that soon after the amendment of law, two things would follow. Firsts that Department of Telecommunications would set up this authority by means of a Resolution of the Government. Secondly the Department would issue a notification that the authority set up under that Resolution is vested with the powers of the Director-General of Telecommunications under Section 4 of the Indian Telegraph Act in respect of certain matters. Once that is done, the authority would be clothed with the powers of Telegraph Authority in relation to its are a of work. However, it would still be a creature of the executive arm of the Government. Later after an year or so it will come before the Parliament with a comprehensive Bill.

In reply to a query regarding the impact of Telecom Regulatory Authority after its inception on working of Telecom Network in the country, the Ministry informed that it was excepted that the Telecom Regulatory Authority would have healthy impact on the working of telecom services in the country, since it will act as a watch dog for telecom sector, ensure level playing field as also monitor quality of services and protect and promote the consumer interest.

Asked whether after setting up the Authority, it would be possible for Government to set aside any decision of the proposed Authority, the Secretary Deptt. of telecoommunications replied in negative. He further added that the intention was that there would be not right of appeal to the executive wing of the Government. The orders issued by the proposed Telecom Regulatory Authority can only be challenged before the High Court or the Supreme Court.

In the light of the Government view known to the Committee, the Committee agree with the amendment of Section 3(6) of Indian Telegraph Act, 1885 for inclusion of any statutory or non-statutory authority within the definition of Telegraph Authority and support the Bill. The Committee hope that steps will be taken to set up a statutory Authority.

**Science & Technology Development**

The investment in Research and Development. (R & D) has increased from a paltry Rs. 20 crore in the First Five Year Plan. Presently there are 214 universities, 400 national laboratories and 1300 in-house R & D centres in the industrial sector. Several Science & Technology departments have been set up in the areas of environment, non-conventional energy resources, bio-technology, ocean development, industrial research, space, atomic energy, defence, health, agriculture and electronics.

Identification and promotion of priority areas in R & D is done by Science an Engineering Research Council (SERC) set up under the Department of Science & Technology (DST). DST supports 12 autonomous research insitutions as well, for furthering research work in several discipline. Technology Information, Forecasting and Assessment Council (TIFAC) has been set up for generating technology forecasting and technology assessment documents and enabling a technology information system that is interactive and nationally accessible.

Industrial research in several diverse fields of scientific activity is being undertaken through a network of 40 laboratories and 81 field stations set up by the Council for Scientific and Industrial Research (CSIR). In the field of bio-technology, more than 24 specialised R & D centres have been developed for pursuing state-of-the-art research. Identical efforts for promoting new avenues of research are being undertaken in the field of ocean development as well.

The Union Budget for 1996-97 has taken various measures to promote R & D facilities. A matching one time grant has been awarded to CSIR and the Indian Council of Agricultural Research (ICAR) for modernisation of laboratories and institutes. The Technology Development and Application Fund created in 1995-96 has been proposed to be strengthened by Rs. 30 crore. A Five Year Tax Holiday under Section 80-IA of the Income Tax Act has been allowed to companies exclusively create for participation in R & D activities. The existing procedure for awarding weighted deduction under Section 35(2AA) of the Income Tax Act on sums paid for scientific research to a National Laboratory or a University or an IIT has been amended, by deleting the condition of approval by an outside body. In order to encourage R & D efforts, goods developed and patented in India and concurrently in specified countries have been exempted from levy of excise duty for a period of 3 years. The exemption procedure for customs duty on import of equipment and consumables for R & D institutions has been rationalised as well.

**Private Sector Partcipation**

The Value added service sector has been open to the private sector since 1992. In respect of value added services, except radio paging and mobile telephony services, companies registered in India are permitted to operate under licence on non exclusive basis. In the area of Radio paging and Cellular Mobile Telephone Services, however, a policy of selection is being followed in the granting of licences through a system of tendering.

A tender for operation of radio paging services in 27 cities was earlier invited and 14 companies have been granted operating licences. For other areas of the country comprising 19 territorial telecom circles, tenders have been invited, and licensing is being progressively done. Commercial service has been started in 22 cities by one or more operators to over 48,000 subscribers and in the rest of the five cities the service will start very soon.

Eight companies have been selected for the franchises of cellular mobile service in the four metro cities namely Bombay, Delhi, Calcutta and Madras. In respect of rest of the country, a tender had been invited. The evaluation of 33 bids for the 20 telecommunications circles, is expected to be completed shortly. Service has commenced in Calcutta and Delhi in September 1995.

With a view to supplement the efforts of Department of Telecommunications in providing telecommunication services to the people, 81 bids received for grant of licence for operation of basic services in 20 telecom Circles are now under evaluation.

The government has decided to create an autonomous Telecom Regulatory body called the Telecom Regulatory Authority of India (TRAI). This will have well defined functions, responsibilities and powers to play the role of a watch-dog body for the telecommunications sector in an effective manner. The Authority will regulate its procedure for conduct of business with the approval of the government and will be expected to ensure transparency and accountability.

Profound changes are taking place in Telecommunication sector the world over and India is no exception. The Government of India has taken bold initiatives to liberalise and expand the telecom network in the country.

Some of the milestones in this direction are:

— 1984

Manufacture of Customer Premises Equipment delicensed.

— 1991

New Industrial Policy permitting private sector to manufacture all types of telecommunications equipment.

Other salient features are:

No industrial Licence is required;

Automatic approval of foreign equity investment up to 51 per cent in the case of manufacturing projects:

Automatic approval of foreign collaboration in the case of telecommunications sector with technology fees up to Rs. 10 million net of taxes and/or royalty up to five per cent for domestic sales and/or eight per cent for exports.

The possibility for more than 51 per cent foreign equity and higher technology fees/royalty in manufacturing projects through special approvals;

All foreign investment proposals for telecommunications services require the specific approval to the Government of India.

1992

Value added services thrown open to private sector participation.

1994

New National Telecommunications Policy allowing private sector participation in basic services announced.

The National Telecommunications Policy announced by the Government would be instrumental in bringing about phenomenal expansion and improvement in the telecom sector.

The objectives of the Telecommunications Policy are:

— providing Telecommunications for all and Telecommunications within the reach of all;
— Universal Service Obligation at affordable and reasonable price;
— Providing telecommunications services of world standard;
— To ensure that India emerges as a major manufacturing base and major exporter of telecom equipment.

The targets laid down in the policy are as follows:

— Telephones to be available on demand by 1997;
— All vjillages to be provided with telecommunications services by 1997;
— In urban areas a Public Calling Office (PCO) should be provided for every 500 persons by 1997;
— Special emphasis on the quality of telecoommunications services provided to the customers will be given;
— All value added services available internationally to be introduced in India, preferably by 1996.

The other important aspects of the policy are:

— Private initiative would be used to supplement the departmental efforts to raise additional resources both through increased internal generation and adopting innovative means, like, leasing, deferred payments, build-operate-and-transfer, build-lease-and-transfer.

— A suitable funding mechanism for indigenous R&D is proposed to be set up;

— Pilot projects will be encouraged directly by the government in order to access new technologies, new systems in both basic as well as value added services.

With low telephone penetration rates, India represents one of the world's most attractive markets for telecommunications service providers and equipment manufacturers. Service sector opening of the basic telecom services to the private sector is the biggest opportunity for foreign direct investment. The growth potential in the basic telephone service in India is tremendous taking into consideration the low telephone density at present.

The challenge in rural telecommunications in India is indeed quite formidable. Out of the 604 734 villages in the country, only 185000 have telephone facility. Over 420,000 villages are still without a telephone facility.

Under the National Telecommunications Policy, one public telephone will be provided in each of the over half a million villages by 1997. Provisioning of a single telephone in each village, as per the telecom policy, may involve an investment of the order of S billion US Dollars. The sub-sector of value added services is already open for private investment. This sector in India represents one of the world's largest opportunities for supply of services and equipment.

The Indian Switching market, which is estimated to increase from about 2.5 million lines now to over 3.00 million lines in 1996-1997 represents-one of the largest market in the Asian region. The digital switching markets in India has witnessed a true metamorphosis since 1991 when the new Industrial Policy was announced by the Government.

A number of foreign companies attracted by DOT's liberalised procurement policies, have set up local production ventures in India. The opening up of the Import Policy in 1992 has opened this largest market to international competition.

The market for providing private networks is also growing very fast. Major international companies have already announced their plans for making an entry in this market.

The Radio Transmission Equipment market in India has undergone extensive changes in the post industrial liberallization period. With the diversification or production of transmission equipment which was earlier limited to the public sector companies, the present production base has expand with the setting up of the manufacturing facilities in the private sector.

With the opening up of Microwave Radio systems to competition, a number of multinational companies have entered the radio equipment market. The digital microwave radio equipment market has potential for large investments since most of the radio frequency spectrum in microwave is still available for deployment.

The investment opportunities in the optical fibre cable and equipment as well as infrastrucure equipment for value added services such as cellular and paging are immense. With the possibility of the entire long distance network being converted to optical fibre media, a number of international companies are getting their products validated at present. The investment opportunities in this area are extremely good.

Another area expected to sustain great demand in the coming decade is VSATs with voice transmission. The steady increase in the number of customers demanding high bit rate data transmission and separate corporate networks has given spur to VSAT development.

With increased availability, VSAT services are likely to get a big push and, therefore, the opportunities in this sector are excellent.

— The gross receipts of the Department of Post during the year 1995-96 were Rs. 1150 crore. Gross working expenses were Rs. 2472 crore and net working expenses Rs. 1810 crore. there was, therefore, a deficit of Rs. 660 crore. During the year 1996-97, as per budget estimates, the gross receipts are expected at Rs. 1350 crore and gross working expenses at Rs. 2616 crore. With net working expenses at Rs. 1962 crore the deficit is estimated at Rs. 612 crore for 1996-97. (BE).

— The Budget of Department of Post has been in deficit continuously over the years, and no dividend is being paid to the general revenue. Modernisation activities, through inductin of new technoloy, has been initiated on a modest scale during the current plan. Its further expansion and spread during the next plan, are likely to improve the service efficiency. A modernised postal system should also be able to provide new value added services to yield revenue. Low tariff on most of the postal services for many years, and inadiquate agency charges for agency functions, are the main factors for the deficit. However, a moderate increase in some of the services i.e., printed postcard from 60 paise to 100 paise and registration fee from Rs. 6.00 to Rs. 8.00 and introduction of cmpetition postcard at Rs. 2.00 each is expected to yield additional revenue to the tune of Rs. 76 crore in a full financial year. The degree of subsidy, as indicated in Table 2.11 ranges from about 1 per cent in respected of money orders to 92 per cent on postcard.

— The network owned and operated by the Department of Telecommunications (DOT) has been generating surpluses, which is utilised for further exapansion of the net work. Net receipts increased to Rs. 4951 crore in 1995-96 (RE) from Rs. 3936 crore in 1994-95 reflecting an increase of 25.8 per cent. Net receipts are estimated at Rs. 5213 crore in 1996-97 (BE). The dividend contribution to the general revenues increased to Rs. 279 crore in 1995-96 (RE) from Rs. 270 crore in 1994-95. The operating ratio, which is a percentage of net operating expenses (excluding the provision for redemption of bonds) to operating revenue earned (excluding registration fee) has come down to 48.7 in 1995-96 (RE) from 48.8 in 1994-95. The plan outlay for Telecommunication Services (including all PSUs) for the year 1996-97 (BE) is marginally higher at Rs. 9874 crore from Rs. 9830 crore in 1995-96 (RE). The entire outlay (except Rs. 5.00 crore pertaining to WMo etc. which is by way of budgetary support) is to be financed from the internal accruals and extra budgetary resources of the Telecommunication sector. Internal accruals amounting to Rs. 7491 crore account for 75.9 per cent of total resources against 79.6 per cent in 1995-96 (RE).

— Though the telecom network in India is fairly large in absolute terms, (in 1994 it was ranked fourteenth in the world) yet the tele density was 1.4 per cent in March, 1996. An advanced and efficient telecommunications system can enhance international competitiveness of the economy. The DOT has been increasing the quantum of resources deployed for the development of the telecom infrastructure, although the pattern of financing has undergoes a sea change. During the first plan DOT received budgetary support which accounted for around 79 per cent of the total resouces deployed it. In the Eighth Plan, 78.7 per cent is expected from internal accruals, 21 per cent from borrowings and other sources, and only 0.3 per cent from budgetary support. In the coming years, substantial investment would be required to upgrade and expand the existing telecom network. The aggregate resource requirements for the provision of basic and cellular mobile telecom services as estimated bny the Expert Group on Commercialisation of Infrastruture Projects is placed at Rs. 1,91,500 crore by 2006. Thee estimates are at todays prices and duty structure.

— Of late, DOT has primarily relied on internal accruals. However, to meet its targets of network expansion, DOT will have to look to a larger resource pool. It will have to devise a tariff structure which largely reflects the cost oriented approach, subject to country's social obligations and thrusts.

— A corporate structure for the DOT will enable it to leverage its substantial assets and raise adequate funds to meet all its investment needs. Corporate structure would make DOT into an autonomous entity owned by the Government. In the short and medium term, the government will remain the dominant operator and provider of telecom services in the countrty. However, with the advent of private operators, the present tariff regime should orient as quickly as possible towards a costbased structure. It is imperative to have the tariffs reviewed to allocate costs for various services and identify the need, if any, of subsidies.

— As per the revised estimates for 1995-96, the total expenditure on Broadcasting was Rs. 974 crore as against total receipts of Rs. 549 crore. This shows an increase of 19 per cent and 20.4 per cent in total expenditure and receipts, respectively. As a result, the ratio of total receipts to total expenditure improved from 55.8 per cent in 1994-95 to 56.4 per cent in 1995-96. The rising trend in commercial receipts in broadcasting activity over the past few years is indicative of efforts being made in this direction. Commercial receipts were Rs. 426 crore in 1993-94, Rs. 450 crore in 1994-95, and Rs. 540 crore in 1995-96 (RE). Further break up of commercial receipts brings to the fore the overwhelming contribution of Doordarshan towards revenue generation. The commercial receipts in case of Doordarshan were Rs. 363 crore in 1993-94, Rs. 384 crore in 1994-95 and Rs. 460 crore in 1995-96.

— The important place commanded by India in world trade in coffee, tea, leather and spices on a historical basis has continued in recent years as wll. In 1994, India accounted for 2.4 per cent, 13.6 per cent, 2.5 per cent and 9.1 per cent of world trade in coffee and coffee substitues, tea and mate, leather, and spices, respectively. Furthermore, there has been a significant progress in export diversification, and India has emerged as an important exporter of iron ore and concentrates, and pearis, precious and semi-precious stones. In 1994, India accounted for 6 per cent or world exports of iron ore and concentrates and 10.9 per cent of world exports of pearls, precious and semi precious stones (Source: 1994 United Nations International Trade Statistics Year Book, 1995).

— During 1950, India accounted for about 1.8 per cent (1.85 per cent of exports and 1.71 per cent of imports) of world trade. After gradually declining to 0.57 per cent by 1980, India's share improved marginally to 0.63 per cent by 1985. The reason for improvement in the share was that while world trade declined in the period 1980-85, India's trade continued to grow. However it came down again to 0.53 per cent by 1991. The first half of the nineties witnessed a sharp increase in India's exports and imports have grown in dollar terms annually by 12.4 per cent and 9.4 per cent, respectively. The corresponding growth rates of world trade was about 5.7 per cent. The secular decline in India's share in world trade has been arrested and reversed, and the years ahead are likely to see a continuation of this increasing trend.

— The trade policy components of the reform process undertaken since July 1991 have been motivated by a full recognition of the important role that trade can play in promoting growth. The utilisation of the expanded scope for specialising in areas of comparative advantage is manifest in the improved growth performance of the economy. Furthermore, while exports have vigorously responded to the removal of the anti-export bias of a protectionist environment, domestic industry appears to have been stimulated by the expended availability of imported inputs and capital goods as well as the challenge of competing in the international market place. The positive response of Indian industry to liberalisation is amply demonstrated by the capital goods sector. The tariff on capital goods was as high as 85 per cent in the pre-reforms period. This has been reduced to about 25 per cent covering about 80 per cent of capital goods in 1995-96. The capital goods industry which witnessed a negative growth of 12.8 per cent in 1991-92, registered an average growth of about 23 per cent during 1994-96.

— The terms of trade, which measure the terms of exchange between a unit of exports and a unit of imports, have been improving in the post-reform period. Two common ways of measuring the terms of trade are the net terms of trade (NTT) and the income terms of trade (ITT). A time series indicating all parameters of terms of trade (TOT) for India since 1969-70 with the base of 1978-79 = 100 Indicates that there have been wide fluctuations in the TOT. The NIT (1978-79=100), which is an index of export prices divided by an index of import prices, improved from 109.3 in 1990-91 to 152.4 in 1994-95. It is

— It may be mentioned that India s purchasing power of exports as reflected thorough ITT has been improving continuously since 1985- 86. The value index of exports at 484 stands much higher than that of imports at 351 and hence, in terms of value, india has gained.But in terms of volume, the index of exports has been much less at 384 in comparison to that of imports at 515. This means that the volume of imports is increassing faster, though India is getting a better price for her exports.

— Compared to the experience of other developing countries, the improvement in the terms of trade for India has been very impressive. The NTT (1990=100), as presented in the UN's International trade Statistics Year Book, 1995, is reproduced below:

— Developing economies, with exports dominated by primary products, lost out to developed econoies,. Relavtive abundance of supply of primary products as well as the superior bargaining strength of developed countries have often ben adduced as two major reasons for the deterioration in the terms of trace. Gains in the terms of trade for India in the comparable period perhaps reflects her diversified export base as well as the relatively low international prices of oil in the relevant period.

India is committed to further liberalisation of its import regime, notwithstanding the dismantling of licensing controls over a wide area. At the same time, there are concerns whether developed nations of the world are implementing in letter and spirit their part of the obligations under the Uruguay Round Agreements. Many contries are resorting to protectinist devices in the guise of environmental hazards and exploitation of labour such as child labour. The obligations of providing access to imports of developing countries, especially textiles and garments, are being circumvented under one pretext or the other, even under the back-loaded integration of Textiles and Clothing into the World Trading System. Such restrictions are designed to keep out cheaper imports.

By virtue of the radical shift from a highly-regulated to an outward-oriented economy, India has attracted immense interest abroad, at both Governmental and private investor levels. India is one of the largest emerging markets, second only to China's, and the country has been experiencing inflows of foreign portfolio and direct investments—thought not as large as in China and a few other countries—which were unthinkable in the world of even 1980s. Economic strength has become the principal determinant of a nation's standing in the international community, and even the most powerful country, the United States of America, looks for market opportunities all over, more especially in the dynamic Asia-Pacific region, as the best shield of security.

With the end of the Cold War, the East-West barriers have broken down. The rapid spread of liberalisation and globalisation is a historic development which has blurred both East-West and North-South divisions. Developing countries have been compelled to adapt themselves to conditions of global interdependence although in the process they run grave risks in the medium-term and rare not assured of international safety nets.

In the rapidly changing world environment, each developing country must certainly concentrate on building its inherent strength and developing areas of comparative advantage and forge alliances with neighbours and, where promising, enter regional blocs which offer greater opportunities of trade and other exchanges to enhance national arena, disadvantaged nations must make common cause and unite to advance their pressing needs more effectively than what has been witnessed over the last fifty years in the post-decolonisation era. This is the only way of securing a post-cold war order which is just and equitable.

India has a long way to go before it could emerge as a strong global player, as currently it occupies the 32nd place as a leading exporter of merchandise, well below several countries in East and South-East Asia. It has to make up for the time lost in its inward-looking route to development which left the cuntry far behind in the international league, despite building a strong industrial base and possessing highly technical manpower, the third largest in the world. Indian planning did not take sufficient note of the gathering pace of global intergration with the frowth of merchandise trade exceeding the growth of output in virtually every year of the post-war period.

In recent years, India has begun to look East, is now a full dialogue partner in ASEAN (the 7-member Association of South East Nations) and excepts to find a place in the Asia Pacific Economic Forum (APEC) by 1999. These should promote greater intra-Asian trade and investment flows even as India strives to gain an increasing share of exports into developed economies of the West such as the European Union and North America. Trade with Russia and Eastern Europe as well as Central Asian States holds prospects of considerable expansion over present levels and a more promising development is the initiative taken by 14 states of the Indian Ocean Rim for an economic cooperation grouping with a Charter expected to be signed in March 1997.

The bilateral and pluralistic approaches cannot, and should not, in any way dilute India's firm commitment to multilaterialism which is the best safeguard against domination of the global economy by a few powerful nations. India's immediate responsibility is to solidify South Asian cooperation through SAPTA and ensure its early graduation to becomes SAFTA (South Asian Free Trade Area) to make it a region of good neighbourliness less prone to conflilcts than at present. With 16 per cent of the world's population, India's weight in the international economy remains negligible, and the building up of internal strength with determination through higher saving, and investments and greater efficiency in the use of resources is a pre-requisite for the country to claim its due share in the global market-place.

**Looking Ahead**

The fifth decade of Independence has triggered investment interest in India as never before. Policymakers should now bring in a lot more clarity on their objectives.

The rules of international trade have changed. Witrh trade barriers getting dismantled by the day, there is need to infuse a very high degree of competitiveness. A major development is the evolution of regional trade groupings like the European Community (EC), the North American Free Trade Association (NAFTA), ASEAN, APEC etc.

Though the south Asian countries have formed the SAARC, progress achieved in free trade among these has been slow. Apart from mere trade flows, potential benefits in terms of the phasing out of poliltical animosities and more cohesive regional developments are immense.... The EC experience proves this. Over the last 50 years Britain, France and Germany, who have been bitter adversaries for centuries, have been bonded together on the strength of mutuality of economic interests. The SAARC union could grow to include China, the Central Asian Republics and the Indian Ocean rim countries, including South Africa, and forge close links with ASEAN and APEC in course of time. The comparable levels of economic development of most of the countries in this region would help in co-ordinated growth.

There is a huge market for such equiptment: there are capabilities in these countries to produce entire range of such equipment–generators, turbines, boilers, transformers, switchgears, motors etc.

The Korean automobile manufacturers—Daewoo Motors and Hyundai—indicate plants for developing India as a major centre for their global operations. Like we did in regard to Maruti, in the assimilation of mass production technology, India should attempt absorption of the high productivity levels of the Koreans, Americans and others; combine this with the strength of the massive availability of skilled manpower to win global markets.

With the progress of economic reforms in many countries of the world and deregulation of financial markets, the importance of private capital flows into Asia has increased from US $ 76.8 billion in 1994 to US $ 98.0 billion in 1995, while net official flows increased marginally from US $ 5.6 billion to US $6.4 billlion during the same period. Similarly, while there were considerable official flows to Mexico and the transition countries in 1995 in support of their comprehensive adjustment programmes, net private capital flows to the developing countries increased from US $ 140.4 billion in 1994 to US $ 166.6 billion in 1995. India has has modest, but increasing, success in attracting a growing part of these private capital flows. Furthermore, much of these private capital inflows into India has been of the non-debt creating variety, and helped to boost the balance of payments as well as the availability of investible resources in the economy.

The international financial community is appreciative of India's economic performance in the last years, but concerns continue to be expressed about the high fiscal deficit, the slowing down of structural reforms, continued restrictions on consumer goods imports, and tariff levels considerably higher than in other countries. Also, references are often made to India's move towards capital account convertibility (with some observers advocating a cautions approach), high level of subsidies, inadequate disinvestment in the public sector, need for further relaxation of rules to attract foreign investment and the continued high stake of the government in the public sector banks. On the whole, the international community is very positive about India's effort to achieve a high rate of growth.

Participants in the India Development Forum (IDF) meeting in September 1996 acknowledged the strong performance of the Indian economy and appreciated the new Government's declaration to continue reform measures to strengthen the social programmes as set out in the Common Minimum Programme (CMP). Various delgates stressed the importance of (i) fiscal consolidation, (ii) sustaining programmes in the social sectors, (iii) infrastructrue, (iv) provety eradication, (v) reforms in agriculture, public sector, and financial sector, and (vi) strengthening of legislation against child labour. In support of India's economic development, the donor countries pledged official assistance in 1996-97 of US $ 6.7 billion. Inclusion of US $ 400 million in long-term finance, promised on a bilateral basis at market rates, will raise this total to above US $ 7 billion. About 33 per cent of the total could be in the form of grants and interest-free loans.

With effect from January 1, 1997, India subscribed to the Special Data Dissemination Standards (SDDS) of the International Monetary Fund (IMF). by subscribing to the SDDS, India ha committed itself to streamilining the tatistical system of the country to produce most of the data categories with a much shorter time lag, improved quality and coverage by December 31, 1988.

By virtue of the radical shift from a highly-regulated to an outward-oriented economy, India has generated immense interest abroad, but it has a long way to go before emerging as a strong global player, opines the author. India's development strategy launched in the 1950s, soon after Independence, aimed mainly at strengthening the industrial base of the country, especially in basic goods and heavy machine-building, and adopted the import-substituation model to achieve self-reliance. Exports were not viewed as an integral part of overall economic development, and such imports as became unavoidable were financed by drawing down foreign exchange reserves that had accrued to India at the time of Independence, in the form of sterling balances held in its favour for goods and services provided by this country during the Second World War.

Export pessimism dominated the mood of the early planners as it was rightly assumed then that until India's manufactures began to be diversified, there was little possibility of exporting manufactures while primary products and traditional manufactured goods faced poor demand prospects in the world market. It was during the later half of the fifties, when the Second Five Year Plan was under way with its emphasis on heavy industry, largely in the public sector, that it began to be realised that India needed to export to be able to finance at least part of the maintenance and developmental imports.

The foreign exchange crisis that was looming by mid-1957 reinforced the importance of export growth as part of planned development. The pessimistic view about the potential for export earnings gave way to a more positive approach in the Third Plan (1961-66) with the introduction of export promotion measures without deflecting from the thrust of import subsitution and industrialisation. It was clear by mid-estimated the import content of the inward-looking path of development opted by India. Pressures on balance of pyaments had already brought into existence the Aid-India-Consortium comprising the World Bank and developed countries interested in providing assistance to India. Renewed emphasis on exports was laid in the Fourth Plan (1969-74) which envisaged porogressive elimination of dependence on foreign aid while the Fifth Plan (1974-79) identified certain sectors such as engineering goods, garments, leather manufacture and marine products for achieving increases in exports.

Thus, as agianst virtual stagnation in the 1950s, export performance improved to an average growth of 3 to 4 per cent in the 1960s, and was more impressive in 1970s with an average growth of 6.3 per cent in volume and 15.9 per cent in value terms.

But in the three decades, India's share in world exports had declined throughout from about 2 per cent in 1950 to 0.65 per cent in 1970 and dropped further to 0.42 per cent in 1980. This was the period when there was impressive growth in world trade and the opportunities were seize by many smaller Asian developing countries as well as the industrialising economies in Latin America to great advantage.

Paradoxically, even as india's export growth was being maintained or marginaly improved upon, her share of world exports was declining. Over the three decades ending the Seventies, the share of exports in Gross Domestic Product (GDP) ranged from 4 to 6 per cent. In a continental economy of India's size, the role of external sector in the development process was under-played so much that it took a successions of droughts, oil price shocks and balance of payments difficulties in the first two and a half decades of planning before the country could begin to see import substitution and export promotion as two sides of the same coin. But heavy reliance on quantitative restrictions on trade through import and export controls and detailed industrial licensing kept India a closed economy.

The Primary issuance of securities has a long history in India. The Indian bond market, measured by the estimated value of bonds outstanding, is next only to the Japanese and the Korean bond market in Asia. By January 31, 1995, the outstanding value of the Indian securities market was estimated to have reached Rs.3000 billion, almost 3.5 times its size in 1986. The size is deceptive as, despite attractive yields, secondary market trading has remained poor with virtually no quotation even in respect of listed securities. The estimated outstanding amount accounts for about 42% of GDP, as at the end of January 1995. Partial deregulation of interest rates in the early nineties and increasing emphasis on monetary policy in stabilization are the first major steps towards the emergence of an active debt market, with government securities spearheading the process. With the issuance of government securities at market determined coupon rates and the use of innnovative products, it has become possible, for the first time, for other issuers to offer debt products priced off the yield on government securities.

The process of financial sector reforms initiated in 1991, is far from complete. The Growth of the Indian Capital Market since Independence has been phenomenal. The number of stock exchanges increased from 7 in 1947 to 23 in 1994. Likewise the number of listed companies on stock exchanges grew from 1125 in 1946 to 7811 at the end of 994. Similarly, the quantum of listed capital registered a growth of about 565 times from Rs.270 crore in 1946 to Rs.152,322 crore at the end of March, 1994.

The basic objective of financial sector reforms is to promote a diversified, efficient and competitive financial system by a policy shift from detailed regulation and controls to one based on market forces. Alongwith dismantling administrative regulation, the goal is establishment of a system of prudential regulation, supported by a mechanism for reporting, monitoring and supervision of the compliance.

Another major plank of reform is injection of new competition into a hitherto virtually government owned financial system. For the first time in many years, six new banking licences have been granted to the private sector all of which have been implemented. The new banks are permitted to have financial joint ventures with fgoreign baks, particularly for accessing modern systems and technology. There has been a mushrooming of Non-Banming Finance Companies (NBFCs), some of whom have already built up a large net-work. Several well known investment banks have established a presence in India. Since April 1993, nearly 300 Foreign Institutional Inestors (FIIs) have been registered with the regulatory authority and quite a few are active investors in the domestic capital market which has been opened up to foreign portfolio investment in a limited way. Several new mutual funds have been set up by the private sector including some by global fund managers. The most spectacular growth has been registered when we compare the share of market capitalization to gross domestic products (GDP) which was 12.9% in 1946, while in 1991-92 it was 57.2% and further increased to 68.8% during 1993-98.

**Trade Policy**

Side by side with the announcement of New Industrial Policy for Promoting Small Tiny and Village Enterprises, the Government have also announced major reforms in the Trade Policy. The main objective of the trade policy have been to progressively reduce the system of administrative controls and lilcences and to link import except in the case of essential items. The major reforms in the Trade Policy are given below:

Exports were in the past allowed replenishment to provide for essential inputs required for the manufacture of products exported. To allow flexibility to enable diversification of export products and also as an incentive for exports, the REP licenses so issued, were allowed to be freely sold. The entitlement for REP licenses also varied from item to item. In view of the flexibility of the REP Licenses Government realise that to treat it as licence is an misnomer, under the new policy the REP licences have been replaced by a new instrument named 'Eximscrips'. Eximscrips will be issued on the basis of FOB value of exports or Net FOreign Exchange (NFE) earnings from exports as indicated below. The main features of the new systems are:

The basic rate at which Eximscripts will be issued against exports will be 30% of FOB value. Exports to hard currency areas will be eligible for Eximscrips valid for hard currency imports while exports to rupee payment areas will be issued Eximscrips valid for imports from these areas only. However, as a measure of transition, exports to rupee payment areas may continue to avail of REP licences valid for hard currency imports at the rate prevailing prior to 4th July, 1991. This transition facility will be available only for exports effected upto 31st December 1991.

Products such as gems and jewellery, handcrafts, newspapers, journals and periodicals and cinematographic films, which enjoyed higher rated of REP will receive Eximscrips at the same rates as before.

The Basis rate of 30% is inadequate for exports of certain products such as value-added agricultural projects, electronics, bulk drugs and marine products, formulations and certain categories of advanced engineering goods. These products will be eligible for an additional Eximscrips entitlement of 10 percentage points, taking the total Eximscrips rate to 40% of FOB value.

For exports made on the basis of duty free imports obtained against Advance Licences, Eximscrips will be available at the general rate of 30% but this will be applied to the net foreign exchange earnings. On the same principle. Eximscrips at 30% of NFE will also be available for all EOU and EPZ units.

The 30% of NFE rate of Eximscrips is also applicable to service exports, including software exports which is a thrust area. The definition of services covered under this category is being ratinallized and extended to include other services such as services of architects, textile designers, artists, management consultants, lawyers etc. The benefit will be available to services exported by resident Indians for which remittances are made to India. The details are being notified separately.

Eximscrips issued to exporters will be tradeable and can be used to import any item in the limited permissible list (Appendix-3), the non-sensitive canalised list (Appendix-5A) and for all OGL, items for actual users (Appendix-6, List 8, Part I and List 10). Eximscrips earned by exporters on their own exports can also be used to import non-OGL capital goods other than those on the restricted list (Appendix-1A). All REP licences issued against exports prior to 4th July, 1991 will continue to be valid for the life of the licence and will have the same import entitlement as the new Eximscrips. Additional licences issued to export houses/trading houses, which were earlier valid for a more limited range of imports, will also be valid for the same range of imports as Eximscrips.

With the introduction of Eximscrips, the system of issuing supplementary licences of raw material, components and spares listed in Appendix-3 will be discontinued except for small scale industries and for manufacturers of specified life saving drugs and equipment. In future, all import requirements of these items (with the exceptions indicated above) will be made through Eximscrips, Similarly items in Appoendix-4 and Appendix-9, which were earlier importable against supplementary licences, will henceforth be importable only against Eximscrips. Import of items appearing in Appendix-2 Part B (list of Restricted Items) and Appendix-8 (List of Scientific and Measuring Instruments Restricted for Import) of the Import-Export Policy 1990-93 will continue to require licences. Such licences as well as licences required for small scale industries and manufactures of life saving drugs/equipment will be called Special Licences as these will be limited and include special cases.

As a measure of import compression and to strengthen the linkage between import capability and exports, two further changes have been made. The category of unlisted OGL has been abolished and these items have been shifted to Appendix-3. They are now importable only against Eximscrips (except for SSI and manufacturers of life saving drugs and equipment). In the case of units subject to the Phased Manufacturing Programme (PMP), many of which benefit from concessional duty on their imports of OGL items, all such items will henceforth be importable only against Eximscrips.

Eximscrips will be issued only after export proceeds have been realised. The procedure for issue of Eximscrips has been streamlined and Government will ensure that Eximscrips are issued within 48 hours of the receipt of the application accompanied by single document, namely, the bank certificate for the realisation of export proceeds.

**Advance Licences**

The system of advance licences is designed to provide exporters with duty free access to the inputs they need to produce competitively for world markets. This is an important instrument of trade policy especially in our situation where tariff levels are still high. The Government has taken the following steps to strengthen the system of Advance Licences as an instrument of export promotion:

(i) The procedures for considering Advance Licence applications have been simplified to ensure that advance licences will be issued within 15 days of application in all cases where input-output norms have been fixed. Where norms have not been fixed, the licence will be issued within 45 days.

(ii) The number of documents accompanying an Advance licence application has been reduced from 9 to 3 where norms are prescribed and to 4 where they are not prescribed.

(iii) Ar present norms have been prescribed for 540 items. This will be increased to over 1000 items by 31st October, 1991 and more items will be covered thereafter.

(iv) Substantial Manufacturing Activity as a necessary condition under the Advance Licence Scheme will no longer be applicable for exports to the general currency area. However, the value addition norms will remain in force. A large number of exporters will benefit under this scheme.

(v) A new Scheme of Transferable Advance Licence has been introduced for GCA exports in selected thrust areas, namely textiles, leather goods and engineering industries. Under this scheme exporters can undertake exports based on duty paid inputs obtained from the market and subsequently obtain advance licences for replenishment of these inputs by duty free imports. These advance licences will be freely transferable. The coverage of the scheme will be extended on merits.

(vi) Advance licence will specify values in free foreign exchange both for the purpose of import and export. The currencies in which such values are denominated will be limited to those notified for this purpose by the RBI.

(vii) The Existing procedure for obtaining Bank Guarantee (BG) and Legal Undertaking (LUT) from different categories of exporters in being streamlined and liberalised as follows:

(a) Export/Trading/Star Trading House and Public Sector Undertakings will have the facility of obtaining advance licence against LUT only without any monetary limit.

(b) All manufacturing units having an annual turnover of at least Rs. 5 crores (including both domestic and exports turnover) during the previous 3 year would also be able to avail of the LUT facility up to a value limit of 50% of their annual production.

(c) A new unit without any production or export performance to its credit would also be allowed LUT facility provided it is promoted by an existing company with an annual production of Rs. 5 crores for more than three years. In such a case, both the new company and the promoting company would have to provide LUT.

(d) Bank guarantee and/or LUT obligation will be concurrent to the fulfilment of export obligation.

(viii) Exporters would be allowed to dispose of the materials imported against advance licences by way of replenishment without seeking prior permission of the licensing authority in cases where no MODVAT facility has been availed of on the domestic material used in exports.

(ix) Adjustment needed on account of fluctuation of prices of imported individual items would be permitted within the overall CIF value of advance licence.

(x) The power of revalidation which presently vests in the Licencing Committee at the Headquarters has been delegated to the Licensing Authorities.

(xi) In case where applications for an advance licence are turned down, the exporter will be permitted to convert to the Duty Drawback regime by the Collectors of Customs so that shipments made in advance can be imported on payment of duty subsequent claims of duty drawback.

(xii) Exporters can obtain advance release orders for domestic supply against advance licences under which the domestic supplier gets the benefit of deemed exports. Henceforth, release orders will be issued across the counter without requiring the name of the domestic supplier, which could be given later.

The adoption of these procedures would reduce discretionary controls and delays and afford much greater freedom to exporters in procuring essential duty free raw materials to maintain their competitiveness in the would market thereby promoting exports from the country.

The export Processing Zone scheme and the 100% EOU scheme were introduced to provide for duty-free enclaves, which would enable entrepreneurs to concentrate on production exclusively for export. However, with increasing liberalisation in the DTA, the duty advantages enjoyed by EPZs/EOUs have become less important. While the procedures of Customs Bonding are very onerous. The schemes have not therefore taken off as expected and they have also not attracted foreign investment aimed at tapping export markets to the extent that was expected. The working of these schemes has been reviewed and the following changes made:

(i) All EOUs/EPZ unit will be eligible for Eximscrips at the basic rate of 30% applied to net foreign exchange earning.

(ii) The duty applicable on DTA sales from EOUs/EPZ units is being reduced to 50% of the normal customs subject to the duty payable not being less than the excise duty on the same product. The extent of DTA sales allowed will be accordance with their entitlement. DTA sales will be permitted in the ratio of 25:75 in relation to export sales in case of units while use of indigenous raw material is more than 30% of production. In all other cases the ratio of permissible DTA sales to export sales will be 15:85. The procedures for clearing goods from the EOU/EPZ units for DTA sales are also being streamlined.

(iii) In order to encourage exporters to set up EOUs or EPX units the net foreign exchange earned by EOUs or EPZ units can be clubbed with the earnings of their parent/associated companies in the DTA for the purpose of according Export House. Trading House of Star Trading House status for the latter.

(iv) The IPRS scheme for supply of steel to exporters will also be extended to EOUs and EPZ units. The

Development Commissioners are being empowered to issue "payment authorities" in lieu of JCCI & Es.

Under the New Industrial Policy, most industries do not require an industrial licence except for a defined list. With a view to bringing about comparable streamlining in the procedure for EOU/EPZ approvals, a systems of automatic approvals is being established for all proposals which fall within certain parameters. Capital goods imports will be allowed under the automatic approvals procedure if they are fully covered by foreign equity or if they do not exceed 50% of the value of plant and equipment subject to a ceiling of Rs 3 crores. All proposals within the automatic approval parameters will be cleared within two weeks. All other proposals will be submitted to the Board of Approvals for consideration and decisions including issue of licences will be taken within 45 days.

A large number of issues relating to the operation of EOUs/EPZ units required centralized clearance in the Ministries of Commerce and Industry. Powers are being delegated to the Development Commissioners so that these approvals can be given on a decentralised basis. The specific approval of the Development Commissioner would not be required in cases of broad banding by EPZ units, where value addition is being maintained. The unit concerned would need only to provide relevant information to the Development Commissioner.

The following specific concessions to EOUs/EPZ units have also been extended:

(i) Allowing entry of imported raw material on "Provisional Assessment" basis, to expedite customs clearance.

(ii) Permitting units under the EPZ and EOU schemes to supply/transfer finished goods among themselves.

(iii) Replacement of multiple bond by a single bond, for obtaining import clearance.

(iv) Increasing the list of items under the "Special Imprest Licence Scheme" on selective basis.

(vi) Clarifying that containers stuffed in EPZ and EOUs are not to be reinspected at other points, as long as seals are intact.

Government have also decided to allow private parties to establish bonded warehouses within EPZs for stocking and sale of duty free raw materials, components, consumables and spares to EPZ units and EOUs. This will cut down delay in obtaining supplies of duty free materials which are in constant and regular demand by exporters. The details of this scheme will be notified shortly.

Other steps announced in the new Trade Policy have been the simplification of procedures for import of capital goods, decanalisation of number of items which were previously canalised, permission to allow established exporters to open foreign currency accounts in approved banks, raise external credits, pay for export related imports from such accounts and credit export proceeds to such accounts, its decision to re-designate the office of the Chief Controller of Import and Exports as Directorate General of International Trade with the principal function being to promote of exports, and facilitation of imports to promote export trade.

The policy changes now being implemented imply substantial reduction in the extent of licensing and in the number of types of licences. Supplementary licences for import of items in Appendixes-3 (except for SSI and manufacturers of life saving drugs and equipment), 4 and 9 of the Import-Export Policy 1990-93 have been abolished. Additional licences which were issued as an incentive to Export Houses and Trading Houses will stand abolished with effect from 1st April, 1992 and the incentive will take the form of an additional Eximscrip entitlement.

To achieve optimal import containment in the context of the present Balance of Payments situation, several steps have been taken. One of these is the shift of many items which are on OGL to the limited permissible list.

With these changes, the policy for import of raw materials components and other inputs needed for production has been simplified. Most raw materials and other inputs (except for those on the Restricted List) can be freely imported either against Eximscrips or on OGL. Some raw materials continue to be canalised but in more of these cases requirements beyond those provided by the canalising agencies can be met through Eximscrips.It is the policy of the Government to move to a situation where imports of essential raw materials and components needed for industrial production are regulated through appropriate tariffs. However, in view of the Balance of Payments position which necessitates continued import containment, this cannot be done immediately. Many items must therefore remain on the limited permissible list, with imports permitted only against Eximscrips.

The medium term objective of the Government is to progressively eliminate licensing and quantitative restrictions on capital goods and raw materials/ components so that all these items can be placed on OGL save for a small carefully defined negative list. This shift is proposed to be achieved over a 3 to 5 year period. The Government will appoint a High Level Committee to work out the modalities of achieving this transition keeping in mind the Balance of Payments position and the need to rationalise the reduce tariffs progressively to provide Indian Industry with an appropriate environment to develop international competitiveness.

**Industrial Policy and Trade Policy of the Government of India**

Over the years the Government of India has been adopting various measures for the liberalisation of the Industrial Policy, for streamling the licensing and foreign collaboration procedures, for reducing the number of agencies which the prospective investors have to approach to get the necessary approvals, etc., with the objective of attracting more investment and technology transfer. On the 24th July, 1991 the Government tabled before Parliament the Statement on Industrial Policy, 1991, which was followed by the issuance of a Notification by the Department of the Industrial Development to implement the Policy Statement and a series of Press Notes to set out the changes in the existing system and procedure for obtaining industrial licenses and approval of proposals for foreign and for foreign testing of indigenous raw materials and products and indigenously developed techniologies.

The new Industrial Licensing Policy of the Government of India has exempted form the requirement of obtaining industrial licence all industries, except those reserved for the Public Sector (Schedule I to the the Notification), those in respect of which Idustrial Licensing is compulsory (Schedule II to the Notification) and those relating to the items reserved for exclusive manufacture in the small scale sector (Schedule III to the Notification).

The exemption from Industrial licensing is also subject to:

The proposed project (except in the case of a project relating to electronics, computer software, printing